KINNAKEET ADVENTURE

TO ALL
KINNAKEETER'S
PAST, PRESENT AND FUTURE...

KINNAKEET
ADVENTURE

STANLEY E. GREEN

GRAVITY WELL BOOKS

NORTH CAROLINA

CONTENTS

Introduction

Introduction is the right word for this preface. There truly was an introduction of *Kinnakeet Adventure* to me when I began reading it for the first time. It was quite a book of mystery. First, I'm not even sure where the book came from. While I have vague memories of purchasing it at a used book store, my wife is sure that I found it at my beach house on the Outer Banks. But that is only part of the mystery.

I knew where Kinnakeet was, of course. Seeing the name of the book, combined with the stock cover image of a teenage boy in obviously late 1960s clothes, head held in his hand as he seems to struggle with a math assignment, did nothing to give away the secrets inside. Nor did I know the name Stanley Green or his claims to an adventure in Kinnakeet. I had to read the book to discover those.

So read it I did. And I was mesmerized by the tales he told. Certainly his struggles to fit in and teach were interesting. I could sympathize with him, as I was a former teacher. What I found most interesting were the many ways he documented both the life of the 1930s on the Outer Banks coast, with all the color he brought into the book with the locals and their various mindsets and talents. He also recorded many specific events from his years on the shore. Stanley was also able to capture a retrospective of the natives of Kinnakeet, as well as document, through the locals and their oral history tales, of the times before them. I really enjoyed the book, because it painted in the details of history around Hatteras Island and the Outer Banks that just weren't well recorded anywhere else. I knew this book should be reprinted.

That's where the real mystery began.

I looked up what I could. There was little about Stanley outside of what he tells in the book and his very brief biography. Even the original publisher, Vantage Press, was nothing more than a vanity press that would print books if paid for them. They went out of business years ago. Stanley passed on in 1996. I had highly doubted the man would still be alive anyway, as I did the math at the time.

But his passing led me another direction. I wanted to republish the book. To do that meant I had to find his descendants, heirs to his estate, children and grandchildren. After a bit of work, I found his grave in Shelby, NC. This gave me some hope. My mother is from Shelby, with family in Boiling Springs, and perhaps they had heard of him. I then looked at his family tree. I was saddened to see that he never married, nor had children. He had several sisters, which meant a bit of a drawn out search for me to see which ancestors still lived, how many might be around to split his estate, and just how many people I would have to contact. It was daunting, but possible.

Then I noticed something. He had a sister named Bertha, who married into the Bridges family. Things were starting to click in my head. Bertha and her husband had a son, named Troy. Troy Bridges.

Uncle Troy.

To be sure, I checked, and yes, he was my Uncle Troy, married to my Aunt Lillian.

I was related to Stanley Green.

I first contacted my mother to check on this, and sure enough, she had met him. So had my brothers. I was too young, I guess, or not born at the time. She remembered him as a pleasant and quiet man, who was happy to meet them and take pictures.

Small world, huh?

It took some time, but I was then able to track down to whom he had left his estate, essentially the rights to the book, and where it sat now. A couple emails from helpful cousins, a note from a distant aunt, and I was in business! This book is the fruit of those labors.

In it you will find a collection of adventures, certainly. They are an assortment of events which may or may not all fall in line, time-wise, and sometimes he leaves a little bit out as he writes, but for the most part Stanley fills in the blanks as he goes. I was initially going to have massive annotations to explain all the parts of the stories, but Stanley does as good a job as I could. You will find I added a few appendixes at the end that explain the broader picture of the Outer Banks around that time. They aren't necessary to finish the story, really. But they do help explain some of the more unbelievable parts of the tales he tells. At least I hope they do.

I would be happy just to accomplish getting this book and all that is in it back out into the hands of new readers. Knowing that Stanley is family makes it even more meaningful. Before there was even a road to Kinnakeet, Stanley built a bridge to the people there with this book. I hope I can do my part to keep that bridge just as strong.

CHAPTER 1

NEW PRINCIPAL AT AVON

On the map, the small village on the Outer Banks, braving the boisterous Cape Hatteras Sea, was called *Avon*. But to those seven hundred souls who lived there, it was invariably referred to by its original name, *Kinnakeet*.

Although I was a native North Carolinian, I found the locale of my first teaching venture as foreign to me as though it were another land, instead of a part of my own state.

When I was still a stranger, a local woman put her hands on mine, regarding me deeply. "You won't believe it now, but if you stay here long enough, you'll learn to love it, too. We call it getting salt in your blood."

She was right. I did not believe it - then! This wild, narrow strip of land, surrounded by turbulent waters was frightening, even as it filled me with awe. But the salt did get into my blood, for I remained in Kinnakeet for twelve years, and what I was able to give as a teacher was negligible in comparison to what I learned from the Kinnakeeters and the Cape Hatteras Sea.

In this region, two oceans meet, and not always on a handshaking basis. The Gulf Stream is working northward, while the cold currents from the Arctic head southward, and the fury upon contact has given the area the reputation of being the graveyard of the Atlantic.

As for myself, I wanted greatly to become a teacher from the time I entered high school, and my avid determination

1

remained during my four years at the University of North Carolina. In my quest for higher learning, I had brazenly borrowed twelve hundred dollars, without foreseeing the Great Depression, which held the country in its grip by the time I graduated in 1930.

In order to stretch the borrowed money, I took any job available, such as yard work, general cleaning, waiting table, and baby sitting. Even these menial tasks were rare after the crash in 1929. Therefore, it was with much anxiety that I frantically applied to a school.

As regularly as I applied, just as often did I get a negative response, and sometimes, none at all.

June came and passed while I stayed for summer school, fortunate that the "self-help" bureau of the university gave me enough work so that I could manage to buy a return bus ticket to Boiling Springs, North Carolina.

September came, and the summer session was over. When I had completed the tasks which would give me the few extra dollars so desperately needed, I had no alternative but to go home!

Never had I known such discouragement; my dreams turned to ashes. How I yearned to teach! Unceasingly, I sent out applications, but in spite of myself, I felt my enthusiasm ebbing.

The second Friday in September arrived with no indication whatever that a great surprise was in store for me. The sky was its usual autumn blue, and the air was invigorating. A mockingbird perched atop a huge oak, trilling happily.

As I dressed that morning, I remembered that the assigned work on campus and in town would soon be finished, and by noon Saturday, I would be through at Mrs. Patterson's in Chapel Hill.

The task she had hired me for was to crawl under her house and remove some scraps that had been there for many years. The rear of the house was scarcely a foot off the ground, so I had to crawl along on my stomach, gathering up bits of rubbish in a huge pasteboard box.

Thus occupied, I heard the telephone ringing above me. Mrs. Patterson answered it, then with quick steps, she walked across the floor.

From the back porch, she called me. It was the university; there was a telegram from home.

My heart raced as I wriggled backwards from under the house. My folks never wired me; it was bad news!

Mr. Lanier of the university sensed my anxiety, for he asked, "Would you like me to open it?"

"Please do!"

I could hear the opener ripping through the envelope, and I scarcely breathed.

"Your father has forwarded by night letter, a telegram sent you at Boiling Springs - it's from Avon, North Carolina." He hesitated. "Green, it's good news!"

Where was Avon? What good news could come from a place like that?

He read me the telegram.

YOU HAVE BEEN ELECTED PRINCIPAL OF AVON SCHOOL, AVON, NORTH CAROLINA. IF YOU ACCEPT, WIRE REPLY IMMEDIATELY.

I was too excited to think. Never, I was sure, had I applied for a position at Avon. How could I be given a job I had never asked for? And certainly, I never applied for a principal's position.

Mrs. Patterson was almost as excited as I. She insisted that the rubbish remain under the house while I went immediately to see what else I could learn.

She did not have to urge me twice!

I insisted I had never applied for this, and Mr. Lanier asserted I must have. When I pointed out the fact it was a principalship, he merely dusted his hands, saying, "You've got a job anyhow, and that's what counts."

"Yes," I agreed, "that's what counts."

But I was still struggling mightily to find some inkling *why!*

Several people owed me money for work, and I spent the afternoon trying to collect it, having decided I would go home on Saturday.

Walking along, I kept wondering about Avon, and in Sutton's Drug Store where I bought a Coke, I asked the druggist about Avon.

"Never heard of it."

A man at the counter sipping a steaming cup of coffee suggested I refer to a road map. There was one on the front seat of his car.

After spreading it out, the three of us searched, presuming it was probably in the mountains of Western North Carolina.

Finally, the owner of the map discovered it, "Hey, it's out in the ocean!" He put a broad finger on the spot.

Sure enough, it was at least thirty-five miles off the main coast of North Carolina, near Cape Hatteras. I couldn't remember the time I did not hear of Cape Hatteras, with its wild hurricanes, shipwrecks and pirates!

What strange pressures a depression creates! What other force would have influenced me on accepting a position, knowing nothing of the locale or other specific conditions? But I was desperate, and as Mr. Lanier had said, "You've got a job, and that's what counts!"

I lost no more time in wiring my acceptance, and the following Thursday morning, after visiting my family in Boiling Springs, I took off for my new duties. My father was no more familiar with that narrow strip of land than I was. However, he was inclined to agree with the others. It was an opportunity I couldn't resist.

Because of its isolation, the journey would take a ridiculously long time, with waits and changes, but the fact that part of it would be by boat delighted me. It was early Thursday night when I arrived in Raleigh. My train for Elizabeth City would be leaving at ten that night, arriving around sunup; from there the Steamer *Trenton* would take me to Manteo. The steamer's departure at one o'clock in the afternoon, would leave me the whole morning to saunter about.

I walked along the Pasquotank River, interested in the ships and sailors. Occasionally, I was able to ask someone about Avon, but their answers were vague; none had been there. I wondered why.

I found a small café on the waterfront and ordered coffee. The place was a hangout for sailors and owners of boats anchored nearby. For the first time in my life, I became aware that seafaring men have quite a different vocabulary from landlubbers.

Starboard, larboard, dory, sloop, portside, tugboat, and rigging! But the two words that puzzled me the most were Kinnakeet and Chicamacomico. Were these parts of a ship?

Settling down with my coffee, listening to the nautical talk, I gradually became aware of a close association between

5

Kinnakeet and the mysterious Avon. They spoke of Kinnakeeters and of Big Kinnakeet and Little Kinnakeet. Were these Kinnakeeters a separate nationality?

"Kinnakeeters are the most beautiful creatures on earth," contributed one sailor.

"They can outfight a tiger," declared another.

A third, commented the only trouble he ever had with a Kinnakeeter was when he jokingly spoke of yeopon, at which time he got the "living daylights" whacked out of him.

I was slightly built, and looked younger than I was. Added to these handicaps was a natural reticence which held me silent among these sturdy seamen. But my curiosity all but caused me to burst. Coming at last to those familiar with the mystic place toward which I was headed, I dared not ask questions!

Would I be meeting the Kinnakeeters when I got to Avon, how could I tell them from the rest of the people?

Daydreaming, I conjured myself walking up to someone asking, "Are you a regular native of Avon, or are you one of those Kinnakeeters?"

I sat there listening eagerly until the sailors departed, then I wandered back out to the street, more confused now than before.

Nervously, I recalled what Montaigne had written, "In the education of children, there is nothing like alluring the interest and affection; otherwise you only make so many asses laden with books."

That was the sort of teacher I aspired to be, giving the students inspiration, arousing in them a desire for knowledge - but these Kinnakeeters - most beautiful creatures on earth, fast with their fists! What was yeopon, and why did it anger them? How many of these queer ones would I have in my classroom?

6

Impatiently, I awaited the departure of the steamer *Trenton.*

CHAPTER 2

I REALIZE MY ERROR

All that autumn afternoon, I stood on deck gazing across the river at the great expanse of flatlands covered with vegetation, interspersed with sandhills.

The water had a greenish hue, which complemented the darker green of the land, the white of the sandhills, and the blue sky. It was enough to put a man in a meditative mood. Not being familiar with the sea, it was hard to realize this was part of my own North Carolina.

Added to this was the fact that I was heading for a position I had not applied for, to a place I had never heard of. But why had a young chip like me been chosen? Everything was in order; they had wired me using my correct name and address, even sending a confirming wire at my acceptance.

There was irony in the situation, since so many experienced teachers were begging for schools. Try as I may, I simply could not fathom why I was on my way to a little town which appeared, as the man said, to be in the ocean.

The boat's captain appeared and suggested I have a bite with him in the galley, but I thanked him saying I wasn't hungry. In fact, I drank so much coffee earlier, it had quelled any desire for food.

He stood there for a moment, then commented, "I understand you're going to teach in Avon."

"Yes, sir!"

He had not referred to me as Principal, and I took a certain comfort from this fact.

The captain frowned. "Son, you look more like a schoolboy than a teacher." There was a brief silence, followed by, "Better eat. There's plenty."

Again I thanked him, declining. Returning to my thoughts. I continued to marvel at the beauty about me when I noticed a young man similarly engaged, his right foot propped on the ship's rail. Somehow, he appeared more approachable than the sailors in the café; maybe it was because he, too, was alone. Summoning my courage, I strolled over to him.

"Know anything about this part of the country?"

He turned. "Sure do. Born and raised here."

"It's my first trip down this way."

He nodded. "Figured that the minute you came aboard. Plain to see you're from up country."

"Western part of the state," I said, proudly.

"Bet I know something else about you."

"Like what?"

"You're a college boy."

I asked him how he knew, and he admitted seeing college stickers on my bags. He thought I was coming down this way to make a special study for a scientific project.

"Before I went into service, several boys came down to Manteo to do a geologic study. They observed the influence of wind and water on land."

He waited for me to commit myself, and when I didn't, said he hoped I would find what I was looking for.

"There must be many interesting things to study in the area," I suggested, telling him that Dr. Collier Cobb, my geology professor at the University of North Carolina, often said the islands off the coast of North Carolina were an unexplored world.

"No doubt about that, but I didn't realize it until I went into the service."

"Navy?" I studied his uniform, uncertainly.

"United States Coast Guard." He pointed to a small white shield on his right arm.

He had been stationed in New Jersey, for about a year. He grinned, saying, "Can't tell you how good these sandhills look to me. I'm thinking of dropping on my knees when we get to Manteo and kissing the ground." He spoke enthusiastically of the many local legends, such as the Lost Colony at Manteo. He believed that the members of this Lost Colony went to Hatteras Island, and the present folks of Hatteras, Avon and Rodanthe were their descendants.

"We're descended from folks shipwrecked over the centuries. We're hardy."

How proud this young man was of his heritage! He talked with enthusiasm about the first air flight by the Wright Brothers at Kitty Hawk, and about the time the area produced enough tea to supply the nation. He claimed proudly that from hereabouts came the most skilled coast guardsmen.

The captain came by, proclaiming, "There she is, boys - Manteo!"

From the boat, appeared a tiny city nestled on an island far at sea. The sun was low in the west, adding to the unreality of the scene before us. It was a strange experience; for a moment, I could have sworn that the vast ocean was talking to me. There was a certain hypnosis which claimed me, and to which I decided to succumb.

As the steamer docked, a crowd of young people, mostly girls, stood at the dock watching the passengers debark. Although I had been traveling for two days, I still had another day before reaching my destination. I was to remain overnight here, but other than this, I had few details.

There was a dark-haired man, dressed neatly, who was watching the exodus, and as I approached him, he asked, "Are you one of the new teachers coming in?"

Surprised, I put my heavy baggage down as I introduced myself and said I was starting in Avon.

A slow look of surprise spread across his face as he asked, "Are you the new principal at Avon?"

I acknowledged I was, and quickly his face resumed a normal expression. He said his name was Johnson and that was Dare County's School Superintendent. "Come along to my office and I'll be glad to tell you about the work."

He instructed the stevedore to deliver my baggage to the Randall House, informing the landlady there, that Mr. Green would be spending the night, leaving early the next morning on the south mail boat for Avon. He motioned me to follow him.

My superintendent possessed a pleasing personality, and I felt encouraged. Perhaps he'd enlighten me as to why I was here!

Falling in step beside him, the pull of the sea was still strong within me. I loved the pungent odor, the noisy flight of gulls, and the roar of the Atlantic. This was a world vastly different from the mellow hills of home!

Superintendent Johnson talked casually as we went toward his office, but I was so preoccupied with my surroundings, I scarcely heard a word he said. We walked up to the second floor of the two-story courthouse, and inside his office he lit a lamp and we seated ourselves.

When he went to a filing cabinet and began going through some records, I expected to be told why I got the job, but he fumbled for a time, then sat down again, regarding me, his brows drawing together quizzically.

"So, you're Mr. Green!" He took a long breath as though he scarcely knew what else to say. "I'm sure you must be hungry after your trip, so I'll be brief. Please feel free to write me if there is anything you wish to know."

"What is generally expected?" I queried, realizing I was vague as he.

Instead of replying, he asked, "Do you know anything about the Outer Banks of North Carolina?"

"Very little, sir. My knowledge of this area is limited."

"Avon, of course, is on Hatteras Island, about six miles north of Cape Hatteras. It is a village of seven hundred people, and blessed with a good percentage of teenagers." With a twinkle in his eyes, he declared the people were noted for large families.

"Then they must have a rather large high school for such a small village."

"They have none at all."

I stared at him. "You mean my work will be in grammar school?"

"Your work will be high school; this year construction will start on a high school building."

"Do the people want one?"

He said definitely, because they realized they had to have one.

"Hatteras Island and Avon, for generations, have furnished some of the country's most outstanding coast guardsmen."

13

"So I have heard!"

This was because of the natives' experience with the turbulent sea. Their educational status had not been of primary importance, but the new requirement was a young man must have a high school education before he could enter the Coast Guard.

Thus, I was to get the high school underway. There would be three teachers for primary and grammar school, while I would do all the high school teaching.

The previous year the freshman term of high school was taught, which meant I would now have both freshman and sophomore classes to teach. Also, there were a few who had gone to high school elsewhere, so the local board told them they could come to Avon this year as juniors. "That saves then the expense of staying away from Avon this year."

How could anyone accomplish such a disparate job? I struggled mightily to conceal my surprise. That anyone would be expected to take on such a burden made me forget, momentarily, the mystery of why I was hired.

Rapidly, my thoughts returned to the twelve hundred dollars I owed and the paucity of jobs. I'd rather stick with this outlandish assignment.

"Sir, what sort of school plant do they have now?"

He said the building was old, and the furnishing poor.

"Where do the students get their supplies?"

There were no bookstores in Avon, thus, textbooks had to be ordered from publishers, while the general stores could supply pencils, paper and notebooks.

He had prepared a list of the required books, suggesting I order them after I registered the students because it would take two or three weeks for the order to be filled. I wondered just what I'd do until they arrived.

Mr. Johnson stood up, and I also rose, knowing he was dismissing me. My boat would be leaving early, I would have to be called at five in the morning. Also he suggested I eat a big breakfast, for I wouldn't reach Avon until tomorrow afternoon.

The mention of food reminded me that I had gone without lunch, and suddenly I felt faint with hunger. Meanwhile, Mr. Johnson gave me the supplies to start off with - six erasers, five brooms, a box of chalk, blanks for reports and records, and four ledgers to keep student records.

I must have appeared dejected, for he added, "Now there's nothing to be afraid of concerning the Cape Hatteras Sea. Folks have been living here for hundreds of years, and as for land tides, the natives have become so accustomed to them, they ignore them entirely."

Why did he presume it was the sea which had upset me? Then my mind did a flip. Land tides? I conjured up a mental picture of the great walls of water rising out of the sea, and I struggled mightily to appear composed, as I followed directions to my overnight lodgings.

The Randall House was an elongated, two story, planked-up affair which furnished rooms and board. Most of the guests were sportsmen and their wives who came from the east mostly, because the Outer Banks was one of the most famous hunting and fishing areas in the country.

My room upstairs was simply furnished with a double bed, a dresser with an oil lamp on top, and one chair. Downstairs, supper had already been served, but the landlady offered to fix me something.

I was famished and said so.

When the plate was set before me, my heart sank. Why hadn't I realized that this was where sea food abounded. The fish was no doubt delicious, but it was the only food I had never been able to eat. I sat there staring at it, my stomach gnawing, while my whole being revolted against this nourishment.

The kind landlady eventually walked by and stopped, staring at the untouched food, she asked if something was wrong.

I began to apologize, realizing she had gone to much trouble in preparing it, but the fish made me sick. "I should have told you."

"Nonsense, I should have asked. There's never too ways about fish; folks either like it or they don't. How about ham and eggs?"

Never had ham and eggs tasted so good, and topped off with fig preserves, the meal was perfection, itself.

My spirits rose, as always after good food, and I left the table for a stroll in the yard surrounding the boardinghouse.

Finally, I returned to the huge front room where most the guests were laughing and talking, with some of the local people. Feeling myself an intruder, I stepped back, seating myself on the porch, deep in the shadows.

Their talk bypassed me, becoming merely background for my thoughts, until a woman asked, "Did you see that young feller who just came in?"

"Now that you mention it, yes," said a man. "Why?"

Another female voice answered, "There must be some mistake, because he's supposed to be the new principal of Avon School."

"Not that little shrimp!" The first speaker laughed. "Why, he ain't nothing but a youngun hisself."

"How do you know he's the new principal of Avon?" the man demanded.

Before she could reply, a male voice said he saw nothing unusual about this. People did enter the teaching profession when they were young.

"Ordinarily, yes, but this is extraordinary." The first woman commented again. "He's not just a teacher; he's also the principal you know. Besides, I hear they had dozens of applications from experienced men." She smacked her lips noisily, and I imagined how she had the attention of everyone in the room.

"A friend from Avon was here yesterday, and she painted quite a different picture of the new principal."

"What's he supposed to look like?" one of the men wanted to know.

"A giant, that's what." She pointed out that the male students had been very unruly, therefore, the local board wanted someone who could govern them with an iron hand. "They think that's what they are getting!"

There in the porch shadows, I clasped my hands to keep them from shaking.

"How could his records be so misleading?"

She said his records were all right and he had been well recommended. It was his own description that was deceptive, he claimed to be six-feet-four, weighing two hundred and forty pounds. He had been outstanding in boxing, wrestling, track and football.

"He wouldn't say such things," came a squeaky female voice.

"My friend from Avon read his letter and she said it was well put and the handwriting, the best she had ever seen."

That description of my handwriting was as far from the truth as were the physical attributes.

I rose and went swiftly down the hall and up the stairs to my room. My world had turned upside down! No wonder Superintendent Johnson stared at me then checked the files, returning empty-handed!

What would happen at Avon, if those lusty, seafaring men awaited an athletic giant who could overpower their young ones with sheer physical force? I shrank into my inadequate body, and tumbled onto the bed, more miserable than I had ever been.

Ordinarily, I wouldn't have slept a wink, but I was too exhausted. The long day on the water, and the heavy, rich meal caused me to slumber without delay.

It is a strange and mystifying thing how some happening, too slight to make a conscious impression on the brain, will come forth from the subconscious, after sleep has taken possession of the mind and body.

While awake, I could not fathom why I was taking this job at Avon. In a deep sleep, it was revealed to me, crystal clear. So great a shock if it, I awakened, startled.

"*Folks in this world!*" I wailed. "What am I to do now?" This was embarrassing beyond description. If only that telegram never had reached me! My pride was of utmost importance; friends and family knew of my acceptance, and I couldn't turn back. Yet how could I go on? I felt as though I were trapped in a cave with all passages blocked.

Sitting up in bed, I nodded slowly. It became as clear as a tall pine tree standing alone on a desolate hill. Thirty days before the telegram came, that tragic joke began.

Since January, the teachers' bureau had sent out applications for me to use in applying for a job. I filled out hundreds with great care, but one Saturday afternoon I was attending to my own neglected correspondence, when a few classmates entered my room.

"More applications?" asked the chap named George, after counting the six letters I was placing in envelopes.

"Wrong! Not an application here." Then I mentioned having received another blank that very day from the teachers' bureau, but it was for a principalship. "You know how I'll have to answer that one," I laughed.

"You mean you aren't going to fill it out?" George exclaimed. "Go ahead, fill it out!" He picked up the blank, "I can just see you as principal now. Here, Ronnie and I will fill it out and sign your name, and we'll even write a nice personal letter giving them some references. Stanley, you are as good as principal right now!"

The boys joked about their elaborate entries while we laughed and talked together. I went out to make some coffee on the hot plate, and when I returned with it, they were stuffing it all into an envelope, finding it quite the lark!

I hadn't mailed my letters until the next day, but by then the incident had been forgotten. The bogus letter must have gone out with the others.

Oh, how could I have been so careless?

Then, forcing myself to calm down, I reasoned that since I had mailed applications for months and nothing had come of them, why had the phony one been accepted? And for a principalship?

I knew the answer - Avon was looking for a brute to beat knowledge into their young men. They wanted their children to be "so many asses laden with books," as Montaigne had expressed it.

At five o'clock, the Randall House was quiet. With my heavy bag and all the school supplies the superintendent had donated, I crept out into the night. A moderate wind from the southwest gave the new day a pleasant coolness. As I made my way to the café near the courthouse, two lamps were lighted.

Here and there were sounds of fishermen casting off for a day at sea, there were no other sounds to break the silence of Manteo.

I stood briefly before the courthouse, the scene of yesterday's session with Superintendent Johnson, and in spite of myself, my whole body began to shake. I was as chilled as though I were wrapped in a wet blanket.

I closed my eyes and tried to overcome this misery which had taken possession of me, grateful for the darkness which still lay over the town.

It passed as quickly as it came, and by the time I entered the café, several fishermen went in before me.

The long day stretched ahead, leaving me no hope for escape.

CHAPTER 3

THE KINNAKEETERS

The south mail boat had developed engine trouble, delaying its departure from six o'clock until eleven. A young fisherman who waited, too, returned to the café with me where we had another cup of coffee.

I inquired if he knew anything about Avon.

"Well, yes and no," he answered.

I had heard so many vague comments now I asked him just what he meant by that.

"I know the women are beautiful; the prettiest girls I ever saw!" He added he came from Norfolk, but was here to help an uncle with the fall fishing. "You going to Avon for a visit?"

I explained what my business was.

"You look too young to be a teacher," He surveyed me critically. "Well, anyway, if what I hear is true, you're going to have yourself a principal you don't read about in books!"

I said nothing, sincerely wishing he hadn't mentioned it.

The young fisherman said he and his uncle were fishing last week in Pamlico Sound, and stopped to help a "feller" with engine trouble. The boat owner was telling a boy about the new principal who was coming to Avon.

I ventured, "How big was the boy?"

He estimated probably thirteen. He started to light a cigarette, but found he was without matches, and went out to get some from the cook. The more I tried to forget my problems, the larger they loomed before me, and I glowered at the seaman as he returned to our table.

The man was trying to scare the *youngun*, stressing this was one year they'd walk the chalk line because of the principal who was goin' to be tough as hell.

"I can't figure why such a good man would want to bury himself in a small school; it don't make sense."

"No," I said. "It doesn't."

"Great big bruiser, wrestler, football player. Claims he can lick half dozen ordinary men any time."

I looked at my watch, glad to start back to the boat.

Among the passengers, I discovered that two of them were my teachers. Although the women said nothing, I could sense they had expected a much larger man. My earlier companion had merely put a package on the boat for delivery, and I was glad to be rid of him. I regarded the passengers who would make the crossing with me - besides the two teachers there was a dignified lady, a sportsman, and myself.

The Sound was not rough, but the surface waves caused by the breeze made the sail an exciting one for me. A boat that was so small the narrow deck was just above the water.

Soon we were away from sight of land.

The five of us began conversing, and the sportsmen, being queried about Avon, and learning that three of us would be teaching there, commented on the dilapidated school building, but admitted he knew little about the town since he usually fished around Hatteras Inlet.

I experienced a certain eagerness to reach my destination, in spite of the awful fate awaiting me there. Perhaps my anxiety was that of a condemned man, who only wanted to get it over with, but I finally stuck my head into the engine room, asking the captain, "How much longer before we reach Avon?"

He said were abreast Rodanthe, from there it was only about twenty knots.

I noticed the small village which had no harbor because the water along the shore was too shallow. The mail boat stopped and a man in a rowboat came out to pick up the mail.

About two-thirty, the captain yelled, "There's Avon on the distance!"

"Where?"

We were told to look directly in a south-southeast direction.

There it was, a tiny city far out to sea.

For the next hour, it grew from a little spot into a real village. There was an attractiveness about it, as if perhaps, the folks in Avon would understand how I was hired by mistake, and that I meant no harm by the misrepresentation of my attributes.

The place was picturesque - I had been prepared to see unpainted, roughly-built fisherman's huts, and a generally unkempt appearance - but it was not so. Even Pamlico Sound was a sight where the sky and sea appeared united. The sky was so blue, its reflection on the water made sky and sea one delightful world of color. The sou-wester had died down to a mere breeze, and no place could have looked more peaceful than Avon that day.

Soon, I discovered what appeared to be a solid wall of varied height, along the south end of the village. As I watched, it seemed to move, not as a whole, but in sections; it ran close to the shore of the Sound.

Was I dizzy? The harder I looked, the more it moved. I mentioned it to the captain. "There's a long wall on the lower side of Avon that puzzles me."

"A wall, did you say? There's no such thing around Avon!"

I insisted it looked like a wall because it was long and narrow.

"Trees and bushes," he suggested.

"No, it's not trees and bushes."

The captain hopped out of the engine room and looked to the south. He shook his head, turning toward me. "Never saw anything like that afore. It's people - just people!"

Why were they at the south end of town and not at the north end?

It was where the mail would be taken ashore.

"But if you've never seen them lined up before, why are they today?"

He chuckled. "Man, they've come down to greet their new principal."

Speechless, I stood transfixed, my eyes glued to the shifting line of people waiting to see the giant hired to teach their children.

I was so fascinated by all this. I almost didn't see a dory with a big man and two little girls aboard, until it was almost up to the mail boat.

The girls were probably eight and ten; their black hair, fair complexions and piercing blue eyes made them enchanting. Both wore blue dresses with small white dots. I could understand why they were considered strikingly beautiful.

"Uncle Tom Meekins," shouted the captain. I studied him, wondering if he were a regular citizen of Avon, or was he a

Kinnakeeter? Somehow I knew instinctively he was a true product of the local citizenry. He was a good six feet, muscular and tanned, typical of the men who follow the sea.

He looked at the five of us, asking, "Is there a Mr. Green aboard?"

I stood as tall as I could, but was dwarfed beside him. I said I was Green.

With great deliberation, he looked me over from head to foot, without the slightest inkling of surprise on his face, and a deep admiration for him filled my soul.

The three women and I climbed into the dory, leaving the sportsman, who was going to Hatteras.

Our baggage was put into the boat, then the mail bags, and several boxes of goods. Surely this was more than the small boat could manage, but Uncle Tom kept rearranging things until he even got a trunk belonging to one of the teachers aboard.

When we were some fifty feet from shore, a horse-drawn cart splashed into the water. The boy driving the cart, and the little girls transferred the small packages from dory to cart.

From this point to shore, the water was less than knee deep. I remembered, later, noticing the women were removing shoes and hose preparatory to wading ashore. But my interest, still centered on the curious crowd waiting to greet us, and I made no move to pull off my shoes and socks.

Then, before I knew what was happening, Uncle Tom grabbed me in his arms and waded toward the shore!

I could not protest, it was all over within such a short time.

Thus, was Principal Green - the giant, the beast, the man equal to any emergency, being carried ashore like a baby by Uncle Tom.

He set me down in the midst of the crowd, saying, "Yore things will be brought to Mrs. Keaton's, yore boarding place." He nodded toward a young boy. "Here's her boy Bill, to take ye there."

Quickly he headed back to the dory.

I glimpsed a young lad with light hair, his lithe body weaving in and out among the villagers, who stood strangely silent. Self-consciously I smoothed my wrinkled suit, but just before Bill Keaton reached me, I heard a small boy comment accusingly to an elderly man, "I thought you said he would be a great big man."

The old man grimaced, and no more was said.

Quickly, I made the necessary introductions and we followed Bill to a great expanse of Pamlico Sound on which was a thick growth of small trees, shrubs and bushes. We turned right at an opening in the greenery, arriving at a wired-in lot, partially grown over with tangled vines and stunted shrubs. From here I saw a large flock of Canadian geese who were creeping through the water, obviously paired off. Our host told us that Canadian geese keep the same mates for life.

The aroma of food cooking reached us from the Keaton home. It smelled wonderful, and suddenly I was starved. Mrs. Keaton stood at the doorway to greet us, tastefully dressed in a lavender dress gaily sprinkled with white dots. I felt myself stiffen against the inevitable - a comment about my size - but she greeted us with genuine warmth, glancing only briefly at us individually.

She escorted the lady teachers to their room, while Bill showed me to mine. It was long and narrow, with a double bed, a bureau, and a small table with an oil lamp on top. Also, it was furnished with a straight chair, and bowl and pitcher on a washstand in which I washed hurriedly before rushing downstairs to eat.

No better compliment could have been paid to my new landlady than show her my thorough enjoyment of that meal. It was hearty, flavorful, and the table was situated in a pleasant spot. Casual conversation was being tossed about as we satisfied our hunger with hambone soup, baked ham, pone bread and cabbage. The pone bread was something new to me; I learned it was made of cornmeal, molasses and salt, which were fermented before being cooked.

In the evening, I strolled around learning about my new environment. However, I learned more than I cared to, because I ran into a cloud of mosquitoes which covered my face, neck, and ankles. Grabbing my hat, I tried slapping them, but soon gave up, and ran back into the house.

Mrs. Keaton brought out a quart bottle of rubbing alcohol. "Douse yourself with this," she instructed, hastening to mention that mosquitoes were not generally about. Weeks would go by with no sign of them, then they'd reappear due to certain weather conditions.

Despite my dread about the future, and my chagrin over the mess I had walked into, I slept soundly my first night in Avon, awakening Sunday morning to step before my window overlooking the village. What an attractive place, embedded as it was on a narrow strip of Hatteras Island, with peaceful Pamlico Sound on the west, and the turbulent Cape Hatteras Sea on the east. How correctly these people could be called "seafarers."

I took several deep breaths before going down to breakfast, resolving that however I felt inwardly, I would put forth a calm exterior. I even compared myself to the churning Cape Hatteras Sea inside, and the peaceful Pamlico Sound outside.

I had just finished my breakfast when my landlady answered a knock on the door. A man's voice declined her invitation to come inside, but she was to send out Mr. Green so he could speak with him!

Mrs. Keaton said to me, "It's Willie Gray, of the Board of Education."

I struggled mightily to maintain the calm of Pamlico Sound as I shook hands with Gray, who wore the uniform of a Coast Guard surfman.

Again I was prepared for criticism about my size, and relieved in knowing that it would happen now.

Mr. Gray said that he was due at the station and had just a minute. George Meekins, also in the Coast Guard, was away, so he would not see me until later. However, Mr. Fields Meekins, the other committeeman, would like to meet me today.

I said I was eager to talk with each of them.

"The first thing I want to impress on you is that we hope to have a high school soon. Your job is going to be a mighty big one, because the boys are rowdy. They have carved the desks, broken window lights, and done other damage. You will have to be a disciplinarian and show them from the beginning who's boss. If you don't you won't ever be able to control them."

I sought some convincing words about my ability, but none came and he seemed not to expect any.

He simply made a statement, that was all.

Turning to leave, he hesitated, adding, "For the past few years, there's been confusion and a lack of understanding between the Methodists and those attending the Pentecostal Church. As a result, many have become indifferent to the school."

Although he had spoken no words of doubt or reproach, a sense of depression came over me. While I could not read his mind, something told me I'd better not try! I felt he was greatly disappointed in me, and I could not blame him. I decided he was advising me to put on a brave front before the students, while he hoped the situation would develop more favorably than it appeared, now.

Back in my room, I sat on my bed staring at my hands clasped loosely before me. Uncle Tom, Mrs. Keaton, Willie Gray, and even young Bill Keaton, hadn't mentioned my not filling the description on the application. I should have appreciated this, and I *did*, but I could not understand it, thus adding to my worries.

A loud knock on the front door brought me to my feet. It was an imperative sound, followed by a thundering male voice.

"Sister Keaton! How 'bout that feller Green? He up yet?"

I found myself confronted by a man who fit the description I wrote about in my cursed letter of application. He must have been six-feet-four, broad shouldered, with a physique that could easily lick a half dozen ordinary men. I was aware of his quick glance of disapproval, while his handshake was enough to convince me that he had cracked some bones.

"Brother Green, I'm Fields Meekins, one of the school committeemen."

He, too, was in a hurry, as he was Sunday school Superintendent at the Methodist Church, making a point to get there before Sunday school started.

"You've taken on a mighty hard job, Brother Green. There's never been a school with more problems to solve - I hate to tell ye this, but we're torn up over religion, while our boys here are worse than Chicago gangsters. You do realize ye have a terrible big job, afore ye?"

This information came as no surprise, and I felt a slow burn creeping up my neck and flooding across my cheeks. Surely, these men meant well, but what was to be gained by each one impressing on me the impossible situation which would confront me in less than twenty-four hours.

I swallowed and kept my voice low and even, telling him the task looked mighty big. This giant made me feel as though he were reading my thoughts. There was a compelling quality about him, and instantly I decided to tell him the truth; that should relieve the pressure building up within me.

But he turned and hurried off the porch, hesitating for a last word, just as Willie Gray had done.

"I must say I'm disappointed in you. Now don't go getting' insulted, you look well enough, but it's your size."

I opened my mouth to explain, but was interrupted.

"Discipline is what we need here; you'll have to use the rod. The boys have gone wild and if you can't control them, they'll run you off. Get ready and come to Sunday school, the Methodist Church is not far away."

This was a command!

I dressed hurriedly and set forth under an azure sky. It was a warm day, caressing, and benevolent, with the roar of the sea serving as background music.

Calmness settled over me as I progressed, then when I neared the church, the general assembly started. The groups were singing their hearts out and had chosen the hymn. "The Cross Is Not Greater Than The Crown." I stopped, standing quietly, to absorb every note of it. Never had I heard such beautiful singing from any congregation.

"And this," I murmured, "is only Sunday school, not the regular church service."

Preaching, I was to learn, occurred only twice a month.

Fields Meekins recognized me and nodded. As I sought a seat, everyone obviously tried to get a look at me. Again I was overcome by the awful sense of being young in appearance and slightly built.

When the singing was over, Uncle Tom Meekins, who had carried me ashore, led the prayer, and could he pray! His enormous faith was evident in his fervor and his words.

By the time I had finished Mrs. Keaton's Sunday dinner, I was ready to admit that her cooking would go far toward keeping me in a placid mood. There was nothing like good food to calm the nerves and put a man in a pleasant frame of mind.

Today, it was chicken pot pie, turnip greens, and boiled cornbread, while the potato salad was the best that I had ever tasted. Bill took pride in the fact that, as usual, he had made it. Dessert was lemon pie and coffee, the meringue on the pie standing in lightly browned peaks.

When the meal was finished, we sat around the table, while I spoke enthusiastically about the townspeople. I had met Aunt Lucinda after Sunday school; a tiny, spry creature in her seventies who appeared as energetic as a teenager. Dressed in black, her hair in a soft knot at the nape of her neck, she was a delight. Also, the sexton, Uncle George Meekins, mentioned to me that he was deeply concerned about the idle local youths. He hoped I would be able to help them.

The fact that I had related well to the folks seems to please the Keatons greatly.

Uncle Tom, they said, was self-educated, and no better predictor of weather could be found. He knew when there would be tides that would flood the island.

Since I was so impressed with the Methodists' choir, Bill felt I should hear the singing at the Pentecostal church, now in session. Sometimes, he said, they sang for hours.

The church had recently been built, and the inside was not yet completed, accounting for lumber piled in the back. We sat down, as the worshipers sang, "It Tastes Like Honey In The Rock." Bill was right, the Methodists had nothing on them. However, the service was soon over, it was their last hymn.

Outside, Bill suggested we go to Cat Ridge. The area where we were now was Dog Ridge. Years before, two gangs of boys who came from these ridges fought each other, this giving the ridges their names.

It appeared that strolling on Sabbath afternoon was a popular pastime. Bill thoughtfully stopped to let me meet the villagers, and finally a girl named Lizzie Price took charge of me for the rest of the afternoon.

"How do you like Kinnakeet?" she asked, and I frowned, not knowing just how to reply. I had decided to keep quiet until I knew more about it.

Lizzie laughed merrily. "It's Avon, to you, but Kinnakeet was the original name for this town. The postal guide renamed it many years ago, but Kinnakeet it will always be to us."

We passed the schoolhouse, and Lizzie said she was ashamed of its condition. I decided as soon as I said *goodbye* to her, I would return to look the place over carefully.

We went to the beach where she showed me beautiful shrubbery calling it yeopon. She said better not mention it in Kinnakeet. I decided then that it was best not to press anyone for information, but to wait until someone mentioned it without prodding.

She took me to her home, where I got my first taste of fig pudding, pronouncing it delicious!

When I returned home, I stopped at the school, and was deeply grateful that I made this initial inspection alone, for I was too disgusted to keep my reactions quiet.

First, I went to the northeast room where I would be teaching, and it was a nightmare. Because most of the panes were broken, planks had been nailed on the windows. While the shattered glass lay on the floor and desk tops.

The partitions were moveable, and when they were opened, they formed the auditorium. At the north end of my room an elevated platform of rough, thick planks stood. The front part of it had never been boarded in and when I dropped to my knees and looked underneath, I saw that junk had been stored there. Suddenly, something flew out, brushing my head, and I imagined any number of creatures, but realized finally it was only a frightened hen that had nested under there.

My door led onto an outside porch full of long cracks. At one corner there was a hole large enough for a pig to run through.

The desks made of soft pine accommodated two and appeared as though they were made a century ago. They were carved so completely, not a square inch remained undamaged. There once were shelves inside for papers and pencils, but those were torn away, while the desks were ripped from the floor.

Wood and coal stoves heated the rooms in winter, but mine was minus a leg, a wooden block served as a substitute.

And as for spitballs on the loft, I knew then I would never again see such intricate designs. Probably grandpa had put some of them there, followed by the generations of sons and grandsons.

On the west wall there once had been a blackboard, but all that remained now were ragged corners. Where the board should have been, someone had written in charcoal, "Let's give the little ol' princ. hell."

I stood in the middle of of all this, when suddenly it occurred to me there was no library; school would reopen without a textbook.

I listed the negative aspects on my fingers - no books, no library, no blackboard, no chair or desk for the principal, and no decent seats or desks for the pupils.

A strapping athlete for a teacher was not all this community lacked to educate its youngsters, I thought bitterly.

Dejection closed in on me, crowding my senses, and causing me to wallow in self-pity. Here I was, having worked and waited until the time when I could teach, and this was it! I confess, I stood there crying until my grief mounted toward hysteria.

Finally, I got hold of myself, dried my tears, and without a backward glance, went out into the little village I now called Kinnakeet, as did the natives who inhabited it.

CHAPTER 4

FIRST DAY OF SCHOOL

It was my idea to be at school well ahead of the students, but as I neared the building, I realized with a sinking heart that every school kid in town had the same notion.

The porch with the long cracks was crowded with children, their heads sticking out the windows which were unplanked, while the school yard teemed with them.

"How could one small village have so many kids?" I asked myself. One more teacher had arrived at Mrs. Keaton's last night, and I wondered if the few of us could cope with such a great number.

"Here he comes!" squealed an excited young voice, which was followed by silence. It was like the quiet before a storm. If all of them hollered at the top of their voice, it wouldn't have bothered me as much.

Should I speak to them loudly?

Or softly?

I settled for a modulated, "Good morning."

A few responded, but most did not.

Several of the larger boys followed me into the building and I managed to avoid looking at them, while simultaneously seeing each one. Some of their pockets were stuffed with seashells, and I knew these had not been brought for the study of marine life, or for decorative purposes.

"Look at Jim," I heard one boy remark. "He's ready for battle, wearing three pairs of pants."

I also noticed a few dirty tow sacks stuffed into the flue of the stove which in turn, was stuffed with paper and rags. Well, since it was a warm morning there was no excuse to ignite this potential trouble maker.

One lad deliberately dropped a paper bag, from which three sand fiddlers scurried, taking refuge under the platform where the hen had her nest. They were ugly looking things, but I pretended they did not revolt me at all.

A few of the girls entered the room, and they made considerable fuss over the creatures, but to these seafolk, I knew it wasn't really fear, but merely an act.

I occupied myself with useless tasks, since there was no equipment to work with, and it was not yet time to start school. I felt sorry for the women teachers who had to endure the filth and lack of materials to work with. As I thought of this, I glanced out the window and saw a young fellow approaching, followed by six admirers. The students inside had seen him too, and their expressions became expectant. The boy, his arms full of tree branches came into my room, and thrust the switches into my arms.

"Mr Green, you'll need something to fight with, so I brought you these. Ought to be enough to start with."

I stood there and looked at him saying nothing while I set the donated horse whips on the raised platform. I was keenly aware that the switches were a subtle warning that war was expected.

It was about then that I realized no adult had come along this morning. Nobody was going to drop by to see how things were going or to wish me well.

They've decided a young principal can't handle the boys, and expect my downfall. The quicker it comes, the better for everybody.

My spirits were too low to convince myself otherwise, and I was ready to agree with the parents.

My teachers were as bewildered and heartsick as I. "Enroll your pupils," I instructed, "and find out what books we'll need. We must talk things over; after an hour, send them home until tomorrow."

They sighed relief, but were not sure they could endure that hour.

One youngster had casually come over, presenting me with a ship's bell. It could be held in the hand, and he thought I might like to use it during the term. I thanked him, but now that it was time to call school into session, my nerves were so jangled, I wondered how I could stand the bell's clanging. I picked it up, feeling like a man headed for the block to have his head chopped off.

Lifting it high, I gave it all I had.

What a boisterous rush! Soon the loose, squeaky, carved-up seats were filled with squirming boys and girls.

Defeat or victory? It had to be one or the other, and this was the crucial moment. Beads of sweat stood on my face, while my body was covered with goose flesh.

Just why I stood beside the stove with the wooden leg was mystery. Perhaps I felt a certain kinship because of its precarious condition. I became keenly aware of the sound from Cape Hatteras Sea, because of the oppressive silence. The youngsters were as aware of this moment as I was.

How should I begin?

What would be the right words?

Or should I give up before I start?

As I stood there, trembling and miserable, trying to put up a brave front, something like a miracle happened. It took possession of me and held me in its grip, and I no longer saw the stove with the wooden leg, the shattered glass on the floor, the ragged bits of blackboard, or the spitballs on the loft.

I saw the children!

And never had I seen such an eager, bright-eyed bunch. They were wonderful! All were clean and neat. The girls were beautiful, and the boys handsome.

I thought of the little beginner who approached me just before I got enough courage to ring the bell. Her blue eyes danced. "Mr. Green, honey, I'm big enough to go to school."

She acted as though this was the greatest experience of her life.

Also, before me sat the energetic, inquisitive, and daring youth that could either build up or tear down our democracy. Here was young America! The type and amount of education they received would depend on me; it was my responsibility, and the power that was mine, charged me with a new energy. If I lost control for one minute, the youth potential would explode. Their looks challenged me. *Here we are! What are you going to do about it?*

Love crowded out my fear, and desire to do something for them burned within me.

Have you ever put up an honest -to-goodness fight for what you believed to be good and noble?

Have you ever dared to go all out for what you believed was right?

Have you ever worked and sacrificed to do something for some youngster you loved?

If you have, you know the incident that happened to me that first day was beyond explaining. I saw the children as wholesome, worthwhile future adults, and I determined that I would fight to get them educated.

And with the sublimation of self came a overwhelming desire to be of service. Thus, another miracle happened - I was no longer Stanley Green, too young and immature to be a principal. Instead, I became a leader; a hero in my own eyes.

I am not able to remember all I said that morning, but I do know that ideas flooded my mind which had not occurred to me before then. All that was noble and inspiring, the ideals that had always been impressed upon me returned then, begging for expression. Actually, it was those persons who had worked so hard to teach me the important values of life, who spoke through me. The boys and girls of Kinnakeet were not listening to one teacher, but to the many who had been inspired and moved by knowledge.

I began in a soft, firm tone.

"For many years I have worked toward this moment, but if anyone told me I would see this, I wouldn't have believed it. I cannot read people's minds, nor tell their character by looking at them, but your expressions convince me that you are the most ambitious group I have ever known."

Walking to the other side of the rusty stove, I talked slightly louder, telling them it was great to have ambition, for it inspired one to fight for what he wanted, although it was not the fighting itself that was important. It was what one fought for that made the struggle worthwhile. "Therein lies the difference between mediocrity and greatness. Some men let their ambition destroy them instead of using it to make them noble."

Their silence was encouraging.

"I believe this morning as truly as I am standing here, that you have everything it takes for a good fight. In your veins flows the blood of some of the most courageous, and ambitious men who ever lived on earth: your forefathers. They fought an heroic battle crossing the wild Atlantic in frail ships, to found a better world. After a long and treacherous voyage, they climaxed their fight in the roaring, destructive water of a Cape Hatteras Sea. The more daring fought their way ashore, and had it not been for their courage, you would not be here today. It stands to reason that you must have inherited that ambition and the question is, what will you do with it?"

I mentioned they had an opportunity to fight for a good education: once that made life worth living, stirring the soul of man. Also, education would deny the forces in the world which would eventually destroy our democratic way of life.

"Many of our great traditions are at stake. Philosophers overseas are becoming monsters, who, eventually, will reach out over the distance dividing us, to destroy our way of life."

I had their complete attention now, putting all I had into my speech.

"Every human has the right to live and drink deeply from the fountains of life. A man who never puts up a good fight realizes nothing, for he must have knowledge, and the more he has, the more he will fight for what he believes."

They might feel they belonged to an isolated world, but never had I felt so close to all humanity as I did now. "From this very room, the whole world parades before us. Only a few miles from here is the greatest highway on earth. All you have to do is open your eyes and look at the ships manned by every creed and color on this great waterway. The route on the outskirts of Cape

Hatteras leads to South America. Also, it connects the north and south, and the east and west, because many ships go through the Panama Canal, then head for the Orient. Never think of yourselves as being isolated!

"Every time your eyes look over the mighty Atlantic, you see a body of water leading in all directions. You are young, ambitious, healthy, and your blood contains a great heritage. Tell me where there are others with the fighting spirit of your ancestors? Seafaring men everywhere are familiar with the word Hatteras, and your ancestors who landed here from the wrecked ships, came not from one country, but from many."

I reminded the youngsters that they were standing at the crossroads since time and tide waited for no man. They would soon be coming up to bat, and what would their battering average be?

No man was spared having to fight during his life. How would he do it--what would he fight for?

I paused, noticing the pile of switches. I had forgotten about them! Pulling out the biggest one, the room remained absolutely silent as I held it up, scrutinizing it carefully. Next, I broke it across my knee, cramming the pieces into the old stove beside the paper and rags. Then I grabbed the remainder and pitched them out a window.

"I refuse to fight you, but if you try to force me, I will walk out that door and take the next boat out. My business here is to help you. I want to fight, all right, but not alone, which is no fun.   Now we are at the crossroads of an unknown destiny. If the future of our country is to be good, somebody will have to put up many good fights. Your generation must realize that America is increasingly becoming a more dynamic part of the world. If you would like to know what real living is, and how it feels to be an intelligent person, then you must fight for it.

"If you are ready to fight hard, a good place to begin is on the issue of a school of which Avon can be proud. It depends on you, for the students make the school. They can tear it down or build it up; degrade it or ennoble it in the eyes of the public. No group has greater influence on the public than the student body and I would like the privilege of helping build an accredited high school here. One is a *must!*"

"We've got to work together or not at all. I know nothing of the Cape Hatteras Sea, but I am eager to learn, and you can teach me about it. Through my educational experiences, I know I can teach you about the world. I am not one to make hurried decisions, so I'll give you until nine o'clock tomorrow to think over what I have said and draw your own conclusions."

I was still sweating, but my perspiration was no longer caused by fear, but from my efforts which were victorious, at least for the moment. During this hour, I had held my ground, but since the tide of battle could still change, I picked up the ship's bell, announcing, "Tomorrow, everyone who plans to aid me in building a high school, please bring notebooks and pencils. We'll improvise until our textbooks arrive."

I instructed them to hand me their names and grade as they left, then rang the bell vigorously.

A stir in the other rooms told me the others were going out into the yard. Yet my students sat and stared at me.

"You are free to go for the rest of the day," I repeated.

They got up and slowly walked outside.

What I was alone, I measured the blackboard size, although I had no replacement, and counted the broken window panes; then I left feeling much better than when I first learned a week before, that I was hired.

I made out the order for textbooks that night and saw that it was mailed.

CHAPTER 5

MILTON

Although it was inevitable that I should be relieved that the brief hour of school had left me in control, I did not, for a moment, try to delude myself that this was the end of the struggle.

It could be considered the first skirmish, and there could be no lessening of alertness or relaxation on my part.

With no supplies other than pencils, paper and notebooks, it was necessary that I assign lessons "out of my head." This, along with daily lectures and opportunities for the students to express themselves, made up our school days.

Handicapped as we were, we did surprisingly well. The students accepted me, temporarily at least, and appeared interested in their studies, as well as my suggestion that the new school building was largely up to them.

For now, until a blackboard and textbooks arrived, I was satisfied to postpone the campaign for a new school. I had managed to get our present one cleaned and disinfected so it was more tolerable.

The first month had not yet ended, and already I realized that as a new teacher I had to learn as much as the students, though of a different nature. Four years of college cannot impress this on a student preparing himself in the education field, as much as four weeks in a place like Kinnakeet.

Teachers have problems with teen-agers because they are weighted down with so many personal problems. It is a time for all sorts of problems, especially emotional ones.

Probably there was no greater task for one guiding this age group than of helping it adjust to a turbulent world.

My first three weeks at Kinnakeet went off without great incident, but on Monday of the fourth week, shortly after my arrival at school, I began to get a hint that something unusual had happened. It was obvious from the faces of the students, although they tried to pretend there was nothing wrong.

The high school students appeared to be more distressed than those in the lower grades. Late arrivals would listen to whispered confidences, their young faces registering anxiety.

I was going to have a problem, no doubt about that! How I longed to ask why they were so subdued and mysterious. Had some great tragedy come to town, or was a hurricane headed this way?

This was not it, of course. One needn't be secretive about anything of this sort, rather it was an incident the students had no intention of revealing.

What convinced me more than anything else that they were completely absorbed in the mystery was the fact that we had a new blackboard this morning, and not one of them noticed it!

It was sent by the County Board of Education, arriving the previous evening and installed immediately. Ordinarily it would have been the focal point of interest, for the room scarcely looked the same.

When I went for the bell to ring, students were paired off in groups, and I was sure that everyone was discussing the same thing.

The old bell sounded unnecessarily loud, as they took their seats. Algebra was the first class. I had been dictating their problems which they wrote down in notebooks. This morning, their problems were on the beautiful new blackboard; I had chalked them up as soon as I arrived. As they took their seats, I added one more, then turned to face the students.

And there was the secret, sitting in front of me! Oh, why was it one of my choice students? Milton Meekins, son of Fields Meekins, Superintendent of the Methodist Sunday school, and member of the Board of Education, was very obviously under the influence of liquor.

The lad was managing to sit at his desk, but it was only through sheer will power that he kept from rolling onto the floor. His face was as pale as death, with eyes twitching as he breathed irregularly.

I rushed to him. "Are you sick?"

He nodded.

"How long have you been like this?"

He mumbled since early that morning.

"Why did you bother to come to school?"

The boy mumbled he thought he'd be cured if he came to school.

"But you're not," I stated the obvious.

"Worse," he said thickly.

The fact that he was terribly nauseated was most evident, and I looked around helplessly, not sure what to do. He began talking again, but his slurred words were not intelligible. Finally, I decided he was begging me not to tell his father.

As I looked around at his classmates, there was unmistakable pleading in their eyes. *No, Mr. Green, please don't tell his father.*

My mind conjured up the stern-visaged Fields Meekins my first Sunday morning in Kinnakeet, when he stopped by my boarding house, commanding I attend church.

For only a moment I hesitated, then I walked to the blackboard, saying, "Isn't that really something?"

My action was rewarded with grateful smiles - from all but Milton, who stared dumbly before him.

"Let's celebrate - will three of you volunteer to go up to the board and write some work on it?"

Two of the students quickly responded, but I waited for a third while the students regarded each other. Then, to my surprise, Milton arose from his seat and wobbled to the blackboard, standing near the first two volunteers.

I dictated a problem to the first boy, then to the second one, while Milton bravely lifted his right hand holding the chalk, but before I could dictate the problem, he began to vomit all over our new blackboard. Finally, he dazedly tried to get outdoors, but gave up collapsing to the floor.

The boys at the blackboard were joined by others who cleaned the board, floor, and Milton as best they could.

There was an overwhelming stench of alcohol which permeated every crevice of the classroom. If there had been any doubt about what ailed Milton, it was over now - he was stinking drunk! The students had known this when they came to school, and now that it was over, the tension on their faces disappeared, and they settled down to work. Milton, who felt much better, sat quietly at his desk and said nothing.

It was usual for everyone to go home at noon, since they lived nearby, and there was an hour for lunch. When the bell rang, everyone rushed out but Milton. I saw a few boys lingering outside, curious as to what would happen to him, but

I stepped outside and asked them to leave, which they did at once.

This was my own private test!

The time had come to settle my first big problem. If I failed, the battle would be lost. Humbly, I reminded myself that I lacked the years of experience which bring wisdom. But then, it was not so long ago when I was Milton's age! Surely this was in my favor, because I had more sympathy for him.

At least, I had made a decision. Right or wrong, I had to do my best.

Milton rose and we met in the doorway. He breathed normally now and the color had returned to his face. He was too embarrassed to meet my eyes, and looked out towards Pamlico Sound, then at the marsh covered with myrtle, yeopon and water bushes. Not far from us, cows stood here serenely chewing their cud.

"If you won't tell my father -" the boy began.

"Right now, this is our problem. If we can settle it, so as I am concerned, it will be ended here!"

He did not see how *we* could settle it.

"Like men," I told him succinctly.

My first question was, "What made you sick this morning?"

"Whiskey!"

"When did you drink it?"

"On my way to school."

"Where did you get it?"

He gave me a quick look; he had found it on his way to school.

"Where?" I pursued.

"In some water bushes along the road."

"Have you ever been drunk before?"

"No!"

"Then why did you drink this morning?"

"I wanted to see what it was like."

"You mean to say you were just walking down the road, saw a bottle of whiskey, and suddenly decided to drink it?"

He said, "Yes, sir!"

"If you and I are going to settle this between us, Milton, I must have the truth." I mentioned that whatever he said was confidential.

"You won't tell my father?"

"I told you, it depends on whether or not we can settle this ourselves."

His lips began trembling, and I could see suspicion in his eyes.

"What you say to me goes no further."

In a small voice, he said he'd answer whatever I wanted to know.

"Who sold you the whiskey?"

"Nobody, believe me, nobody."

"Who gave it to you?"

He stared at me dumbly.

I repeated the question.

"Please don't make me tell you that."

"Someone did give it to you?"

He nodded.

"Did you ask for it?"

"No!" His tone was emphatic.

"Then why was it given to you?"

"They wanted to have some fun by getting me drunk."

"Why? They knew you were on your way to school."

"They wanted to see what the teacher would do about it."
So that was it!

"Did they make a bet with you that you wouldn't do it?"

"That's right!"

"Now, before I state my verdict, I'm going to give you a chance to plead your own case."

"Mr. Green, to tell you the truth, I don't really know why I did it. It sounds crazy, but that's how it is. They dared me and I did it. If you won't tell my father, I won't ever make any trouble again. Please tell me what my punishment is, and let me get home before they wonder what's keeping me."

"Hurry along," I told him. "We'll settle this after school today."

When we found ourselves the only ones in the building that afternoon, I walked up to him, saying, "You've made me a promise, and I've made a promise. We have an agreement with each other, and it is truly my belief that both our promises will be kept." I offered him my hand and he shook it firmly. "Go now, and all I ask for you is to remember our mutual promises."

Without a word Milton turned and left the room.

As I locked the building and trudged forward, I remembered an afternoon in September when the woman fondly known as "Miss Omie" kept me in to give me advice. I had not been impressed with it then, but now it returned to me so strongly, I wondered just how much of my wisdom in handling Milton had been prompted by this kind woman.

It has been unusually hot that day, and when the school was finished, all I could think of was getting to Mrs. Keaton's and having a drink of water. There was none available at the school because our surface pump near the building was out of order.

"Miss Omie," actually Mrs. Omie Meekins, lived near the schoolyard, and as I hurried past, she called to me. Because of my thirst, I hesitated.

She mentioned the water - if I could arrange for someone to fetch her water, we were welcome to it for school use.

I thanked her.

Then I realized she had another motive in hailing me. "I hope you won't think I'm interfering, but you look so young, and your job is so big, I want to tell you to guard the fighting spirit within you, Mr. Green. You must be determined never to give up."

I nodded, my throat too dry to speak.

"You probably know there is a religious conflict here, with considerable talk about the churches. You'll hear much from both sides - some of it true, some false.

"But you can't afford to be taking sides. Be a good listener and keep it all to yourself. Kinnakeet needs someone like that, and you're the logical one." She looked at me sharply. "Young man, that applies to individuals. Treat them *individually* and they'll worship you for it. Embarrass them in public, and they'll despise you! And remember, let all these things be confidential. Think about this and come to your own conclusions before you condemn me for being just a bossy old woman."

I had long since passed her house earlier this afternoon, hurrying along toward Dog Ridge and my comfortable accommodations at Mrs. Keaton's, but I recognized it had been her sound counseling which had influenced me in dealing with my first big school problem.

"Thank you, Miss Omie," I said aloud.

CHAPTER 6

NO HIGHWAYS

More and more as the days passed, I was learning, but much of my new-found knowledge could be readily classified as unbelievable!

The matter of drinking water was one example. The lack of it at school was a great drawback, even though "Miss Omie" offered us hers for the taking. Since all of us did go home at noontime, it was not as though we spent the entire school day without water.

But a major revelation was that the drinking water in the home was rain water, caught during each storm and stored in oaken barrels.

No less startling to me was the fact that Hatteras Island was without roads when I arrived there in 1930. That is to say, there were no highways or roads maintained by means of public taxes. Because of this, nobody was required to have a car tag unless he drove his car to another vicinity where there were public roads.

There was no shortage of cars and trucks on this sandy island populated by two thousand people, and somehow the sturdy seamen managed to negotiate their vehicles. It took some doing!

The occasional streaks of grass made such places difficult to maneuver. Folks traveled by the moon, too. During decent weather, along the ocean's wash at low tide, driving conditions were anywhere from good to excellent. Just as the tides were ruled by the moon, so was the driving of a motor vehicle.

When it was high tide, or poor weather conditions at low tide, one had to drive through the soft sand in places, or not at all. When driving on the "inside," that is, not in the wash, dry weather was the worst possible time, because the sand was loose. It was a peculiar fact that travel was better on the island in wet weather than dry.

Gradually I was able to compile a list of observations regarding the males who had to drive away from the wash in dry weather.

First, driving under such conditions developed powerful muscles in the arms, legs and back. The drivers had to get out of their cars and onto their hands and knees, scratching away the sand with a piece of debris from the beach. This could happen several times within a few miles, and their nonchalance stunned me at first. Many of them had never left home, and were unfamiliar with highways and decent public roads. They accepted these inconveniences as a way of life. To them, the world was made of sand and water, while the salt was in their blood.

The second advantage of driving on a dry, sandy beach was the resulting patience of those involved. It was a deep, enduring patience that evolved, because its alternative was that of becoming a complete nervous wreck.

I felt that the third result of driving in the sand was much more important than the first two put together. It was the feeling of human kindness, which was something that didn't merely show on the face, or in the heart. It was a credo put into action! During all my years on the island, I never knew of anyone being passed by who was having car trouble, in dry sand or elsewhere. A helping hand was always there, and I was willing to bet such a record could not be bettered elsewhere.

Before I had become accustomed to no highways, one of my students told me about her first ride on a highway during a visit away from the Outer Banks.

"I never had such excitement," she began.

"You mean it was good?"

She said she couldn't imagine how a highway looked until she had actually seen one.

"But surely you had seen pictures of them?"

She had, but they looked nothing like the real thing. Anyway, it was not the looks, but the experience that mattered!

Sincerely wanting to know her exact reaction, I asked how it was different from riding along the open beach.

Her hands emphasized her points as she said, "It was so *smooth* - no bumps. We went so fast, while cars came toward us just as fast, and passing so close."

How could these people and I both be native of North Carolina, I wondered. My geology professor, Dr. Collier Cobb, who had mentioned these islands off the coast, called them "the foreign land at home," and I was beginning to understand why.

On Friday afternoon during the fifth week of school, I had scarcely arrived at my boarding house when a group of youngsters came by and invited me to accompany them to Hatteras, a village on the south end of the island.

Some of them were my students, quite a number were not, and the fact they had cared enough to include me was a pleasant and reassuring surprise. I lost no time in accepting their twenty-mile trip invitation.

The sun was low in the sky as thirty-six of us piled into six cars, setting forth, with a movie as the evening's goal. I wondered why it was necessary to go so early since the show started at eight. I did not care, particularly, suspecting they had some other plans to utilize the time until eight, which I would learn on the way.

Our six cars spread out all over the beach, each vehicle making its own roadway. They were not going fast.

Twice before reaching the Cape, the car in which I rode, stalled in the sand. All but the driver hopped out, and the car was able to thrust forward.

Before we reached the forest west of Cape Hatteras, known as Cape woods, the sun had dropped below a smooth Pamlico Sound. Scattered clouds in the sky caught the sun's reflections and the west was a riot of gorgeous color.

It was my first experience in the Cape woods, and I was amazed that palmetto palms grew in North Carolina. There were huge oaks, too, and stately, long-leafed pines intermingled with myrtle, yeopon, cedar and dogwood. The scene was so beautiful, I forgot about the lack of public roads until we came out on the opposite end of the woods. In no time, three of our cars bogged down in the soft sand. I was a passenger in one car; everybody got out, but it did no good.

"Got to scratch out," one boy called, whereupon the occupants of the mired cars dropped to their knees and scratched frantically around the wheels.

Not wanting to shirk my part, I got busy too, promptly slashing my hand on a piece of oyster shell. I wrapped my handkerchief around it and got back to work, and it was not long until we were merrily on our way again.

Three more times before reaching Hatteras, we stuck in the sand, but the drivers were able to pull out without "scratching."

It was fifteen minutes before eight o'clock when we reached the movie theatre.

After the movie, we sauntered into a nearby store where everybody had soft drinks, cookies, fruits or candy as their appetites dictated, and it was exactly eleven o'clock when we finally started north to Kinnakeet.

It was a gorgeous night! The few clouds at sunset had disappeared and there was a caressing quality to the air, as a half moon shone in the eastern sky. It was high tide, so we couldn't possibly drive in the wash. Back we headed through the loose sand!

This time, as the motorcade neared the place we had to scratch out, they gave it all the gas they could, determined to sail through this time, or else. For two of the cars, it was "or else," but I was in a car that made it.

The stalled drivers tried to race their engines, but the spinning wheels on one got two blowouts, and the other one, as a result.

"How many spare tired we got among us?" somebody wanted to know, A survey showed we had none. So now, the two cars were not only stuck, but were without tires.

Luckily, a few cars not belonging to our caravan made it through the soft sand, promptly coming to a halt on solid ground. The drivers tumbled out, and hurried toward us.

One car was from Buxton, called The Cape by the natives, while the other was from Rodanthe, on the north end of the island, called Chicamacomico locally. Not one of these strangers abandoned us or complained about the delay until both cars were scratched out of the sand, placed on hard ground, their tires patched, and ready to roll.

Never before had I witnessed such cooperation and humane consideration!

Even the girls in the group contributed by getting together and singing, "Carolina Moon, Keep Shining." It was a treat to hear - no wonder the boys worked with a will!

When we were on our way once more, I asked, "How do you get to Hatteras when the weather is windy or rainy?"

"Kinnakeeters don't go to Hatteras when the weather is bad," they chorused. All the more, I could appreciate what this evening's fun had meant to them.

From the Cape woods on the return trip, our cars went to the open wash of the Cape Hatteras Sea. Heading north right at the ocean's edge was the most exciting part of the jaunt, and how we sped along! In no time at all, I got out at Mrs. Keaton's, trying to tell the youngsters what a wonderful evening I had.

Mrs. Keaton catered to transients as well as regular guests, and it was the following Monday evening, that I accepted an invitation from a salesman spending the night, to accompany him on a business trip to Buxton. We went south on the wash again. The tide was really too high, but he went anyway. Several times, I thought we'd plunge into the ocean, but I hung on and said nothing.

His business appointment was soon finished and we started north towards Kinnakeet. Now, the wind had risen, and even this daredevil would not try the wash.

On the beach, near Big Kinnakeet Coast Guard Station, we got stuck in the sand. We scratched sand to no avail, until finally my companion got into the car and started the motor while I pushed.

The endurance and strength of the local males were not due entirely to their vigorous life as fishermen. The endless pushing of cars had contributed to their muscles. However, my arms ached unmercifully, and my breath came in gasps.

Just as I was ready to collapse, I heard the sound of a Coast Guard truck, and two coast guardsmen jumped out and pushed. In seconds, we were freed.

"How did they know we were on the beach?" I asked the salesman.

He guessed the lookout in the watchtower saw us and reported it. Also there was never any charge for the service.

"Well, I think it's a shame there aren't any roads on Hatteras Island."

After hesitating, he said, "I've been coming down the Banks for fifteen years, and I figure it's a blessing."

His answer annoyed me, then - not now. I argued that cars were needed here, because the water on the Sound was too shallow for transportation. While on the east, the Cape Hatteras Sea was too treacherous for a harbor.

He nodded agreement. Looking at it from a standpoint of development and convenience, they did need roads. However, he was looking at the Kinnakeeters themselves. The sharing of troubles, and the willingness of the natives to give of themselves was a tribute to the adage, "love thy neighbor as thyself."

"It's as simple as that. Hardships and isolation make for strong characteristics that get diluted in more sophisticated places. You're new here. Start sitting around in Gibbs Store, and observe the Kinnakeeters. You have to look deeper than their faces, and really study them. Do it, Green, and you will see what I mean, that the lack of roads is a blessing."

All that week, I found myself thinking of what the salesman said, and the next Saturday morning, I did go to Gibb's and perched on the counter. This was the big shopping day in Kinnakeet. The *Daily Advance* from Elizabeth City lay there and I pretended to read it, but instead I watched the people.

It was moderately cold and there was a small fire burning in the coal stove. Gibb was seated where he could gaze into it. The fire and his tobacco chewing engrossed him completely.

When a customer entered, he would cheerfully say, "Good morning," while the Kinnakeeter would wander about the store waiting on himself. I had not been there long when a woman entered, going behind the counter, and rummaging through the yard goods. After deciding what she wanted, she cut from three bolts, measuring carefully. Next, she folded the loose end back against the bolt, and stacked it neatly, as it was before she made her selections.

"How much is a yard?" she called, holding up her purchase.

Gibb told her, and she figured the amount on a scrap of paper. Then she entered it in an account book he kept for that purpose.

She had to be a relative, I reasoned. But if this were so, why didn't she forget the charge?

A fisherman came in, weighed some sugar, picked up about a dozen canned goods, and was able to figure the price of all but one can. He held it up for Gibb's inspection, and going to the cash register, put in a ten dollar bill, took his change, picked up his purchases and left.

Meanwhile, Gibb still chewed and studied the fire.

Next, a boy in his teens rushed in, "I just put three gallons of gas in my car," said he, dropping the correct amount in Gibb's hand, he hurried out.

I spent the morning there, and by twelve o'clock, I knew what the salesman meant. When the folks have common hardships, and each feels obligated to help his neighbor, whether it concerns loose sand, hurricanes, or ordinary sickness, he learns the true meaning of loving his neighbor as he does himself.

Their philosophy was similar to that of an Outer Banks man who was queried about the whys and wherefores of the frequent hurricanes. He quoted from the eighth verse, third chapter of St. John. "The wind bloweth where it listeth."

The life of the Kinnakeeter was one of acceptance and enduring patience. And I, for one, found myself loving them for these qualities.

CHAPTER 7

YEOPON

Lizzie Price, with whom I talked that first Sunday in Avon, was the first person to speak of yeopon to me, or rather, I asked what the shrub was with the glossy green leaves and red berries.

She had been to Raleigh, having taken a business course there. The fact she knew another section of her home state gave her an enlightened perspective.

Yeopon, she said, was also spelled *yeowpon*. It was a species of holly, but I shouldn't ask about it of any Kinnakeeter. They had their peculiarities, and queries from outsiders about it was one.

Quickly, my kind, new friend changed the subject, leading me a short distance onward, into an ancient cemetery. Here were human bones, bleached and weathered because the winds had blown away the sand covering the graves.

"We don't bury on the open beach anymore; these are the remains of ancient burials." Nowadays, they choose a high sandhill, or bury their dead right in their own yards.

The stones in the graveyard were so eroded, many inscriptions were no longer readable. I did make out the name Pharaoh Farrow, and the tombstone next to it, marked the resting place of his wife, aged eleven years and eleven months.

As I was about to exclaim over this, Lizzie said, "He was a notorious early pirate of the Outer Banks."

This area, it seemed, was the world headquarters for pirates. Several hundred years ago, they found refuge in that isolated place, and buried their gold and other treasure in these very sandhills. Much of it presumably was never found.

"But what about Pharaoh Farrow," I reminded her.

She frowned. Many folks living here were naturally his descendants, so again, I was not to prod about him. I was an outsider, and although he was one of the worst, he was a native of the locality.

It was rumored he used shipwrecked men as slaves, and that he once beat a slave to death in a fit of temper.

Pharaoh's great love was for gold, and he kept robbing ships until he acquired a great chest of gold nuggets. He was so adamant that none would take it away from him, that he blindfolded a slave, making him carry the chest to a secret burial place. Pharaoh died suddenly, and the hunt began, with everyone digging for the chest.

My curiosity about this colorful character had been somewhat satisfied, but not regarding the yeopon. It was strange that it was considered bad etiquette and maybe a bit dangerous, to ask about it.

During the second week of school, I overheard the children talking, and one boy exclaimed to a little girl, "You've been drinking too much yeopon!"

Instantly, a silence fell as they studied my reaction. I pretended hearing nothing unusual, but the remark only whetted my desire to unravel the mystery.

How could yeopon be drunk? What were its aftereffects? Could it influence the brain?

It was when Gibb's store had become a popular hangout for me that I heard it mentioned again. Having sat for hours with my legs dangling over the counter, I barely jumped down and was gazing out the front window when the men in the store began talking about yeopon. I had not caught what they said, but suddenly they became silent all looking at me.

Gibb said, "Do you know anything about yeopon, Mr. Green?"

"No, I don't."

The men looked silently at each other, and becoming aware that I was an intruder, I quietly walked onto the porch, down the steps, and headed back to my room.

Another day, as I was writing science questions in a notebook at school, I heard a group of high school boys outside mention the word. Usually there was much laughter in the schoolyard, but when I glanced out, their young faces were very serious.

Suddenly their voices became angry and one boy yelled, "You just let him throw that word at me, and I'll knock his teeth down his throat."

Another said, "Hell, Joe came near doing the same thing. Thought he was goin' to kill 'im."

And still another voice, "How did this fellow know anything about yeopon? Never been on the island before, was he?"

The first boy presumed somebody had bet him he wouldn't do it. Besides, he must have had several drinks in him.

A girl standing on the porch yelled, "But he didn't know anything about yeopon! Besides, some of the Capers put him up to it."

At least, I consoled myself, I did know that a Caper was a resident of Buxton.

A boy commented, "He'll know better next time when he finds out we won't take that from anybody. If he ever tried it again, he won't be able to another time."

I rang my ancient ship's bell, and not another word was said about yeopon, at least, that I heard. I did observe one of the boys who had entered the conversation was nursing a black eye, so there must have been a fight the previous night.

Yeopon occupied my mind throughout the day - how could it be otherwise when I merely looked out the window and saw sandhills covered with it? In fact, a bush grew so close to the building its branches swept against the pane when a strong wind blew from the northeast.

It was only a few days later as I passed through the village just before sundown. Some old women were cutting branches from yeopon bushes on the very path I walked on

Glancing up, they saw me while I was about two hundred feet away. They ran behind the bushes and when I reached the spot they had been, they had disappeared.

This mystery, whatever it was, must have gone on for centuries, but I couldn't understand why I had never heard of it before.

The following Thursday evening, six travelling salesmen were guests at Mrs. Keaton's. After supper, we sat chatting in the living room and one asked how school was progressing, and when I thought the new building might get under way.

After answering him as best I could, he leaned close, and whispered, "Know anything about yeopon?"

Shrugging, I bantered, "Should I?" Considering my gnawing curiosity, I was pleased with my indifferent attitude.

"Don't ask questions about it, not until you know these people better," He surveyed me. "Green, from what I hear, they like you. Don't go spoiling it by acting nosy."

This was getting disgusting. "Suppose I did, what would happen to me?"

He hitched his chair close. "I'll give you an example - fairly recently an Avon man was in Norfolk, Virginia, walking down Granby Street, when two fellows from Norfolk, recognized him as being from Avon. One dared the other to as him about yeopon.

"'Hey, fellow,' the darer stopped the man, 'Got any yeopon?'"

Instantly, he lay sprawled on the sidewalk, out cold, while the Avon man walked stiffly down the street without a backward glance.

I had a feeling the salesman might have told me a few enlightening things, but just then some girls entered looking for Mrs. Keaton, and the other salesmen gathered around while the opportune moment passed.

From then on I thought about yeopon until I was sick of the subject, but the greater I fought to expel it from my mind, the firmer it became entrenched.

Soon afterwards, when I had come from school one evening, tired and discouraged, Mrs. Keaton invited me into the kitchen to visit her and her son Bill while they cooked supper. Bill was creating his unbelievable potato salad again, while his mother was stuffing a wild Canadian goose with oyster dressing.

We talked casually for awhile, and she told me of various sportsmen who had come down to hunt and fish. They spoke emphatically of how good looking our young folks were.

"Haven't I said the same thing?"

She nodded, "And you say they learn fast, too."

Bill mentioned proudly, in spite of poor schools or none at all, there were only two folks in Kinnakeet who were illiterate.

Mrs. Keaton popped the goose into the hot oven while pushing a stray lock of hair from her forehead. "How'd we get off the subject; I called Mr. Green in, for just one purpose."

I looked at her, surprised.

Bill said, "I bet ye're going to tell him about yeopon."

Mrs. Keaton noticed my startled reaction, and asked, "You've heard about it?"

"All I've heard is that I shouldn't hear about it," I told her disgustedly.

"You never tried to find out?" Bill inquired.

"Never!"

His mother said, "Good!" She gazed out the window, "You're not a Kinnakeeter, and it won't be easy making you understand. You'll have to keep an open mind about it."

"I promise!"

"If I can make you understand why we feel so vehement about yeopon, I'll have done something that's never been done before."

I didn't comment, wondering if I could restrain myself until she got around to disclosing the secret.

According to her understanding, there was no place on earth as suited to the plant's growth as Hatteras Island.

For hundreds of years before the white man came, the Hatteras Indians became renowned for the tea they brewed from yeopon. And the natives came from great distances to partake of it. Tribes made annual journeys from the backcountry for this purpose.

"Tea!" I exclaimed. That partly explained the conversation I heard on the schoolyard. "Do you folks like it?"

"It is a favorite Kinnakeeter drink."

"What does it taste like?"

"Bill, pour him a cup."

I couldn't believe I was actually going to drink some of it!

I took a swallow and almost strangled. How could anyone drink it?

Mrs. Keaton and Bill laughed, "You'll learn to enjoy it if you stay around long enough," Bill predicted.

Mrs. Keaton continued telling about the Indians who attended the yeopon party. They believed the tea to be a great health builder and, after arriving, would remain for weeks, drinking so much yeopon, they ended up in a stupor.

"I still don't see why it's so mysterious," I prompted Mrs. Keaton, while staring belligerently at the cup which sat before me.

"The background is necessary because you're a stranger," she opened the oven door to check on the bubbling goose. To her there was no mystery, she was proud to be a Kinnakeeter and felt the way they all did about yeopon. People on the mainland, thought it was extremely foolish, but that was only because they had a narrow outlook.

"I'm sure I'll understand."

"Well, I'm taking so long, because I can't decide if you are merely curious, or if you sincerely want to know."

I had to admit I was curious, but it did go deeper than that. I felt I should know; that it was essential to my understanding of these people.

Mrs. Keaton was glad to hear this.

Back in the early days, tea was not found in the American colonies. The colonists needed tea, and searched the forests for an herb to make a refreshing drink.

Since the Indians had been drinking yeopon for hundreds of years, it was inevitable that the French and British colonists would not become familiar with the yeopon found on Cape Hatteras Island. It did, in fact, rapidly become quite an important industry.

For a time, Kinnakeet yeopon was famous up and down the east coast. Hundreds of acres were covered with the shrub. The small branches and leaves were chopped and dried. The more that was cut, the more abundantly it grew.

Mrs. Keaton said it was there for the taking, and folks made money that way. They salted fish, trading it for corn before, but now the curing of yeopon surpassed this as a moneymaking enterprise.

"There's a reason for everything," said Mrs. Keaton, "and that's why a Kinnakeeter won't stand for abusive talk about yeopon. It shouldn't be like that. If folks understood, it would be a compliment to a Kinnakeeter, not a disgrace."

It was time to check the goose again, and I sat impatiently. The plant was beautiful, and the natives enjoyed tea made from it, and if it brought money and fame, there were only blessings surrounding it. *Why, then, is the Kinnakeeter angry?*

Wiping her fingers on her apron, Mrs. Keaton sat down. "We don't mind folks asking about yeopon, if it's done respectfully. Outsiders use the word as an insult. You revere the flag?"

"Naturally," I told her.

"If anybody was to insult it, you'd be angry."

"Of course."

"You don't feel it's ridiculous to be so emotional about it?"

"I wouldn't have it any other way."

"Let's start from there. You will agree that it was not the flag itself that caused you to ge angry, but rather what flag stood for. It symbolizes the people of the United States of America. Now do you have a high regard for Americans because they represent the flag, for what it represents, or do you think that's silly?"

"Of course it's not silly!"

"Would you respect a man who fought for what the flag symbolized, as long as there was a breath in him?"

I nodded.

"Then you would respect a Kinnakeeter who would do the same thing when anyone maligned the word *yeopon*. We furnished most of the tea in early America. It was an industry that included men, women and children, and the word was synonymous with Kinnakeeters and everything good and noble. Up and down the coast, folks never thought of Kinnakeet without thinking of yeopon. It was an honor, and they were proud."

Bill quietly occupied himself in the neat kitchen, preparing food for the huge table which would be groaning in a little while. Mrs. Keaton leaned back against her straight chair, with one capable arm resting on her work table.

It had all started back in the year 1801. Uncle Edward Scarborough was one of the most loved men who had ever lived. He stood for everything good, and like all Kinnakeeters, he chopped and cured yeopon for commercial purposes.

When a boatload had been prepared, it was taken to market. Thus, the day came when Edward and his son, a lad of

71

about twelve years, took a cargo of yeopon up the Pasquotank River to Elizabeth's Pothouse, near Elizabeth City, tying up at the docks that evening.

It was dark when they arrived at the pothouse, and Mrs. Keaton interrupted herself to point out that Kinnakeeters were also noted for their fighting ability. Oh, not unless they were aroused, but they were handy with their fists if necessary. Probably many men along the coast had been whipped by a Kinnakeeter, which naturally would not add to their popularity.

The pothouse was quite a meeting place, and no doubt Kinnakeeters were as famous there for their fighting ability, as they were for their yeopon.

When the loiterers hanging around the pothouse saw a lone Kinnakeeter accompanied by a small boy, they must have been delighted. They had him outnumbered, making it one time a Kinnakeeter would take a licking from them.

They began to toss insults at Uncle Edward, but he paid no attention. He was a huge man, but was mild of character, and God-fearing, who abided by his religion in his contacts with his fellowmen. It was not easy to anger him.

Then it happened when Uncle Edward saw a dirty fist shaking under his nose. A raucous voice shouted, "You Kinnakeeters ain't nothin' but damned ol' yeopon eaters! You're ignorant! Don't know nothin' but to chop yeopon!"

Uncle Edward must have been very tired after his long trip up the river. However, the man's profanity showed his disrespect for Kinnakeet, and yeopon took on an ugly meaning. The word became synonymous with denigrating the people and the town he loved.

Suddenly, a mighty fist came up and took the man full force. He spun, seeming to float in the thick pothouse air, and his inert body came to rest on the far side of the room!

Uncle Edward casually asked, "The rest of you have anything to say?"

Of course they did not.

He took his son by the hand and marched out.

"Come," he said, "we'll sell our tea elsewhere."

It was the lad who spread the story when they reached home and Uncle Edward became Kinnakeet's hero. All Kinnakeet was insulted and angered, and folks soon learned it was not sensible to throw yeopon at them, unless they were ready to fight.

Determinedly, I took another sip of the cold yeopon tea, restraining a gag.

"Three cheers for the Kinnakeeters," I said.

It was several years after this pleasant evening in Mrs. Keaton's kitchen that I learned who had knocked down the man in Norfolk, Virginia, whom the traveling salesman mentioned. It was Fields Meekins, the Methodist Sunday school superintendent and school board member whose son, Milton, put me to my first test at school.

And it was he who approached me eventually, slapping me heartily on the shoulders. "Brother Green, have you learned to like yeopon?"

Perhaps by then, *tolerate* would have been more accurate than *like*, but I had no intention of arguing.

"Yes sir!" I exclaimed.

"Then here and now, I declare you a full fledged Kinnakeeter by adoption."

He could have said nothing that would have made me happier.

CHAPTER 8

EMOTIONALLY TRAPPED

The knowledge I had recently acquired regarding the mysterious yeopon certainly put a stop to my gnawing curiosity, and also increased my fast-growing respect for Kinnakeeters. I admired people who would fight for their dignity, and for that which gave them their livelihood.

But, fate was determined to give me no chance for peace, and I found my problems mounting. The unfortunate part was the fact it was an inner struggle. On the surface, there was no indication that all was not well - with me and my work.

Glorious autumn was upon us! The hurricane season was over and the pesty mosquitoes had gone. The sky was without clouds and the sea breezes were blandly invigorating. Great flocks of wild fowl clouded the sky in their migration south, and Canadian geese visited in abundance, for our locale was their way station on the Atlantic Flyway.

For the first time in my life, I saw large ripening fig trees. Also, the small home gardens abounded with collard greens, tomatoes and turnips. Mrs. Keaton's garden was second to none in Kinnakeet.

Here was a small world of peace and plenty, even to the succulent black grapes which abounded in the forest and were ours for the picking.

Even Kinnakeet fishermen were having extraordinary luck, getting unusually high prices for their catches.

All this, when the rest of the nation was going through a great depression.

How could I live in such a rosy world and still be unhappy?

I suppose I was just lonely. I was a stranger in a new environment. These people had accepted me, yet I did not really belong. I had come here during their religious conflict and was determined to remain neutral. This actually made me an outcast to either side.

The fact that I had no girl friend affected me because I was young and liked female companionship. Yet I had been subtly warned that the Kinnakeet men tolerated no outsider flirting with their beautiful women. Kinnakeet men were as tough and strong a bunch as they were seaworthy. I knew their hints were true, because the boys at school furtively watched me when the girls gathered around to discuss some school subject, or just talk. My constant vigil against wrong impressions made me self-conscious and nervous.

I even went so far on a rainy Friday evening to ask Mrs. Keaton about a handsome blond giant I saw riding in a truck with other Kinnakeeters. Was he, too, an outsider? She thought she knew him. He was definitely a Kinnakeeter, but serving in the Coast Guard, he had just come home. "A nice boy until he gets to drinking, then he is a jealous, fighting fool!"

"You could say that about most of them," I observed. My eyes watched a half-dozen Canadian geese walking through the tall collards in the garden. I thought how Bill mentioned they coupled off, remaining true to each other forever. I was jealous of them because they were so sure of themselves, and contented with their way of life.

"Leave the girls alone and they won't bother you, although they've quit worrying about you in that respect." She laughed, embarrassedly. "They've decided you have a girl back home, and are speculating on what she looks like and when you will be sending for her."

I made no comment, let them think what they would.

Mrs. Keaton told me about a handsome young principal who had ignored the warnings about the local girls. One night, the boys ganged up on him, recalling his mentioning his fear of graveyards. They blindfolded him, whirled him around until he was dizzy, and carried him to the old cemetery where they tied him to a tombstone, and removed his blindfold. To add to his fright, a heavy electrical storm arose.

This conversation only drove me to harder work at school, but at least my efforts were rewards by seeing a gradual awakening of school spirit, an attempt by the pupils to put forth greater effort.

Slowly, I sensed a conflict between the boys and the girls. As always, this was kept from me, but there was too much grouping together, and too many whispered discussions.

By Friday afternoon, it became clear that something was about to break. During the latter part of the lunch hour, the students stood outside the fence, verbally battling it out. Apparently the girls won, for when they sat down, they looked elated, while the boys appeared defeated.

A girl came to me saying there was a matter which needed discussion.

"Is it that important?"

She said it was, and her young face showed concern and anxiety.

The boys sat sullenly.

"Does the entire class feel a discussion at this time is necessary?" I queried.

Every girl responded affirmatively, while the boys remained silent.

I stood there, reluctant to let a discussion get started because the controversy might get out of control. But what would happen if I quelled it? The alternative struck me as being equally perilous.

"Suppose we take thirty minutes of the last period," I proposed. "That is, if we can concentrate on our work until then."

The boys fell into studying, while the girls struggled to settle down.

I would have spent the entire afternoon trying to guess what the excitement was about, without even touching the matter.

Sharply at a half-hour before dismissal, I waited for whoever would serve as spokesman. The same girl who approached me after lunch said, "It's simply this. Our schoolroom looks worse than a cow barn, and we want to get donations to improve its looks!"

I was flabbergasted!

"At first the boys didn't want any part of it; they still don't, but they've promised to help."

"And a Kinnakeeter keeps his promise," I said stoutly.

One lad spoke up rebelliously, "They want us to do the beggin'. When they want ye to do somethin', you might just as well do it. I hope they never get after you."

The others roared with laughter, and there was a lessening of tension.

"Just what does this begging involve?"

"You walk up to someone and say you want somethin' for the school, then ask how much he'll give."

I had been telling myself all fall it was too soon to hope for a definite commitment on a new school building, and knew it was going to be difficult to get the project rolling. These people were thrifty, and worked hard for a living. Also, with the two religious factions to consider, the new building seemed remote to me.

"How do people react?" I wanted to know.

The boys shrugged, saying, "They'd all react differently. Some will donate a little, while others would only growl."

I decided to ask, "What did you girls have in mind by way of improvement?" I glanced about me without admitting anything they did would improve it.

I was in for a surprise. One girl stood with a paper and pencil, while the others called out items, and not one was for anything frivolous. They wanted a floor mop, floor oil, cleaning cloths, wash pans, soap, paint and brushes. Also, yardage for curtains, and the broken panes replaced. They needed lumber to build me a table and chair. There were certain basics needed - stove polish, and a new pipe for the rickety stove, a coal box, and also if they could acquire a few pictures, they'd be grateful.

"Well," I said, heartily wishing I already had that chair to sink into. Finally, I said we could hardly expect to get all these items, but we might manage some of them.

Still bewildered, and a bit excited, I told Mrs. Keaton what had happened, but she did not act surprised at all. "An old Kinnakeet custom," she explained. "Nobody knows how it started, but folks expect it. Oh, there's always a few who resent being asked, but most folks don't mind at all."

Monday morning, the boys divided into groups and were dismissed about an hour early to start their "begging."

I could scarcely wait until the next morning to see what they had gotten. Without expecting much, I had to admit this new project was just what I needed as therapy for my loneliness.

Never had I found it necessary to do such an about-face as I did that morning. Every item on the list stood before me, and instead of lumber for one table, there was enough for two. And in a corner stood a beautiful begonia plant full of red blossoms, in a dark earthen pot. When I caught my breath, I asked, "How long were you - soliciting?" Somehow the word "beg" sounded much too crude.

"Two hours," answered one, and there was no mistaking the pride which all shared in their success.

The girls were astonished, too, and while excitement was at its peak, we decided to postpone some of our classes and get busy cleaning-up.

It took all that week.

I helped wherever I could, cleaning first with the girls, then with the boys doing general repair work. We removed the spitballs that had studded the loft for years, and the rusty stove was scraped and polished. The pipe was replaced with the new one, and the floor was mopped and oiled. The window panes were replaced, and two small floral pictures hung on the wall. Part of the lumber was made into a small table for me, and the remainder used to repair the porch. Also, somebody donated an old, but adequate, char for me.

But nothing gave us as much trouble as when we replaced the old stovepipe, even though it was too rotten to put up resistance.

The Meekins boy and I were elected to do the job, which appeared simple enough. George was six-feet four and went at it enthusiastically, but we spent two hours getting the joints of the new pope together only to discover it was far too long. Therefore, we had to remove a joint and cut it in half.

But we had done too good a job at putting it together, and the harder we worked to get it apart, the tighter it stuck. By supper time we were desperate. George and I were the only males present, but the girls volunteered to take one section of it, while we grabbed the other. At the count of three, everyone was to pull with all his might. Standing in the middle of the room, I counted.

"One!"

"Two!"

"Three!"

We gave a quick jerk, and it separated with such force that George and I landed in one corner, while the girls lay piled in the opposite one.

I would never give up such an experience where we howled with laughter. The stilted relationship I had tried so hard to maintain melted quickly. If I could not know my female students, socially, at least we could be better pals at school. I had striven to maintain a safe barrier, without actually alienating them. I was sure my attitude would help my nerves and lessen my loneliness.

When we stood back on Friday afternoon, surveying our week's work, I wondered if any of them realized how sorry I was that it was finished. Now only the old carved-up desks remained, and there was nothing we could do about them, other than build a roaring bonfire. In my heart, I sensed that never again would there be another carefree episode, such as this had been. I had loved every minute of it and dreaded Monday, when we returned to our old routine.

CHAPTER 9

AND PHYSICALLY TRAPPED

With the excitement at an end, my need for companionship deepened until it was a thing of torment. I wanted girl friends, just as any other young chap my age, yet I was even more keenly aware of the need to stand apart. One false move, and I was done for. How could a normal young man live like this?

Saturday morning, I went to Gibbs' store for want of something better to do, and because my emotions threatened to conquer my judgement I had to keep busy.

Being their regular shopping day, most people were out, and many stopped to talk with me about the improved schoolroom, or how glad they were about the good job I was doing.

I should have been elated, but today it only made me more aware of my responsibilities, and of the wall that divided us.

One woman said, "And we do appreciate your not bein' girl crazy. First time I saw you, being so young and all, I said you'd never make it, that you'd become crazy about our girls. But bless your heart, honey, you're the nicest thing in Kinnakeet!"

I wanted to scream out that I *was* crazy about her girls, and I detested acting aloof, setting a good example for everybody.

There was malice in my soul, as I spent the afternoon grading papers in my room. After supper, I went into the living room and turned on the radio, but a man's voice spoke of his broken love affairs. Angrily, I shut it off, going outside to walk off my frustration.

I went rapidly in the darkness to the shore of Pamlico Sound, some two hundred yards away. Down here, there'd be privacy, since I was not fit company for anyone tonight.

The sky was partially cloudy, with intermittent patches of stars. The shoreline was scarcely visible, but I could hear the waves sloshing lazily against the sand, and they soothed me. Even the usually acrid odor of rotting seaweed was barely noticeable now, as though nature contrived to give me a pleasant stroll.

About a mile south, I came upon a wide creek which had probably been washed out previously by a hurricane. Just east of where I stood, there was a thick growth of brush and there was no way of telling the depth of the creek. Since my way was checked, I turned to walk back up the shore.

Just north of the creek were three sandhills, shaped like tiny oblong mountains, their peaks probably ten feet high. These were covered with yeopon, myrtle and water bushes, except on their north sides. The sandhills were in a straight row, running parallel to the Sound.

Curious, I climbed the sandhill next to the creek, and even though the other two were between me and Kinnakeet, I could see the village lights.

All that broke the rhythmic sound of the waves were the fish jumping in the creek, and an occasional cry from a sea gull. Here atop this sandhill, I watched the revolving light of the Cape Hatteras lighthouse, and thought of the destructive forces of the Cape Hatteras Sea. How many lives had been saved by this circling beam, and how many thousands were lost regardless of it?

It was good to escape from myself. There was a temptation to remain among the shrubbery all night, but as usual my sense of responsibility dominated. Would the Avon principal condone such a ridiculous escapade? My place was back in my room, and I had better return before this soothing atmosphere got the better of me.

I began working my way through the bushes when car lights sent forth a shaft of light, heading toward Pamlico Sound, and the narrow strip of sand where I was.

Why would a car be coming here this time of night? Or, for that matter, at any time? It was saturated here with bullrushes, cattails, and the usual yeopon and myrtle.

The car came bouncing through the vegetation, and when it struck the soft, dry sand of Pamlico, the wheels began spinning and the vehicle came to a standstill. The more the driver spun the wheels, the deeper they sank.

A voice bellowed, "Hey, you fellers, get outa the car and push."

"You son-of-a-gun, I told you not to drive out here. Sheephead! You wouldn't listen. What did ye expect?"

Three of them got out, though. My eyes made out their vague shadows as they pushed. As quickly as the car was freed, it headed south, toward the hill where I lay hidden on the yeopon bushes. The lights seemed intent on shining right where I was, and I wished heartily I was elsewhere. If they found me skulking here in the middle of the night, no good would come of it.

The car stopped in front of the middle hill, north of where I lay shaking fearfully. The lights went out, and one of them took something from the car. He put a match to it and instantly flared the light of a lantern. Now, I recognized one boy as a student of mine, and the other two were Kinnakeet fishermen. The fourth man stood in the flickering light, and I caught my breath. He was the handsome chap whom Mrs. Keaton had identified for me - the coast guardsman who became bellicose when drinking.

They went to the hill on the north and Joe held the lantern while the others dug through seaweed and bushes. Finally they pulled out one quart jar from the sand; two more followed later. I was sure I was getting my first view of Kinnakeet home brew.

They walked to the shore's edge and seated themselves on the sand. As the party progressed, they talked faster and louder, but none could outdo the one they called Sam.

Men are men the world over, I thought. *They can't keep their minds off women.*

It was now after midnight, and a sudden realization struck me. Supposed they came searching the other sandhills, and discovered me instead of home brew? I tried to figure a way of crawling out, putting some distance between us, then dashing home. However, the dense growth to the east made escape impossible that way, and Pamlico Sound was on the west, the creek to the south. The water looked too deep for wading, and I couldn't swim. To the north were the men.

Always subject to hay fever, I now felt an attack coming on because of the damp ground. This would mean a series of sneezes which simply could not be stifled.

The fact that I became the subject of their drunken conversation did make me forget the hay fever. Sam had wobbled to the water's edge, taking another swig from the jar.

"Where the hell is that li'l principal that's supposed to be such a giant? He ain't bigger'n a bug. Where's he keepin' himself?"

My student, a lad named Joe, staggered to his feet, saying the teacher must be sick "or sumpin."

"Shoulda brought him with us and filled him full of home brew. I could lick the hell outta him any time."

I was proud of Joe. "Aw, sit down and shut up. He's a nice guy, and he makes school work interesting. I like him."

Sam sank back onto the sand relating how the folks had bragged about how the new principal Kinnakeet was going to have - wrestler, boxer, football player.

They all laughed.

Joe told them about a traveling salesman for a supply house who had come to school, asking for the principal. "When Mr. Green said he was principal, the salesman said to quit this foolishness."

Again they laughed, loudly and boisterously. That Kinnakeet home brew was potent!

The fishermen said nothing so far, but now Sam grew belligerent. He stood up, and squared off, doubling his fist. He'd like to beat the hell out of the teacher.

"Then why don't ye quit talkin' and do it," one suggested.

Sam was ready. They would go to Kinnakeet, and call him out of his room; he'd show him.

Joe said, "Why the damn hell don't you pick in somebody your size?"

With a cat-like swiftness, big Sam slapped Joe so hard he went reeling into the Sound. Joe struggled out, soaking wet and whimpering, "Damn you to hell!"

87

Sam went to him and I thought he'd strike him again, but instead he put a huge arm across Joe's shoulder. "You know why I must lick him, kid. It ain't because he's small, or a good teacher, or the color of his hair, or whether he drinks home brew. I got to make it clear he ain't to flirt with our girls. It always happens and it will this time, too." He must have sensed that Joe was going to defend me again, for he added, "Oh, it ain't happened yit, but just wait, it will."

Joe grabbed Sam, "Let's go home."

"Keep your damned hands off me."

I rubbed my upper lip by way of diverting or preventing a sneeze. I had scratched my nose, too, but my throat had filled and was bursting with the need to cough.

The four of them were still talking, but what they said wasn't important. It was so unfair of them, after I struggled to retain my dignity and act the part of a teacher, when I had sacrificed so much pleasure, just to give them no cause for criticism.

And now it looked as though my doom was sealed because I couldn't prevent sneezing and coughing.

They came, one following the other, with the force of an explosion. Simultaneously, I rolled down the hill, plunged into the creek and remained underwater until I had crawled onto the open beach some distance away. Fortunately, the creek was no deeper than my shoulders, but when I went into it, I didn't care if I drowned or not.

The foursome must have been startled, but I had the advantage of being sober while they were drunk.

Dawn was breaking by the time I reached my room. Well, I had contemplated spending the night on that sandhill, hadn't I? Teasing myself about it did no good; I was beyond laughing at the episode and I was mentally and physically miserable. If they had seen me, I would never be able to face them again. I could only hope that the darkness and their condition combined to hide my identity.

CHAPTER 10

THOSE MIGHTY OBSTACLES

Rugged though the first month at Kinnakeet was, I suppose, if it were otherwise, I might not have remained a teacher; a decision I would have always regretted, because working with the younger generation has compensations no other career can offer.

The next Monday morning, with Saturday's experience still too vivid for comfort, I went into my schoolroom and stood admiring it. There was a quality about it which magnified the horrible conditions remaining. The building was still a disgrace, completely inadequate to our needs, and would remain so until we got a new structure.

In Kinnakeet were progressive people, and I couldn't understand how they tolerated such a deplorable school building!

Have you ever attempted the impossible? Made a bargain with someone who fulfilled his part of the bargain, but you promised more than you could deliver? In your heart was the determination to carry out your promises, or die trying.

This was the way I felt at the beginning.

That first month did more to make a teacher out of me than anything else: it colored my entire teaching career. Had I never come in contact with Kinnakeet and its problems, my entire life would have been vastly different.

For anyone to undertake teaching freshman, sophomore and junior grades under the best conditions, strains the imagination. Furthermore, my school started with nothing by way of supplies, not even a dictionary!

The pledge I made them that first morning was that I would not fight against them, but with them, and if they stuck by me in building a high school in Avon, I would remain with them until it was an actuality.

They had accepted the challenge, but at the time I had few notions about how to deal with the situation.

My teacher's certificate was beautifully new, and the University of North Carolina was one of the best, as were many of its professors. I had been taught practice and theory, but nothing gave me an inkling as to how I could teach all subjects of the first three years of high school, and serve as principal making the endless reports required and be the janitor. All this without materials, and in a disgracefully shabby school, besides.

Aside from these handicaps, and surely not the least of my troubles, was the lack of social life which I knew would be my lot for a while until I had won the Kinnakeeters' confidence. At the university I socialized with my classmates and dated as frequently as I could spare a few coins to take a girl out. Often though, we hiked or sang, merely enjoying each other's companionship.

I had a habit of jotting down any problems on paper, believing I could sit back, regarding what I had written, bringing it into sharper focus. Thus it was, that balmy September in Avon that I had enumerated my ten major obstacles. The minor ones were too numerous, and anyway, if I didn't get the big ones licked, they'd lick me.

After much crossing out, and rewording, I came up with my ten "working" problems.

It was a rather staggering list.

1. Four subjects were required for each student. This meant twelve subjects to be taught each day for the three classes. This would make each session, twenty-five minutes. Much too short a period!

2. Books and school work go together like the head on a body. How can I manage without books? I'll have to remain standing all day, for there is neither table nor chair in my classroom.

3. At the university, my special fields were physical and social sciences. Here I will be teaching those, as well as languages and mathematics-and without books.

4. These are not ordinary students, and ordinary teaching methods won't arouse and hold interest. How will I manage this?

5. What can replace extra-curricular activities since there are no funds and no provisions for any?

6. Discipline by force is out. These boys are huge and tough, and I must constantly be be on the alert to control them in other ways. We are without a law officer in Avon, besides.

7. How can I teach sciences with an open mind? The parents are conservative, religious, and I'm sure science looks to them like the devil's handiwork.

8. The religious conflict going on cannot be overlooked; it puts me in a spot, for I am sure there are good folks on both sides.

9. How can I be one of them? I sense that this will be deeply important to me.

10. Above all, the problem is how to help these ambitious young folks develop their potentialities. They have such possibilities, but they lack the proper guidance.

Now, as the first month of school drew to a close, I brought forth my list. I wanted to check it to find out just how many problems I had solved completely, and which ones had been partially resolved. Shuddering. I knew I had to face up to somewhere I was not making headway.

I worked out the first problem by having a five period schedule in four class periods of seventy minutes each, instead of twelve periods, because each student must study English and literature, social science, mathematics and physical science. General discussions were for the entire school, but sophomores were supposed to do more than freshmen, and juniors more than sophomores.

This system enabled all the students to be occupied for the first four periods, thus, eliminating disciplinary problems.

I reserved the last period for discussions and reading, and it turned out to be one of my most valuable educational projects.

As for problem number two, in English I selected certain grammar rules, giving examples. The students took down this information, then wrote their own examples. This was similar to writing their own grammar books! They liked it so well, I suspected it was something we would continue after receiving our textbooks.

For the physical sciences, I took up interesting questions from various studies which we discussed until we had satisfactory answers. These were put in essay form and the students wrote their own science books. Many scientific ideas had never been introduced here, and the students showed great interest. Also, I handled social science in a similar manner.

Mathematics was taught by making up problems and letting the students work them out. Their favorite was algebra, where each progressed at his own speed.

My third problem gradually adjusted itself. From my high school studies, I had enough math and English to manage these subjects, now.

As for the fourth obstacle, creating interest was not a problem because my students possessed good minds, and the excitement of learning was pleasurable to them.

The last period of reading and discussion served as the recreation which concerned me, originally. Discussion occupied us entirely at first, for it took me a while to obtain a book enabling me to read to them. These general discussions benefited us greatly.

That way Joe defended me that night on the Sound spoke eloquently against disciplinary problems. From the very first, with few exceptions, my students stood by me through thick and thin, just as I was ready to stand by them.

My scientific ideas were carried home by the students and probably related with considerable excitement, and I had no doubt but that repercussions would soon be manifesting themselves.

The matter of religion was a problem I feared more than the others. Although, at the end of a month, by keeping quiet and making no comment about either faction, neither side chastised me, even though they rejected me me for my neutrality.

The matter of becoming one of them bothered me, and would continue doing so for a long time. It was something I had to work on, hoping in time I would became a Kinnakeeter, too.

And what about problem number ten? My big one! How could I get them started along the right path, inspiring them to develop to their fullest capacity?

I was beginning to believe this problem was solved, too. After all, they were intelligent, easy to teach, and eager to learn. What more could I ask?

Kinnakeet was unique because so many of the men were away. Fathers, older brothers, even grandfathers might be in the United States Coast Guard, which kept them away from home much of the time. Regular employment for young boys was limited, as was supervised recreation. Therefore, it was inevitable that the children got into mischief.

With the writing, note-taking and discussions, my school day was organized so the boys hadn't an idle moment. And neither, of course, did the girls, but they presented no problem that way. They got together and sang, but the boys' evenings were too empty for their own good. I felt I should at least send them home from school weary from a full day of studying.

I prided myself on the way I did this, and since students and parents were not familiar with other schools, they accepted it without question.

The fact that they spent idle evenings continued to trouble me, and I devised the idea of suggesting to each one, separately, that we get together. I began this project by loitering around their hangouts, eventually asking one casually what he was doing that night. The answer was invariably, "Nothing!"

"I need exercise. How about hiking down the beach with me?"

He would accept eagerly for want of something else to do.

It worked rather well; the boys appeared curious, wondering, no doubt, what we would talk about. I never repeated to a boy what another one and I had discussed.

I approached the leaders first, and we strolled, talked, played, fished or wrestled in the sand. Although, when we were in the schoolroom, their respect for me as a teacher was all that I could possibly want.

All this worked out better than I dared hope it would. We talked of everything-ridiculous and serious. Our relationships became intimate, and I hoped, permanent. I reminded myself that friendship was something one could not force. Try to, and you make an enemy. However, I began to discover there were ways of developing friendships.

I must first help a boy trust me, then encourage him to converse in the sort of way that reveals his innermost feelings, not only about himself, but about everyone with whom he comes in contact. This is the basis for a lasting and sincere friendship.

My ten obstacles listed when school opened already were looking far less formidable.

CHAPTER 11

THE SERMON

Perhaps because the sciences had been my specialty at the university, I was especially enthusiastic about teaching them. Our discussions ran the gamut from what makes the wind blow to the possibility of man's flight to the moon.

My students began to act as though a whole new world opened up. We looked forward to these sessions, even without any laboratory equipment.

By the time October cast its golden blessing over the island, I formed the habit of going out on Friday nights gathering with the men to talk and socialize. About six weeks after school started, I was amusing myself at Gibbs' store.

The conversation concerned the autumn wild fowl hunting; then one of the men began to tell jokes. Suddenly, I saw a fisherman looking at me. When he caught my attention, he nodded, motioning me outside.

Without talking, we fell in step and headed for the sea. I was more curious than frightened at his behavior.

He had youngsters in school but there had been no trouble.

He broke the silence, with a harsh, unpleasant question.

"What the hell you been teaching the younguns at school?"

"Nothing except what is supposed to be taught," I replied without sarcasm.

"The hell you hain't!" He didn't refer to history, English, or spelling, but, "You been makin' them believe a lot of nonsense."

I said, "Perhaps you mean our science discussions." This was one of my ten listed obstacles.

He assented.

I reassured him, "Nothing other than proven scientific facts have been studied."

He objected to science being taught, saying I should stick to something that made sense.

I was baffled because there was no common ground on which to base our discussion. Why did he assume that science, of all studies, didn't make sense? Inwardly, I bristled because he was attacking my favorite subject. Besides, his own boy was one of my best scientific thinkers. I decided he and his son had been arguing about some of the issues discussed in class.

We had arrived at the wash of Cape Hatteras Sea, while a bright second quarter moon threw its mellow beams over land and sea. I studied it, part of my mind thinking how beautiful it was, while the rest was with the immediate problem. I asked, "What was I teaching that was so bad?"

He needed no further prodding - if I never said certain things, I was to say so, but if I did say them, surely I hadn't meant them.

I waited.

His boy said if and when man learned to split the atom, he could go to outer space, as far as the moon.

"Now saying such a thing is bad enough, but when the younguns asked you if man would some day fly to the moon, you said "yes!" Now you know perfectly well the Lord will never let a man do a thing like that. You've got my boy believing your damned foolishness."

We were so close to the Sea now, the exploding breakers, made it necessary for him to shout to be heard. There was such worry, and sincerity about him, that I felt my anger die, and I knew I must respond to his accusation.

"Before I studied astronomy, I felt as you do, and the more I study about the universe, the more interesting and mysterious it becomes. The harder I study and try to learn, the more I find my knowledge is pitifully limited. There is so much I do not understand." I added, there was much more we didn't understand, than we did.

"You trying to wiggle out of things you said?"

I told him that had been furtherest from my mind. "Look at these bursting breakers. To move so much water with that speed takes a mighty force. Look at the moon, which is 240,000 miles away in outer space; yet it causes the rising tides twice a day. You can't remember when you didn't believe this. We know this great force exists, yet we do not see it, feel it, or hear it."

I gave him a chance to express himself, but when he remained silent, I reminded him that many people who never saw the ocean would not believe the moon was so powerful. And we who knew it, could not understand it. Yet the fact remained that the tide rose and fell in with the moon's actions.

"You claim the Lord would not let a man fly to the moon. Don't I have as much right to believe that He will? You believe the teachings of the Bible?"

He most certainly did!

"How about Genesis, where we are told men are the children of God? Doesn't that give man a kinship with Him?"

"Certainly!"

"If man does fly to the moon, won't that prove that men are the children of God? Wouldn't that be a miracle? And wouldn't it require someone with a kinship to God to carry out such an act? Do you believe that jut an ordinary animal could perform such a feat?"

He made no reply.

"We live in a wonderful universe, but the more we study it, the more bewildering it becomes. However, there is nothing to fear in the study of science. I have a feeling you believe that science will destroy the religious faith of youth. Nothing could be further from the truth."

Probably there was no place on earth where the weather could change as rapidly as here on the Outer Banks. Dark clouds gathered, hiding the moon, and a vigorous wind whipped sand so that we pulled our coats close, hiding our faces in them for protection. Then we hurried back to Kinnakeet; the man returned to Gibbs' store, while I went up the street.

When I reached the Methodist Church, the moon was out again and the wind had abated. Branches from giant oaks lay strewn on the ground as a result of the freakish storm. Passing the schoolhouse, I thought how unreal it looked in the vague moonlight.

A bridge made of poles sunk into a soggy marsh separated Dog Ridge from Cat Ridge. A I walked across its creaking boards, a man's voice asked, "Hey, Mr. Green, is that you?"

I turned to find Uncle George Meekins, the church sexton. He said his brother Fields had been searching the town for me because he had an important matter to discuss.

My nerves were a bit raw from from my recent encounter. I was so enthusiastic about teaching science, and delighted with the receptive young minds with whom I worked. Now, the parents were going to ruin all I had accomplished, killing whatever I hoped to teach in the future.

"What does he want to see me about?" I asked bluntly.

He shrugged; the Methodist church had appointed him, was all he'd say.

I sighed, it was wise that I waited for Mr. Meekins to find me, although I was in no mood to defend science again.

The two of us sauntered along making small talk, when Uncle George said, "Brother Green, there's lots of talk about what you're teaching in your science classes."

"What are they saying?"

"That you teach lies!"

Wearily, I assured him, that we had studied nothing which was not science fact.

It was obvious he was embarrassed, for he admitted having no schooling, but the boys told him boiling water would be hotter in Kinnakeet than in western North Carolina.

"I have told them that - several times."

"It doesn't make sense to me. Can you prove it? You know, all our children are in your science class, and them younguns comes home and repeats everything you say. They try to convince their parents, but mostly they don't succeed."

"Uncle George, did anyone ever explain any scientific principle to you?"

If they had, he didn't recognize it by that name. "Suppose you tell me about this boilin' water, even though I won't understand it. Seems like boilin' water's the same the world over."

Seeking for simple words to prove my statement to my student, I asked if he believed in the Gulf Stream, which flowed only twenty miles east of us, was a river of warm water running north through the cold Atlantic, regardless of the weather or how hard the wind blew.

My companion said that any Kinnakeeter believed that as surely as the sun rose and set.

"Do you feel if the temperature dropped to zero tonight, the water in that great river would still stay warm?"

"Of course it would!"

"Wasn't it you who said that if a freezing north wind came from the southeast instead, off the Gulf Stream, the freezing weather would change to summer temperatures?"

He chuckled - Oh, the times he had seen this happen!

"Do you believe the Gulf Stream causes it?"

He was sure of it.

"Have you ever thought about the thousands of people who wouldn't believe that? You could find folks in western North Carolina who'd be very dubious!"

"I know from experience!"

Now, could I make him understand about the boiling water?

"Let's suppose all the boards on yonder bridge were here beside us in a heap, and you're lying flat on the ground. If someone put a plank on top of you, even with your eyes closed, you'd know the plank was there. How?"

"Because of its weight."

"Now pretend we have a big tin washtub, and we cover the bottom of it with an inch of water. Will that water have any weight on the tub's bottom?"

It would!

"Let's fill the tub full of water. Is there more weight on the bottom now?"

Uncle George said anybody with an ounce of sense would know there was.

"You know that boards have weight, and that water has weight. So does air - the more air, the more weight. When heat is added to water, the particles that make up the water start moving faster and faster, and the hotter the water gets, the faster the particles move. If enough heat is added, these particles move so fast, we can actually see the water moving. Then we say the water is boiling.

"The more weight there is on the water, the more force it will take for the water to move, or boil. Now, air has weight, and the higher we go from the center of the earth, the less air there is to have weight. Atop a mountain there is less air than at sea level. Therefore, water boiling in an open pot on the coast would be a little hotter than water boiling on a mountaintop."

Slowly my elderly pupil nodded his head, and without a word, he offered me his hand which I shook vigorously.

I might have returned to my room feeling somewhat better about my science classes, had I not met one of my pupils. He confirmed that Fields Meekins was looking for me, appearing very excited. When Fields left Gibbs' store, the men said he probably wanted to see me about those science lies, and a long discussion ensued about what I taught. The feeling, I gathered from this lad, was plenty bitter!

From Gibbs' store on Saturday morning, I went over to the school where there were papers that needed grading. It would be much better to meet Fields Meekins here rather than be confronted by him at the store where others could overhear our discussion. I felt depressed, with no inclination to convince Kinnakeet that I was teaching fact.

By lunch time, I headed home, although I was not hungry. Soon the roar of Fields' car and his booming voice hailed me.

The amenities over, his smile faded while he said, "Anxious to see if all the bad things I've been hearing about you are true."

The blood rushed to my face as I stood dumbly before one of the most influential men in town - churchman, and member of the school board. How I dreaded losing my job, but I had no intention of backing away from the truth.

Suddenly, the huge man burst out laughing. "Don't take me so seriously," He slapped me across the shoulder. "I've heard only great things about you!"

He was chewing gum with his mouth closed, and his sudden change of attitude stunned me.

"You're teaching plenty we don't understand, and our children tell us it is because we're ignorant. Milton has explained much that he understood and I didn't."

I still found it impossible to compose myself. Apparently whatever he wanted to see me about didn't concern my science class.

I waited while he took a deep breath.

"A group of us Methodists met yesterday to select someone to fill the pulpit because our preacher will be away tomorrow, and we decided on you!"

"Me? You don't want a sermon?"

That was usually what was expected from the pulpit, he said, assuring me that the vote had been one hundred percent for me.

"But there is so much controversy about my teaching."

He shrugged, conjecturing some of them wanted me for that very reason. It was my chance to show them how science and religion meshed together.

If I had been in a storm before, I was in a hurricane now. Even if there was a month for preparation, I still would hesitate to appear.

It seemed, however, that it was not my place to accept or reject. Mr. Meekins hopped back into his car, waved a huge hand, and headed his vehicle toward the "northerd." He called back assuring me that folks were looking forward to hearing me.

I went to my room forcing myself to stretch out in bed, since I couldn't relax, I made an outline of my speech, and it was a terrible piece of work.

Mrs. Keaton was fixing lunch in the kitchen and I joined her, seeking sympathy.

When I had told her my predicament, she tilted her head and laughed merrily. "Is that all? You looked as though you were going to be hanged. Shame on you, a man with a university education, when most folks in the congregation haven't even been to high school. There's so much you can say to them, and in an eloquent way, too."

"Well, *folks in this world,* I'm not sermonizer, or a preacher. Where is the sermon coming from?"

Convinced that I was serious, Mrs. Keaton told me to pick a scripture, read it, and comment about it.

That afternoon, I wandered about town, returning to my room more miserable than before, because even the children were excited over the fact that I was preaching the next day.

Too many of the adults believed me to be a charlatan, while the teen-agers were convinced I possessed true wisdom. I was in a predicament - if I refused, there would be many who would say, "I told you so." And the youngsters would be deeply disappointed, because I had failed them.

One fact I learned about Kinnakeeters was their lack of sympathy for a coward. Right or wrong, if a man *thought* he was right, he had to fight for it.

I might know science better, but the Kinnakeeters had me when it came to the Bible. Most of them could probably quote it backwards and would detect any error. They'd declare that if I didn't know science any better than the Scripture, I shouldn't be teaching.

Far into Saturday night, I tried one idea, only to discard it for another. I finally went to sleep fully clothed, exhausted.

On Sunday morning as I shaved and dressed, I decided just to read the First Psalm and make a few comments. However, I wasn't happy about this, because my congregation would be disappointed and disillusioned.

After Sunday school, the men and boys invariably congregated under the great oaks in the yard. I joined them feeling numb, with an advanced case of stage fright. After the men walked away, I was grateful. Trees soothed me; I drew comfort and strength from them, and on this hot Sunday morning in October, I was grateful for their shade.

Soon, I was joined by my pupil, George Meekins, who spoke proudly, but shattering whatever composure I had.

"Just look up toward Cat Ridge; they're really coming to church today."

He was right, and as I faced Dog Ridge, crowds poured from that direction, too.

"This is awful," I said.

He pulled himself to a full six-feet-four, "I think it's wonderful. We been telling them how well you talk, Mr. Green. Pour it on. We like rip-roarin' sermons; get excited like in science class and let'em have it."

I lifted a hand in protest. "George, I'm not a preacher. I don't even have a sermon prepared."

"What are you scared of? What's the difference between talking to old Kinnakeeters or young ones. All us younguns is fer ye. Let'em have it, right between the eyes."

Uncle George rang the church bell. Folks filed into the building, but I remained leaning against a sturdy tree trunk. Everyone had gone inside, and there were only oaks and me, remaining.

I must have been a rather pitiful picture as I slithered down the aisle, wondering why I found it necessary to wait until everyone was seated, then enter so all eyes could see me.

In the pulpit, I peered out over their heads, and if the music for the opening hymn hadn't started, they would have heard me groaning.

It was the same hymn they sang my first Sunday in Kinnakeet. During the chorus, I sat back, my eyes closed.

"The cross is not greater than His grace.

The storm cannot hide His blessed face.

I am satisfied to know with Jesus here below

I can conquer every foe."

Uncle Tom Meekins, who carried me ashore the day of my arrival, now led the prayer. He was a true product of Cape Hatteras Island; none questioned his integrity. He had studied the powerful elements of nature around here developing a profound belief in God's ways.

After another rousing hymn, I rose to read the First Psalm. The singing had served to calm me, and I was grateful.

"Blessed is the man that walketh not in the counsel of the ungodly, nor standeth in the way of sinners, nor sitteth in the seat of the scornful, But his delight is in the law of the Lord; and in his law doth he meditate day and night. And he shall be like a tree planted by the rivers of water, that bringeth forth his fruit in his season; his leaf also shall not wither; and whatsoever he doeth shall prosper.

"The ungodly are not so; but are like the chaff which the wind driveth away. Therefore the ungodly shall not stand in the judgement, nor sinners in the congregation of the righteous. For the Lord knoweth the way of the righteous; but the way of the ungodly shall perish."

Closing the Book, I gazed at them, and suddenly my meager plans lost all meaning. These people were expecting something unusual. I was the man who was suddenly blessed with a great host of guests who came to visit, expecting a great feast. But lo and behold, the tables were bare.

Rapidly, I found myself dividing them into groups, there were those who expected me to exhort, but I was no preacher. Some wanted oratory, but I was not a public speaker. The largest group, I felt, wanted me to defend my science teachings, but what could be accomplished in thirty minutes? I decided not to get involved.

In the front row, some of the younger girls sat, beaming at me in their Sunday best. In the third row, Aunt Lucinda in her usual black. How straight she sat, with her eyes on me expectantly.

Then I saw George Meekins sitting on the back bench. He was so tall, his head was visible over all the others.

"Give it to 'em right between the eyes, just like you do us younguns at school."

Why pretend to be a profound philosopher when I wasn't?

Or try to be an orator.

Or attempt a big argument about scientific principles, which would only result in confusion.

I would be myself. Anything else would be pure sham. I had become too anxious and excited; Mrs. Keaton had assured me of this. Young George wanted to know the difference between talking to kids at school or their parents in church.

They were so receptive, and in such a state of anticipation! It is incredible what an audience can do as a speaker. A window was open, and the oaks spoke to me, offering me their strength. How many hurricanes had they withstood? Yet they were confident and serene. My thoughts returned to that First Psalm.

"There is no need to look to the past for good examples by which to live on this beautiful morning," I began. "Or reach out to the various parts of the earth seeking something by which to steer our lives, when we have perfect examples here in this church."

As they began to gather the significance of my statement, I continued.

"Just a quick glance toward the east, and we see examples that can teach us something about real life. I mean the aged oaks that have been a real joy from the first time the shipwrecked Europeans laid eyes on this very spot, long before the time of the American Indian."

Kinnakeeters loved their trees, and were proud of their heritage. The fact that I had observed and expressed tribute to the oaks drew me nearer their hearts.

"Each time we look at a tree, we see a truly miraculous creation of God. We do not have to return to Biblical times for miracles wrought by God, they're with us constantly. When God made the tree, He created a living miracle to be with us, always. This is not guesswork, but scientific fact.

"Thus, it is a wonderful compliment for any man to have his greatness compared to a mighty tree. But the truth is more of us never give thought to the miracle of one tree, to say nothing of all we see this morning in their magnificence.

"No tree starts off great, just as no man is ever born that way. He must grow into what destiny prescribes. A tree achieves greatness by starting as a tiny seedling, and in its youth prepares for maturity. How is this done? It builds, as God intended, a great root foundation that sinks deep into the earth."

I was encouraged by a mumbled "Amens" from the older people, and my confidence increased.

"The roots must take hold before the tree can partake of the underground rivers God prepared for it."

It was possible for me to speak more forcefully, now. I stepped from the pulpit, getting closer to the congregation.

"Its great root foundation gives the tree security against the storms it encounters, just as the staunch trees beside the church have witnessed innumerable gales and hurricanes from the most turbulent sea in the world.

"And now as never before, young men and women must set their goals high and work for them as though their lives depended on it. In many parts of the world there is seething unrest; revolutions are developing that may overthrow democracies if the rising generations do not prepare for these conflicts. Young people will have to face situations unknown to their parents, and our civilizations will depend upon the next

112

generation more than most of us realize. If youth doesn't prepare through study to carry on our great democratic way of life, then may God have mercy on us."

I turned toward a group of young people midway in the church. "Like the mighty trees, you require a solid intellectual foundation as well as a strong physical one. You were given a mind, and God meant for you to use it."

More "Amens" flowed through the congregation.

"I emphasize repeatedly that now, as never before, young people must learn from the psalmist, and let the trees in our midst teach a lesson.

"The only way I know to delight in the Lord's law is in deep meditation. To enjoy the spirit of His law, one must study all his life. The more intelligent a person is, the more he can carry out God's law. Obviously, all men seek rewards, and what will be the rewards of those who delight in the law of the Lord, and who meditate upon that law? They will bear much fruit, and whatever they do will prosper. What more can a man want?

"Never forget the words recorded in the First Psalm. Let them penetrate your heart and inspire you, now and forever. His delight is in the law of the Lord, and in His law doth he meditate day and night, and he shall be like a tree planted by the rivers of water. His leaf shall not wither and whatever he doeth shall prosper."

When I had finished my talk, surely it wasn't a sermon, I felt a certain elation, as though drawing inspiration from my own observations. I had strengthened my own thinking, which I hoped had been transmitted to those expectant ones.

The little church was strangely silent when I finished speaking. I picked up the hymnal and started to announce the closing hymn, when dear Aunt 'Cinda rose from her seat, shouting "Hallelujah!"

Her soul was filled with faith and love for God, and the rising generation of Kinnakeet. Now she appeared to be bursting with unspeakable joy, which was infectious, for many wiped their eyes.

Repeatedly, she shouted "Hallelujah," and such approval from one so devout, seemed to me then, as it did forever after, the real sermon that day.

She preached the greatest sermon, ever, and without words, other than the shouted "Hallelujahs."

CHAPTER 12

THE NIGHT OF THE STORM

It was usually hoped the hurricane season was over, but I was to learn this was not the case. On Friday of the eighth week of school, the wind at noontime was of gale force and there was a danger of a land tide, so school was dismissed.

In the afternoon, the ever-increasing wind brought tons of seawater from the wild Atlantic into the village of Kinnakeet.

With the night's approach, dark clouds swirled, and blackness engulfed the town earlier than usual.

It was my first experience with one of these notorious storms, and the constant noise of wind and sea sent chills chasing up and down my back.

There was nobody at Mrs. Keaton's that night, other than the good landlady, her son Bill, and me.

"The tide might do more than flow under the house," Bill informed me cheerfully. "Water might come into the house."

Carefully, we began to raise all the downstairs furniture above the floor level. What an odd sight it was, after everything moveable was put up on wooden or cement blocks, planks, and boxes of various kinds.

The south door of my bedroom was in the opposite direction to the wind, so it was kept open. If the tide rose rapidly, water would enter the house, flooding the downstairs; this should prevent Mrs. Keaton's home from floating out to sea.

I had to forgo lights in my room, since the wind coming from the opening would quickly extinguish them. Therefore, I sat in the living room with Mrs. Keaton and Bill, beside a flickering oil lamp.

There was something upsetting about their calm, and I told myself Kinnakeeters had many peculiar traits. My own nerves were jumping, yet here they sat, serenely, as though a breath of air hadn't stirred.

When midnight came, Mrs. Keaton suggested we retire. Surely she must be joking. But when she handed me a flashlight, I realized she meant just that!

In that piceous room, there was nothing to do but stretch out on the bed while the winds shook the house, and the rising tide slushed under it. Frequently, I turned the flashlight to see what was happening outside, only to find the water had not yet entered the house.

Then I recalled a remark of Bill's, saying there was little danger of the tide flooding unless the wind switched suddenly from northeast to northwest. At least, this gave me something new to speculate on. Cold sweat enveloped my body, as I imagined the wind was changing!

I tried to calm myself by thinking of something other than the storm. I attempted to force out one thought by filling my head with a different one.

These local people had endured these storms for years, I told myself. Certainly I could manage it, too.

Then something new happened; lightning filled the landscape, followed immediately by the loud roar of thunder. That flash of lightning revealed what appeared to be the middle of the Atlantic Ocean.

By one o'clock, I was resigned to the fact that I couldn't sleep, and I made myself think of my school work.

I relived that period when we labored without textbooks, and I marveled at the slight difference they made. Oh, we used them, but had adjusted so well to discussions and note-taking, that we felt quite independent without them.

I should have known it would be inevitable, but I was able to think of the schoolroom without remembering a pretty young student. In these eight weeks at Kinnakeet, she had become very dear to me, and it had taken sheer will power for me to conceal it. She was studious, but also, delightful to see and hear. Her dark head would be bent over her studies, but as I passed, she would look up with laughing blue eyes, and lips parted in a smile.

There was a small age difference between myself and students, and I was in love with my pupil, Marie. I dared not admit my feelings to myself, but tonight, I wondered where it was calm, for the storm outside was not much greater than the one raging within me, now that I dared to think of her.

I realized the good will I had established here was largely because I avoided the local girls. I needed respect and cooperation of my male students, if they turned from me, I was finished here. Of course they'd rebel if I fell in love with one of their classmates.

I forced myself to dwell on other aspects of my teaching career, but it was a losing game, for repeatedly, I thought of the girls. I needed a sweetheart just as other boys did. They took girls for granted. However, I must pretend they didn't interest me in the least.

Loneliness and fright conspired tonight, and it was a relief when I finally noticed it was four o'clock; morning was greatly anticipated.

Suddenly the wind switched; I was totally aware of it. It no longer came from the northeast, but from the northwest. There was a hint of daylight, and I noticed the huge live oak east of my bedroom window. All night its twigs and branches had slammed against the house, but now it was bowing to the ground.

"Green," Bill roared, no longer serene, "Get up. Put on your hip boots. The tide's rising."

I had sent for my boots from a mail order house, and this was the first time I wore them, but felt no elation about it. By the time I struggled into them and reached the living room, water was flooding through the house.

At least, dawn was upon us; that fact consoled me. In another hour, the wind subsided slightly, and the water receded until it was only three feet deep but there were fish ranging from two to ten inches! However, I was in no mood to joke about getting out a pole and bait.

Eventually Bill made coffee and we stood in water above our knees, eating breakfast. We went upstairs and looked out the east window to a rare scene. All of Kinnakeet was under water except for the sandhills and the higher ridges. Houses looked like a fleet of ships at sea, with the sandhills and ridges serving as islands. Some of the fishing boats had broken from their mooring and floated idly through the village.

Herds of cattle and wild ponies had taken refuge on the higher places, some completely out of the water, others standing in it belly high. They were secure, could return soon to their accustomed places, but many wild ponies floated about, drowned. My heart was sad for these poor, unfortunate creatures.

Another two hours and the sun broke through the clouds. Then we had a pretty scene. Only a strong breeze stirred, and the water receded so rapidly, it looked as though Kinnakeet were rising up from the ocean instead of the water returning to the ocean from the town.

By noon Kinnakeet was high and dry, and not even a fish remained in Mrs. Keaton's house.

Bill explained what happened as we cleaned the floors. When the winds blew from the northeast, thousands of tons of water were carried through the inlets and low places into the Sound. This process might take from twenty-four to seventy-two hours. Then, when the winds suddenly shifted to the northwest, all the water that had transferred from the ocean to Sound did not have time to return through the inlets. It had to flood the island, covering it.

How much damage had it done?

Mrs. Keaton replied, "It has killed all the vegetables, except the onions and many of the shrubs and plants."

Bill tried to minimize the damage, saying that was probably all, though.

"It will be a while before folks can drive on the beach," I commented.

They laughed. It was only a matter of hours, because salt water quickly soaked into the sand.

"You mean I could walk over to the ocean tonight and not get stuck in the sand?"

It would be perfectly alright, Bill said. "The moon was full night before last and it'll be nice on the beach, although there'll be some water in the low places."

After lunch, I went onto the screened porch and sat down. I was in a land world again, only a short time ago it was a water world. Before long, I wandered over to the oak, standing in all its majestic beauty, as though it had never bowed its head.

Pamlico Sound was smooth and peaceful, but the Atlantic Ocean was having trouble settling down. It was rough and angry, as though it still resented the hurricane's abuse.

I headed for Gibbs' store, just east of the house. The road was dry on the surface, but ditches along the side were full of running water, flowing to the Sound, from whence it came.

Folks were mostly digging out, so nobody was inside the store.

Gibbs said, "Now you've seen it!"

"And felt and heard it," I added.

"Sleep well last night?"

"Sleep well!"

This pleased him mightily, and he chewed his tobacco strenuously. Suddenly he laughed merrily, "You stick it out, son, and one of these days you'll be a reg'lar Kinnakeeter."

I returned to my boarding house, and after supper, sat again on the front porch. The wind came now from the southwest, scarcely moving the few remaining poplar leaves out in front. They had not withstood the storm as well as the oaks did.

The lilting notes of a mocking bird were heard, no doubt in a clump of yeopon bushes near the Sound. After my sleepless night, I should be anxious to retire, but the beauty of the evening stimulated me. How little these folks realized my need to live a more normal life.

The sun had disappeared, and as I glanced up and down the shore, I witnessed a strange sight. It looked from the front porch as though a tree were bottom side up. I hurried to the shore of the Sound, and sure enough, a tree had been uprooted farther up the island. The tides floated it abreast Kinnakeet, where its roots were raised into the air, while its top was nestled in the sand.

As I sauntered back, oil lamps were being lighted, and sitting in the porch chair again, even the gentle southwest breeze had disappeared, and the world was enclosed in a muted silence.

Then all at once, there was the glorious sound of singing. What melody and harmony! There was no doubt that the chorus would be composed largely of my students, and it sounded as though they were near Gibbs' store.

My first impulse was to head there, joining them, but I became cautious and concerned about maintaining my dignity.

My landlady came out, put a lamp on the old table near me, and said she was going over to Sis Mitt's for a spell.

As soon as I saw her enter her sister's house, just down the street, I rose and paced nervously, from the porch to the yard.

I stood on the top step and looked up at the stars wondering what would become of me? How could I manage to continue living this way?

I could hear the voices now, and see an occasional flash of a light. People came to the gate presently, and making a tune of it, they chorused, "How do you do, Mr. Green, how do you do?"

They surrounded me, all talking and laughing, and I was overwhelmed by their attention. I could not resist looking for Marie in the dim lamplight, and when I saw her at the back of the group my heart pounded.

Young Vance Gray explained, "We came for you. At school yo're the captain and your word goes, but tonight, we demand you join us."

If that boy realized what he was offering me, he would have been amazed. It was not easy to pretend I was considering their proposal.

They pulled me off the porch and broke into song again. I never ceased to be amazed at the number of songs they knew, and not just the chorus, but completely.

Perhaps it was not a wise thing I was doing tonight, but right now I didn't care. I needed to start living again.

George Meekins suggested, "Let's take him out to Breeze Inn."

This was a hangout for youngsters not far from the school. I never had been there, but knew it was well managed.

One of the girls added, "We'll go to Breeze Inn later, but now, let's take him through Lover's Lane."

"In Kinnakeet?" I marveled.

The girl's brother said it was right above their house and they knew all about it.

"Why haven't I heard about it?"

They exclaimed, "You ought to get out and learn something about our town!"

And if I learned too much, I would be finished among you, I thought.

They became silent, then a boy asked if I wanted to know why it was so named.

Obligingly, I asked, "Why is it called Lover's Lane?"

"You can't take a girl through there without kissing her."

"But surely there are exceptions."

"Never, especially on moonlit nights."

We passed Gibb's store and the usual number of loafers leaned against the front porch.

I heard one say, "Ain't that the teacher with them younguns?"

The reply was inaudible, but I was gripped with fear that this might have repercussions. I forced myself to bury the thought; tonight I was gay and happy!

On we went, passing the Methodist Church, then the grove of live oaks to the east, and finally arrived at the schoolhouse.

"Almost there," said Vance. "It's just north of here, where the sandhills begin."

It was a narrow, sandy path winding through many sandhills covered with the usual shrubbery.

Vance took a flashlight and showed me the path. He went ahead while the rest of us followed. At best, only two of us could go at a time, and there was only one fellow who did not steal a kiss as we made the trip - the school principal.

Breeze Inn was a small frame building with a counter at one end where soft drinks were sold, and benches ringed the room. It was the only place of its kind in Kinnakeet.

The warm night, the soft drinks and ice cream added up to fun. I was one of them. I talked with everyone, except the one I most wanted to be near. She appeared shy, and I kept telling myself it was better this way, but that did not satisfy the needs of my heart.

They next went to watch the moon rise out of the ocean. When we arrived, it was already over the Cape Hatteras Sea and the sight was indescribably beautiful. Was it only last night this land was beset by a hurricane? The Sea had many moods; she could be nasty, but tonight she showed us how wonderful she could be.

We stood huddled together, drinking in the beautiful scenery. Finally singing again, we headed toward the lighthouse, its revolving light adding to the charm of the evening.

I felt as though I had transferred to a fairyland of love and beauty. What could be lovelier than the Cape Hatteras Sea, unless it was the Kinnakeet girls. All night, I hadn't spoken directly to Marie, but I constantly watched her. The other girls had caught my arm and walked with me, but not her!

We were having so much fun that before I realized it, we were almost at Big Kinnakeet Coast Guard Station, four miles south of Kinnakeet. It was getting late, so we turned, rapidly heading to home.

The young folks of Kinnakeet began to pair off now, and I was resigned to the fact that I would be alone. However, such was not my lot, there were three girls left over, one of whom was Marie. The others disappeared and we walked together on the beach to a section of partially-built dyke that was being thrown up between Kinnakeet and the Cape Hatteras Sea. A deep ditch was dug, but the girls did not know about it, since it was so recent. This made it necessary for us to go farther south to get into Kinnakeet, unless we chose to go farther north, returning as we had come, earlier.

We chose to go around the ditch at the south end, then up Dog Ridge. This took us through the old cemetery where I recently inspected the aged tombstones. Our talk naturally turned to Pharaoh Farrow, and pirates in general.

First, we came to Sue's house. She checked the time for us and it was midnight! I hurried on to the upper part of Dog Ridge, presuming both remaining girls lived there, but after Betty said goodnight, I learned that Marie lived in the section north of Cat Ridge, at a place the teen-agers called Spain.

I was alone with Marie!

My heart pounding, we passed the schoolhouse, then headed through Lover's Lane; the nearest way to Spain.

Kinnakeet was asleep; not a lamp showed. The moon flooded the village, and I was so excited I couldn't believe my luck!

The local girls were supposed to be in by ten o'clock, but here I was, the principal, walking one home after midnight.

Not only that, but I was with the one I loved.

When we negotiated the narrow Lover's Lane, I took her hand in mine and I was ecstatic! The fact that it was compulsory to kiss made me very daring, and before we came out onto the beach, I took Mare in my arms and kissed her full on the lips.

She did not remonstrate, but said nothing. Neither did I. When we reached her front door, we stood for a moment, holding hands, then she smilingly patted my cheek and said good night.

Marie occupied my thoughts as I attended church services the next day. However, I was not prepared for what took place afterward out in the church yard. A handsome young sailor put his arm about her shoulder possessively, and they walked off together!

By Monday, I had learned from many sources that I took Marie home the night before, but the most reassuring part was that nobody minded in the least. The Kinnakeeters liked me and trusted me.

I knew then I could be their "captain" at school, and their pal outside of school, which was good.

CHAPTER 13

FOURTH AND FIFTH GRADERS

By my second school year at Kinnakeet, I was very aware the Cape Hatteras Sea afforded enough episodes to fill many volumes. However, what occurred at school the last Friday in November, 1931, would probably never be duplicated again.

For three days previously, a northeast gale had stirred the sea into a fury, but the tides did not flood the island, postponing school. The greatest handicap was the struggle the pupils endured fighting the powerful wind.

On Thursday night, the winds lessened, temperatures dropped, and blue skies prevailed. Everyone felt happier on Friday morning when the sun shone again and the capricious Sea was its usual beautiful azure. There was a sting in the air that morning, and the Kinnakeeters went out wearing more than their usual number of garments.

There was no doubt about it, children worked harder on crisp days like this. I swung along, breathing deeply, shoulders back, head high, telling myself this was going to be a *good* day, one of study and accomplishment.

The first class was still general science, and the question to be discussed this morning was, "If a tree far away from any living creature were to fall suddenly, would there be any sound?"

Their opinion was unanimously - yes!

"I dislike disappointing you," I differed, "But there definitely is no sound under a circumstance like this."

They bristled, and George Meekins argued, "That may be true, but I ain't got 'nough sense to understand such stuff."

Another student has just started to express an opinion when there was a loud banging on the door. This was my favorite class, and I hurried to the door reluctantly, hating the interruption.

Miss Wood, the fourth and fifth grade teacher, stood there, pale and drawn, looking as though she had turned to stone.

"What happened?"

I shook her a little, and she began waving her hands about frantically. "It's too awful. Don't let your students know about it."

She tugged my sleeve and I turned to my class asking them to excuse me. I closed the door softly behind me.

"Tell me," I begged as we hurried along.

"Send for their parents as fast as you can, Mr. Green."

At her door she paused dramatically. "This is the end of everything."

I shook violently, and what disturbed me most was the silence in Miss Wood's room. Forty-six fourth-and-fifth graders minus their teacher should never be *that* quiet. Had they all died?

Miss Wood hid her face in her hands and just stood there. I touched the door knob, and never had I dreaded anything as I dreaded that!

As I gave it a quick jerk, the door opened wide.

What a sight!

The room was always pitifully overcrowded, and most of the children are boys, whom I now found draped over their desks, unconscious. What few girls there were sat, eyes wide, with handkerchiefs over their noses, and vomit everywhere.

There was unmistakably the foul odor of alcohol, and a brisk fire was burning in the stove.

I rushed to the windows and opened them, letting in the cold wind. The first boy to show signs of life was quickly given the cold-towel treatment in the face. "Tell me what happened," I demanded.

Sobbing miserably, he stated, "They drank out of a keg."

"What keg?"

"On the beach - it's full of 'em."

"You mean they washed ashore in the storm?"

He nodded, hiding his face in his folded arms.

My first thought was wood alcohol, which had many commercial uses and was usually shipped in kegs. If I had been frightened before, I was paralyzed now. With no doctor available - but what did it matter? If these boys drunk wood alcohol, death was certain.

If there was such a thing as Hell on earth, I was there for the next few minutes. Finally, I turned to Miss Wood, who, poor thing, was doing her best to clean up the mess. I mustn't let her know my fears, and I disliked alarming the parents until we were more certain just what it was.

The room turned cold now, and nothing could have helped   the boys more than this. Gradually, they regained consciousness and I talked to as many as I could, as fast as possible.

Soon, we were satisfied that it wasn't wood alcohol, and classes resumed, but I was anxious to check on what the Cape Hatteras Sea had tossed at them now.

The story gradually evolved-the recent storm had necessitated the crew of a distressed ship tossing overboard part of their cargo, which consisted of hundreds of kegs of unadulterated alcohol! They floated, of course, and the strong nor'easter blew them landward, casting them ashore on the beach just east of the Kinnakeet schoolhouse.

Kinnakeeters rise early, since the men are mostly coast guardsmen or fishermen. Also, they breakfast early, which leaves considerable time for the children to romp before school starts. They usually started ridiculously early, playing until the bell rang.

So, this morning on the beach, they saw the kegs. The coast guard had just patrolled, and it would be another hour before this unusual cargo would be discovered by the authorities. The boys excitedly rolled a keg away from the wash, set it upright, and knocked the head out with a piece of bedstead that had washed ashore.

Now, just as though they were having an ice cream or watermelon eating contest, they tried to see who could drink the most alcohol. They ran to school afterwards, and the warm room did the rest.

CHAPTER 14

SECOND YEAR

It was in February, 1932 when I met old Preacher Price one evening as I hurried home from school. The day was unseasonably warm for winter, and I commented, "Maybe we won't have any more cold weather. This is too good to be true."

"Young man," said this oldster, endowed with spiritual as well as empirical wisdom, "you just said something that is a great philosophical truth."

"I never considered myself a philosopher."

He leaned against a tree, "You said the weather was too good to be true. It is! You may depend on it, foul weather will follow."

My spirits were dampened, "Oh sure, there'll be bad weather before summer."

"It's not the weather, Brother Green, but life."

I joined him against the tree.

He predicted most of my life was ahead of me, adding, "Your success in Kinnakeet has gone beyond what anyone expected. I have heard you say the same yourself. Your work has gone so well we can compare it to this beautiful mid-winter day. There will be a change in the weather, and likely it will be violent. The longer it is in coming, the louder the bang!

"Similarly, one day your good luck will change, and for a while, the storm will blow. Be prepared to weather it; keep your head up. The whole world may seem against you, but stand up and fight for what you believe in, as long as there's breath in ye. If ye go down fighting, ye'll belong to men of the honorable class." He peered at me over his glasses. "Promise me that, eh?"

"I hope I will be able to weather adversity."

He felt I was sincere, but lacking in practical experience. Also, since I had been so lucky here, he was afraid I wouldn't understand what he was trying to say. He said I had made a good principal, but that did not necessarily mean that I could handle bad things. Many a smart fellow had found himself incapable or unwilling to overcome reversals that were his lot.

"Don't brood about what I say, but consider it seriously."

He walked slowly back toward the parsonage, while I stood pondering his words, no longer cognizant of the warm February sun. Finally, I sauntered over to my rooming house.

On March 6th, there was an educational meeting in Manteo. It was on a Friday night, and I had to return Saturday, since no mail boat ran on Sunday.

The warm weather held, and the sail up the sound was a delight. The Hotel Raleigh was crowded, mostly with sportsmen brought out by good weather, and I was grateful I had a room reservation.

This meeting lasted no more than an hour, but when I came out, heavy clouds swept angrily across the sky and the temperature dropped so much it was as though we had been transferred to another locale. Nobody worried about it, except to comment briefly, for bad weather and winds were expected in March, and the hurricane season was late summer and early fall. And anyway, hurricanes arose in the Caribbean Sea.

The wind built up rapidly to gale force, and rain fell. My room was on the north side of the hotel, and I looked forward to sleeping as late as I pleased the next morning.

The room was warm, and the rain too heavy for an open window, so I pulled only a sheet over me and fell asleep. At daybreak, I awoke shivering. The wind and rain had increased, and to my amazement there was ice on the windowpane!

The electric wires were blown down so there was no power to the furnace. I dressed and went below, where men and women huddled in the lobby, wrapped in blankets.

There was no use pretending any longer, the wind had reached hurricane force, and Kinnakeeters taught me if it switched from northeast to northwest, water would pour in from Pamlico Sound.

Right on cue, no sooner had I thought this, a man at the front door of the hotel yelled that it had changed.

I ran to a south window and saw the elm tops almost touch the ground. A warehouse roof blew off, and suddenly the streets looked like swiftly-flowing rivers, the water rising to the second step of the hotel.

Kinnakeet was in a much worse position than Manteo because it was isolated. My mind visualized all sorts of mishaps there, and I suffered for the Kinnakeeters.

A woman in the lobby approached me, "Aren't you the principal at Avon?"

I assented.

"You're fortunate to be here; I understand it's washed off the map."

I became miserable.

Soon the wind began to diminish and the coast guard contacted, but the telephone lines had been blown down so no report was available, and rumors added to my concern. Strange now, only a short time ago, I had never heard of Avon. Now it was all that mattered to me. There was nothing to do but wait until the first mail boat, that I would surely be on!

I was the first one to board the small boat, and lost no time in asking the captain, "What about Avon?"

"Very little news from there, except the schoolhouse has been destroyed."

Closing my eyes, I stood there aghast.

The shabby little building had furnished us with a place of learning, in spite of the awful carved-up desks, the old stove, and rough porch boards.

When I spoke again, I asked if any lives were lost, but the captain did not know.

There always appeared to be a penitent attitude from the weather after a hurricane, and today was no exception. The way down the channel was perfect, without even a breeze. Eagerly I watched for sight of Avon, and at first nothing seemed different. Avon was not swept out to sea, but as we drew closer, I could see houses pulled from their foundations, and the usual animals strewn along the shore.

Uncle Tom picked up the mail, and I was the only passenger to debark. Usually he had much to say, but now he only nodded at me.

While I pulled off my shoes and rolled up my trousers to wade ashore, I asked him if any lives were lost.

"None! The Lord saw to that!" Then he looked woefully sad, "Have you heard about the schoolhouse?"

"Yes."

Ashore, the pupils awaited me and walked beside me enroute to Mrs. Keaton's.

One girl exclaimed, "They're saying we can't have any more school this year, which makes me so mad I could fight.

Now we'll have to sacrifice a whole year's credit when we only had nine more weeks."

"Who's saying that?"

"Everybody!" they chorused.

Without realizing it, I walked faster. In fact, some of the girls were running to keep up with me. And all of them were begging me to do something about not stopping school.

At the gate, they departed. Inside Mrs. Keaton's, I found the primary teachers waiting for me; each had her little say.

"Just think of having to repeat the same grade next year. My pupils have cried about it."

"Even the first-and-second graders are frantic. Who'd have thought such tots would take school so seriously?"

The third teacher said somebody ought to do something, and obviously she believed I was the "somebody."

Mrs. Keaton, preparing a hot lunch, asked, "Don't ye think these younguns are the most important thing in Kinnakeet?"

"There is no doubt of it."

"Then don't you think they're worth fighting for?"

One of the teachers said under such conditions, how could one put up a fight.

"I'm willing to fight, but I can't make any promises," I told them. I had heard nothing except the matter of the school from the time I debarked. Lack of sleep, and the food I had just eaten, merely served to confuse the issue.

"You go to bed," said Mrs. Keaton.

"And don't call me for supper, please. I'm not coming down until morning. If anybody wants me, he'll just have to wait!"

I had barely entered my room when a group of students arrived, and while I disliked rejecting them, I was in no condition to talk to anyone.

Morning found children playing in the streets. The day was beautiful; and it should have been a school day, but there was no school. The children were restless, and their parents wanted them to attend school. The teachers wanted to teach, and the principal wanted school more than anything else.

But there was no place to have school!

I spent the day talking with people, and this included members of both churches. Nothing but discouragement prevailed regarding the school. I was more discouraged at the day's end than I had been when I set forth that morning.

The building still stood, after a fashion, but it had been condemned, because it was unsafe.

My thoughts turned to the two church buildings. To conduct school with room dividers for the various grades would ordinarily be a problem, but not here in Kinnakeet. The religious conflict between Methodists and Pentecostals had by now reached a climax. My loss of rapport with either side meant that neither church building would be considered.

Disgustedly, I told myself there was still the long, sandy beach with the sky above for cover!

That first day of suggestions, discussions, and defeat, had unnerved me. I had worked hard for Kinnakeet, and felt I had done much for my children, exercising patience and expending energy unstintingly. Now hate and love fought to claim me. I did not want to talk with anyone by the time I returned to Mrs. Keaton's. How I wanted the privacy of my room, door locked.

But it was not dark yet, so I couldn't do that. Also, I suspected some of my pupils would be along before supper time.

I made a quick decision to walk toward the Sound, where I would be alone, and perhaps the soothing sound of water lapping at the shore would calm me.

Finding a protected spot, I sat down as was my custom, but without the usual pad and pencil, I began enumerating the pros and cons.

Parents had reluctantly given up, and the students accepted their verdict.

Teachers had given in; the board of education had proclaimed the school closed until next fall.

The North Carolina Department of Education did not protest the decision.

Yes, defeat had been accepted all the way from the state department to the first grade child.

Actually, a hurricane forced the decision, and they received it without a fight. Why couldn't I do the same?

The easy way out would be to finish my reports tomorrow, pack my clothes, and leave for summer, forgetting the whole thing until the Fall.

The more I thought, the more I refused to give up. A feeling of determination crept over me, much like the one I had that first morning of school. I faced what looked like an impossible situation then, yet a workable solution had come out of it.

If it happened once, why not twice?

But this was different, the whole town was on the other side of the issue now, even the state department!

I argued mightily with myself, trying to talk myself out this foolishness. If I kept on persisting, all of Kinnakeet would reject me in disgust. The final decision was already made.

Maybe that's how it was today, but tomorrow was coming and I would be a lion compared to a kitten today.

I got up and began to walk, rapidly, thinking how reserved I had been today, showing great respect, pleasantly listening to all that negativism.

I thought of that first-day promise of last year - of a new school building if they'd stick by me. They stuck, hadn't they? I was going to fight, regardless of how hopeless things looked. Now was my chance to win the rest of the term.

A year's credits meant much to most students, and nobody was able to measure the extent at this point. To some it would represent a curse to society, which could have as well turned out a youth who'd have been an asset.

Fight, I told myself. My emotions had merely smoldered today, but now they were flaming. I would take this to the governor if necessary. Madness? Perhaps, but the national and world situation in 1932 cried out for educated youths, for leaders capable of stopping the rampaging dictator.

Suddenly, I happened to think of Preacher Price, who only last month talked to me under the oak tree. He wanted to elicit my promise to be man enough to weather the storms that came, I sensed that he was praying for me now.

That night I slept fitfully, dreaming I was before a court, pleading for the young folks of Kinnakeet, I felt the need to put my emotions into written words, and getting up, I lit the oil lamp.

"Oh, Kinnakeet," I wrote, "you have what it takes to build empires, and that which can either crush or build a great nation;

you are able to conquer the seas and the air, and stop oncoming evil. This growing power can can make life as black as the dungeons of hell, or as bright as the portals of heaven. It can tear down governments or build up great democracies!

"Do what you will, but neglect youth, and your history will fade from the minds of men. Develop and cultivate their abilities, and you shall be known throughout the world. If you could only realize youth can be more powerful than great stores of ammunition, or greater than the powerful ships that connect the trade routes of the earth.

"Oh, Kinnakeet! You are too indifferent to your youth. Oh, Dare County! You have been inconsiderate or too long. Oh, North Carolina! You have underestimated your youth! Oh, America! The greatest nation on earth, you have taken youth for granted. To a great extent, all you're asleep; would that I could awaken you from your slumber."

At breakfast the next morning, Mrs. Keaton said I looked "pert."

Briefly I told her of my determination to fight for a chance to finish the school term.

The expression on her honest face said plainly she thought it was suicidal. At least she couldn't accuse me of being without an appetite, because I devoured an unusually large amount of food, feeling this was essential to my preparations.

Afterward, since she undoubtedly would have visitors dropping in, the three teachers and I went to their room, where they sat dejectedly on one of the beds, while I stood before them.

"Are you willing to try something that's probably unheard of? If you are school can start tomorrow."

"Tomorrow?" they chorused, talking amongst themselves. They had packed and finished their reports, ready to depart for homes.

Then Miss Wood looked at me, speculatively.

"Is it anything that might land us in jail?"

I laughed, "Nothing like that. It would be more a matter of inconvenience. However, the weather is fairly good, and we have to trust it will remain that way, because I would like to start classes tomorrow on the beach."

Their mouths flew open.

"I know it's crazy, but no more than giving up school. Besides, there's no law against it. If it accomplishes nothing else, it will put Kinnakeet on the map. The world'll talk about it."

Miss Wood giggled, "I'm willing. I always did like spectacular things."

I smiled agreeably, thinking how she had dramatized her little drunken boys.

The other two nodded slowly. "Count us in."

I sent word to all the pupils to meet me at the old building after lunch. They came in eager groups, running from Dog Ridge, Cat Ridge, and from Spain.

Standing on a box, I asked, "How many of you would like to see school continue for the rest of the year?"

Every hand went up; that was all I needed.

"Then, let's show the world we want school. Action is stronger than words, so tomorrow, we commence classes on the beach. We'll be there, and you be there, too! See you tomorrow at nine!"

What a scampering ensued as they took off in all directions, yelling.

Thus, school began on the beach, under a clear sky. The old seats had been drug out of the building, and I remembered how I imagined them floating out to sea, as I returned from Manteo. I would never have believed they'd look so good to me.

And what was going on in Kinnakeet? Talk, and plenty of it. Folks could hardly believe that classes were being held, and the students were having a wonderful time.

By the time our first day on the beach ended, a message came that there was a home in Cat Ridge with a large empty room, suitable for the first and second grades. All it needed was a stove. I reported this to Fields Meekins and we removed the stove from the old school. Fields furnished a length of pipe, and we rushed to the house. Curtly the owner said he changed his mind, and firmly shut the door.

I apologized to Fields, feeling I had played the fool, but he was so obviously discouraged, he didn't even reply.

I had no need to be depressed, discouraged, for that evening brought miracles. Three women came to see me, one of whom said she couldn't bear the children attending school on the beach. It would inconvenience her, but she would turn her living room over to us for the rest of the year.

The second woman had seven children, and I knew how she needed every inch of space, but she insisted they'd live packed in a corner while donating their living room.

The third woman had an old house that had been her grandmother's. It was empty for years, but she'd fix it up so, at least, it would be a temporary shelter.

All this influenced Mrs. Keaton so that she insisted we use part of the house next door, in which some of the rooms were for transients.

The nine remaining weeks simply flew by, and I felt I was doing some of my best teaching. How unimportant are adverse conditions if teacher and students are properly motivated!

I met Preacher Price one day, and peering at me over his glasses, he said, "Young man, you have helped develop some of America's foremost citizens."

I felt guilty because I hadn't made it a point to call on him to thank him for his advice, but I had been too busy. I offered him my hand now, and he clasped it in his own.

"You know whose words came to me when everything looked darkest," was all I said.

CHAPTER 15

NEW SCHOOL BUILDING

All that summer of 1932, I dreamed of how wonderful it would be inhabiting a brand new schoolhouse next fall.

I was to be notified when the building was completed, and September found me watching students and teachers go to school. Repeatedly, I told myself there hadn't been enough time because the Kinnakeeters had postponed this endeavor too long. Just as the elements had made the old building unusable, so would the forces of nature furnish much of the needed lumber. The sea, in one of her more benevolent moods, would cast lumber onto the shore, from some unfortunate ship which had sunk in a storm.

October was beautiful here at home where we observed the mountains in the distance, but I kept thinking of October in Kinnakeet. Even with the likelihood of hurricanes, this golden month of Pamlico Sound was not one I liked to miss.

It was November when I was notified that school was to start November 21st. I could scarcely wait to return!

As usual, it was Uncle Tom who met me and patiently tried to answer my eager questions. Because of the isolation of Kinnakeet, transportation was slow, impeding progress. Then too, it had been a mosquito ridden summer. Materials came from Elizabeth City by way of sailboat, and due to the shallow waters of the Sound, transportation was difficult. Also, the swarms of mosquitoes tormented the workers so much, they were forced to leave the project to flee the pests.

I reached Mrs. Keaton's about noon Saturday, and school would begin on Monday. As soon as I had eaten a hasty lunch, I headed for the school. Even before reaching Gibbs' store, students surrounded me, the girls embracing me, and the boys shaking my hand. They tagged along, bursting with excitement, wanting to accompany me when I first glimpsed the building. Our old school was within the village, while the new one was on the open beach east of Kinnakeet. When I glimpsed it, my heart pounded with joy. Four large stove flues pointed heavenward, while a wire fence encircled the yard, and a cement walk led from the gate to the entrance.

The building itself was a long frame structure and looked very modern. We fairly tiptoed inside, nobody saying a word, as we progressed from room to room. I strained to see everything.

Four large classrooms, and a small one, an office, a wide hall, and amazingly, it had an auditorium! Considering how small our village was, this addition was more than adequate; how everyone was going to enjoy it!

In my office, and in each classroom was a new stove, a coal bucket and shovel. The classrooms had ample blackboards too, and adequate cloak space.

The windows were high, and from mine, I got a great view of the Atlantic!

Gradually the young folks left, while I stood alone, observing much that was still lacking. I had to check just how handicapped we still were despite the building, itself.

The office was completely bare, not even a chair in it; while neither library books, nor laboratory equipment was to be found anywhere.

But what annoyed me more than anything else, was that there was not a single new desk in the entire building! Anything that held together from the old building had been placed in the elementary classrooms, and the small high school room. An extra teacher had been hired for high school, and I was grateful there would be someone to help me carry the load.

But what about my own classroom? There were no seats in it, at all. Were we starting school with no place to sit? The auditorium had none either, but that could wait.

I inquired of the school board, and was told the students would have to bring chairs from home. The truth was there were no appropriations made for seats.

School opened on Monday, and because the students hadn't any chairs, they sat on the floor, forming a neat circle. I suggested bringing chairs from home, but few did. Three straight chairs were found in our classroom, three nail kegs, and one chunk of wood block.

It was not lack of interest which kept them from bringing seats, rather, it was because they were too interested to care whether they were on a chair or on the floor. These youngsters were *motivated.* The boys were anxious to get their high school diplomas so they could join the coast guard, while the girls just naturally wanted to learn. They did good class work, and had a thirst for knowledge, and so they learned.

The senior year was not provided for at Kinnakeet, so students transferred to a larger school to graduate. The fact that they held their own upon being transferred was a great satisfaction.

At first, some of the pupils complained of backaches and doing so much written work from this unfamiliar position. But weeks turned into months, and gradually they accustomed themselves to it, and I heard no more.

One morning, as I prepared to go to school, the radio told of a new school building on the mainland. What a satisfactory thing it was! The announcer enumerated its advantages, then spoke with great eloquence about America and how it never stinted when it came to learning. Nothing was too good for America's youth, and nowhere was there a lack of facilities.

I switched off the radio angrily, and as I proceeded to the school, I fumed! Why had I been complacent for so long? We still had no drinking water, and my students were on the floor. Even the lower grades could not find those dilapidated desks and seats very comfortable.

For the first time, our school had become accredited, and next spring would see a group graduating from Kinnakeet, with official high school diplomas. But would the audience be forced to stand in the auditorium throughout this meaningful ceremony?

The first assignment each morning consisted of written work, and the room was always quiet. I wandered about should there be questions and help needed, but actually my mind still seethed. Why, some of my students were on their stomachs, head propped in one hand, and writing with the other! It was a pitiful outrage. Savagely, I began trying to blame this condition on various people, but finally admitted that nobody was at fault as much as the principal! It was not easy to face up to it, and at first, I refuted it. Why had I accepted this without finding a way to overcome it?

It was on my mind the rest of the day, and evening. I took it to bed with me, and when sleep finally came, I still was without a solution.

Suddenly, upon awakening in the morning, I had an idea. It might be fantastic, or even no good at all, but at least, it was a beginning. I felt that something should be done so that the press heard my class was sitting on the floor! Nobody would believe it, but let one news reporter come and see for himself, and it soon would be read by millions. Reporters loved something unusual, which would grip the emotion of the reader.

I chose two young ladies, calling them aside before school started. Would they like to have some seats?

They would, indeed. In fact, both of them complained simultaneously.

They were almost ready for graduation, and had to sit on the floor!

It was ridiculous! No other school had to endure this sort of situation. They bet we were the only school in the country subjected to such indignity.

Purposely, I had elicited their feelings, for it was my intention to try to stay in the background, making it appear spontaneous, without my guidance.

"Do you want seats badly enough to try out a wild idea?"

They said they'd try anything.

"Very few people from up-country come here," I said slowly, as though the idea was vaguely forming in my mind. "But many of them who do come are wealthy and highly educated. I refer, of course, to the sportsmen of whom there are many fishing in Pamlico Sound right now. They come here from Washington, Baltimore, and New York, and if they'd discover our situation, they would be telling the others, or even the press, directly. If eventually it made the newspapers, we would startle people into action."

I could see they were dubious, and I was disappointed.

"Why can't you just ask some of them to tell the press we don't have seats to sit on?"

"Yes," chimed in the other girl. "Tell'em we sit on the floor and write our lessons by resting our textbooks on our laps."

I shook my head. "No, that's the easy way out. And that way never works, it's too blunt and too obvious."

They looked at each other, "You want us to go down to the Sound and tell them?"

"Men will listen to charming young ladies like you," I pointed out. "They will sympathize, and be attracted to you and your problem."

The other girl protested they were too shy. They would simply die, but I was patient, assuring them they'd be good actresses if they tried; they might even manage a few tears.

Finally they agreed, but were filled with misgivings. I couldn't blame them. Perhaps I should call off the whole thing, maybe it was just a wild idea. These girls were my responsibility, and it was possible their parents, if they heard of my plan, would object.

But we did so want those seats!

I watched as far as I could see them trudging off towards the Sound, to where the sportsmen had their boats docked. These men would be curious about the girls and would take time from their fishing to talk with them, never worry! Surely at least one would come and see for himself.

But I was filled with misgivings. Why hadn't I mulled it over for a few more days? Surely, if I had done so, I would have come up with any number of reasons not to send them on such an errand.

I rang the bell for school to begin, and when one student asked about the missing girls, I reported they had business in the village. No more questions were asked.

I thought of other reasons for not sending the girls. The men would see through the scheme at once, thinking me the biggest coward in the world to send two young girls begging for seats.

And suppose there just might be one who was not a gentleman, and would insult the girls? I could scarcely continue with my classes.

At the end of thirty minutes, I kept working my way to the door where I could observe the direction they had taken.

The first hour passed, and still no girls; another thirty minutes, then another. Surely, they didn't have to stay this long!

My nerves were cracking. I would wait no longer but would excuse myself from the room and tear off toward the Sound, praying fervently I was not too late.

Then as I paused in the doorway, what a sight I saw!

The girls were coming, accompanied by a tall, distinguished-looking man, obviously a sportsman. He wore a long-billed cap pulled well over his forehead and held his head high. He walked so rapidly, the girls almost ran to keep alongside him, while the dry sand flew as be progressed.

I hurried back into the schoolroom and rapidly told the students the story, suggesting they be very busy when the stranger arrived.

It was only seconds before a loud, demanding knock sounded on the door. The girls slipped quietly into the room, taking their seats on the floor, while the man regarded me sternly.

"You the principal?"

I assented.

"These girls tell me they have no seats to sit on, and I don't believe it. That's why I'm here."

"It's true, sir. They sit on the floor."

"On the floor?" he boomed. "And what do you sit on?"

"I stand, but I don't have time to sit, anyway, because I conduct more than one lesson simultaneously. They write most of their assignments while I go checking them."

"How can they write without desks?"

"Come in and see," I invited, opening the door wide.

I had never been prouder of my students who misrepresented nothing but did a fine job of getting down to their studies without staring at our visitor. Everyone of them had an open notebook and was occupied with written work. Two girls were using the nail kegs while three others shared the old straight chairs. One girl put her notebook on tip of the wooden block, while others were on the floor, and some leaned against the wall. However, most of the boys were in their usual position, lying on the floor.

He stared at the scene as though he found it hard to believe what he saw. Next, he stepped back out into the hall, and I followed him.

"How nice of you to take an interest in us." I tried to sound casual. "Have you time to see the rest of the building?"

I showed him all of it-the battered seats in the lower classrooms, and the shining new auditorium with no seats at all. He said little, but when we returned to the front entrance, he offered me his hand, thanking me for showing me around. Then he left.

Well, at least we had tried!

The days fell into a pattern again-one week passed, then two. Nothing about our situation appeared in the newspapers. I was deeply disappointed, because the sportsmen had seemed so concerned, and he was such an intelligent chap, too.

On Monday morning of the third week, school had barely started when a coast guardsman delivered a telegram that had arrived for me at Big Kinnakeet Coast Guard Station.

A SHIPMENT OF ONE HUNDRED FIFTY SCHOOL DESKS HAS ARRIVED FROM NEW YORK CITY AT DEPOT ELIZABETH CITY NC FOB

I sat down weakly, on the floor, too excited to stand up. This wonderful person had sent us the desks and chairs, even paying the freight on them!

We were further delighted to find he had included a great number of books and periodicals, the start of our school library.

And we didn't even know his name!

CHAPTER 16

KINNAKEET CHRISTMAS

Mrs. Keaton was a great help to me in many ways during my stay with her. Just as she had divulged the mystery of yeopon, so she familiarized me with the prevailing customs of Christmas.

"The students shower their teachers with gifts the day before Christmas vacation," she said, about a month before. "I thought you'd want to know, because if they don't receive a treat in return, they're going to be awful disappointed."

I exclaimed, "I should say I want to know!"

She quickly added, "Now, Mr. Green, *what* you give won't matter. It's just that you remember them."

"It never would have entered my mind, to exchange gifts, and how embarrassed I'd be. But what do you mean by showering their teachers? Up country, I never heard that expression."

"I mean *shower!* There probably won't be a student without something-no telling what. Perhaps clothing, toilet goods, candy, or books."

"Well, I've known teachers to receive something from a few students, but this-!"

"We're different," said Mrs. Keaton.

"In a nice way," I replied.

I lost no time in procuring a mail order catalog, and thumbing through it carefully, I selected Eversharp pencils, ordering one for each student. When they came, I wrapped them in gay holiday paper with plenty of ribbon, putting them aside until the last day of school, before the holiday.

By then, the youngsters were immersed in the holiday spirit. But I ignored them until I heard them talking about parades.

"Parades at Christmas?" I asked incredulously. "Never heard of one. Can't see how you could scare up enough participants in such a small place."

They felt I was to be pitied because I had reached adulthood without hearing of such a thing.

"We Kinnakeet younguns just get some old tin pans, pieces of tin, whistles, any noisemaker, and run up and down the roads sounding them," a young man explained.

"It must look crazy."

"Perhaps, but no one can see us."

People would be sure to *hear* them, though, so I asked what kept them invisible.

"It's dark. We get up at three a.m. and parade up and down until day breaks, then we go home to bed."

"The morning before Christmas?" I guessed.

"We do it every morning except Sunday for three weeks, and it's almost time to start."

I puckered up, then released a long, low whistle. "How do the grownups stand it?"

"Oh, it *mommocks* them a lot, but they put up with it."

I had been in Kinnakeet long enough to have learned that *mommock* meant to fret or worry a person, just as "from can to can't" meant from dawn to dusk, and "family favor" meant simply the general family characteristics.

After that first night of being awakened, I began to ask how this got started, but none could enlighten me. All they knew was that it had occurred for many years, and did have the redeeming feature of carols. Surprisingly, after the first few times, I was able to turn over and go back to sleep.

This was a time of homecoming; so many folks would return who had not been here since last Christmas. The United States Coast Guard, and other armed forces in various parts of the world claimed so many of our stalwart men, it was said the sun never sets on the Kinnakeeter.

I was well aware of another reason why Christmas meant so much to everyone. They were strongly Christian and were imbued with a deeply religious feeling. The churches kept the children busy after school, rehearsing Christmas programs. And there was another observance here, none left church after the program without having received a gift, church members saw to that.

A week before school closed for the holidays, students came to me to discuss their plans for the last day of school. They intended to sing carols, along with a suitable program, which of course included the giving of gifts.

Mrs. Keaton had not exaggerated! Teachers received exactly as many pleasing gifts as they had pupils! I felt overwhelmed with delightful presents.

The custom prevailed while I stayed at Kinnakeet as teacher-principal, but the day before the Christmas holidays, my third year there, left imprints still vivid in my mind.

We had moved into our new building that November, and to make it a very special celebration, the students wanted to start school at the time the parade would ordinarily start.

"Three o'clock in the morning?" I cried. "What in the name of common sense do you want to start school then, for?"

They had their arguments ready-one was they would be dismissed earlier.

"You don't know how good it would make you feel."

I admitted never starting school at that time, but I greatly doubted if it would make me feel good.

Eagerly, I though of an argument, "There are no lights; we can't have school in the dark."

"We planned having our program first, except for the giving of gifts. By the time we get around to studying, we'll be able to see."

"And I suppose you don't need to see in order to present the program."

"Lanterns," they explained, "will add to the festivity of the occasion."

Unanimously, they chorused they'd be on time. After three weeks of getting up to parade, I had no doubt about it!

Students and teachers discussed their proposal, and finally a compromise was made. We settled for five o'clock, instead of three, but even this made me yawn just thinking of it. I had experienced so many unusual things here in this isolated village that I was reaching the point where I would try anything once.

With boundless energy the students began decorating the building. They bought crepe paper at the local stores and from the forest at the Cape, they came with arms filled with cedar and holly, as well as the beautiful yeopon with its red berries.

Thus, the morning of the last day arrived, and it is one which my memory will cherish, always. I pity those who have not experienced something similar, at least once.

I told Mrs. Keaton I would be leaving so early, I'd have to forgo breakfast. She only laughed at our plans without comment. At four o'clock I arose and as I made my way toward the schoolhouse beyond the village, I was unusually aware of the beauty around me. The night had no moon, but the sky was studded with twinkling stars, and the thunderous roar of the wild Atlantic filled the air, as I neared the school. Located as it was, on the open beach, we benefited fully from the roaring sea.

The school building loomed dark just ahead. The silence was profound at five o'clock, and I was confident none would be tardy.

There was the flickering of lights from oil lamps in various homes at the village, which increased with startling rapidity Shortly, two boys arrived carrying lighted lanterns. They built a roaring fire in the cast-iron stove in the auditorium, which outdid the roar of the sea. Going to the door, it seemed to me that lights were moving through Dog Ridge, Cat Ridge, and that northern portion called Spain.

Accompanying the lights was sound, the pleasant noise of laughing and chatting, and generally making merry. What an environment! Onward they poured, until they were close enough for me to distinguish between the voices of the first-graders, those of the elementary grades, and my high school students.

Not one youngster had failed to wake up, and few missed bringing a lantern. There were big ones, small ones, and ordinary sized ones.

The auditorium was still without seats, but we had a piano. The students sat along the walls, or gathered in groups across the floor with little folks leaning against the bigger ones. Everyone was merry, while the heating stove glowed red hot. The lanterns cast eerie shadows on the new white walls, and each pupil brought his gift, the result of savings and sacrifice. He presented it with a loving heart.

The kindergarten teacher sat at the piano, beginning to play, "Joy To The World."

I felt no place on earth had more good voices than Kinnakeet and now, as they burst into song, I was absolutely convinced.

They put their young souls into it, especially when they reached "And heav'n and nature sing," the bigger boys coming in on the bass. I wiped tears from my eyes, unashamedly.

We sang one Christmas song after another, until it came time for "Silent Night," then, they turned the wicks of their lanterns so they emitted only the merest trace of light.

Gray dawn was creeping in now, dissipating some of the magic. We went to our classrooms, but routine study and recitations were impossible. We simply went dutifully through the motions. It was a relief when the time came for our exchange of gifts, and dismissal of classes until after Christmas.

This first year in the new school building was different in another way, too. Because the opening of school was delayed until late in November, we were going to forgo our usual holiday. School would resume immediately after the Christmas weekend. Thus, I remained in Kinnakeet, attending the program at the Methodist Church on Saturday night, regretfully forgoing the Pentecostal one, since it was held simultaneously.

Sunday gave me the opportunity of attending the Methodist morning services, while going to the Pentecostal services that evening.

By the time we tasted Mrs. Keaton's wonderful Christmas dinner on Monday, all of us around her bountiful table agreed this was one of the best Christmases we had ever spent.

But I was unprepared, when school started again on Tuesday, to hear the students talking of a coming Christmas celebration.

"It's on the fifth of January, up at Chicamacomico," they chorused at my query.

They insisted that it was important I accompany them to the town on the northern end of Hatteras Island.

"Why the celebration?" I wanted to know.

"They believe in celebrating *old* Christmas, and feel it comes properly on the fifth of January, instead of the twenty-fifth of December. It is their belief that Christ was born on this day."

Thus, I accompanied them to help the folks at Chicamacomico observe Christmas. It was not at all unlike the one we just enjoyed in Kinnakeet, and I found that celebrating two holidays was twice as much fun as celebrating one.

CHAPTER 17

MY FRIEND BUD RANS GRAY

Mrs. Keaton's Sis Mitt, who lived close by was a great source of comfort to Mrs. Keaton, and I had not been in Kinnakeet long before I began to feel similarly about her husband, Bud Rans Gray. He was an excellent story teller and his tales of this part of the country were colorful and, I was convinced, true. I never missed a chance to spend an evening with him, hoping to be well entertained.

One particular Friday in October, although the hurricane season should have passed, the wind and water had reached alarming proportions by the time school was dismissed. I arrived at my boarding house soaked despite my raincoat; I had the sensation of having flown there instead of walking.

Mrs. Keaton was placidly preparing one of my favorites, chicken potpie served with steamed cabbage, and pone bread. I changed into dry garments and sat where I could see, through weaving fig trees, the madness which was Pamlico Sound. I looked wistfully over at Bud Rans' house; water ran off the roof in a torrent. It was going to be a long evening, so decided after supper, to spend it with him.

"Surely you wouldn't venture out on a night like this," exclaimed my landlady.

"I have become a Kinnakeeter, and a true one would go out in such weather."

She lifted her hands and laughed.

Hip boots on, head and body wrapped in a raincoat, flashlight in hand, I made a dash for it, guided by the mellow lamplight shining through their kitchen window. Even then, I had to follow a wire fence which would take me to the only door they'd be able to open because of the wind. I pounded but they didn't hear. Kinnakeet doors were always unlocked.

"I've come to be entertained," I admitted. "I felt blue, and you know so many interesting stories."

I knew he was as eager to relate them as I was to listen, but he had to be coaxed, protesting that he might repeat something he previously told.

"If you do, I'll stop you."

"You never told him how some of the inlets were formed." his wife prompted him dutifully.

"And I have often wondered."

"Bud Rans, honey, tell Mr. Green what happened when Hatteras and Oregon Inlets were cut."

Nobody ever addressed him as Bud or Rans. It was always Bud Rans!

Sis Mitt turned to me. "We sat for hours when we was younguns listening to the old folks talk."

He said it was hard to believe, and folks from up-country would accuse him of lying, but it *was* long before his time, even though he'd heard exactly the same tale from many oldsters who were alive when it happened.

"How long ago was that?" I prodded.

The Oregon and Hatteras Inlets were formed in the same year, 1846.

I asked him how many months it took, and he laughed heartily, slapping his knee with is broad hand.

"They were cut out in one night."

I stared at him, unbelievingly.

My host said he couldn't remember all the details, but he leaned back in the old rocking chair, folded his arms, and crossed his legs.

Back in the old days, folks had to be their own meteorologists, and mostly did a commendable job. But on the night of September 7, 1846, came a storm that baffled them.

He straightened. "Now remember, Stanley E., there were as many people on the island then, as now. Been folks aplenty here for four hundred years."

At that time, the land where Hatteras Inlet was situated, and the area surrounding it, was one of the most populous places on Hatteras Island. He estimated there might be a thousand people, who lived in good homes, with bounties of oak and long leaf pine timber, not to mention the wealth of building materials from shipwrecks.

Bud Rans emphasized the beauty of the homes which stood exactly where the inlets were cut. The gardens were a sight to see. I questioned him about such greenery on sandy soil, and it seems they had wonderful fertilizer. They brought rich humus from the Cape woods, and used tons of fish from Sound and Sea. Also tons more rotted seaweed washed ashore. The villagers were proud of their orchards of figs and peaches.

Sis Mitt brewed coffee which she poured now, steaming hot and strong. The house shook and creaked.

"On the day before the storm, folks sensed it coming, and did what they could to prepare for it. Just afore nightfall, dark clouds boiled up out of the sea and covered the island. The rain came so hard, it was like the sea had risen up and fell down again."

He interrupted himself to explain how folks were gathered in crowds when a storm approached.

I nodded; I had noticed it was so. "Fear," I observed.

He thought not, because often the storm would last three days, and it was more for social reasons.

On this particular September night in 1846, they gathered in homes at the northern end of Hatteras village, having first shuttered and battened down their houses as best they could. After all, they had experienced many a storm, and survived them in good shape.

They brewed yeopon tea and visited, laughing and singing, finally spreading quilts on the floor trying to sleep. The storm raged unabated, and they were reconciled to the fact their gardens would be ruined and their orchards damaged.

At daylight, they looked out, and there was no southern part of town! The inlet that cut across the island was three miles wide and proved an average of twenty-five feet deep.

It became a great connecting link of the Atlantic and Pamlico, without a loss of life.

He stopped, waiting for my reaction, and I admitted it beat anything I ever heard.

"You still haven't told him the most important thing, Bud Rans, honey."

"No man can explain it," he said, "but similar things have been happening for four hundred years. It must be a Higher Power."

"You mean folks were guided to the northern end of town?"

He nodded. Since Columbus, it's been common knowledge the Cape Hatteras area is the most destructive place on earth. Yet, it is also the safest place to live. The losses in property and lives around Hatteras Island and in the Hatteras Sea were tremendous. Yet, other than a six-month old baby, there were no deaths from abnormal forces during the past four hundred years.

The mother of the baby became frightened and tried to reach the house of a neighbor. The wind threw her down and the baby drowned; had she remained inside, nothing would have happened.

Sis Mitt poured more coffee, and looking reflectively into the cup, I said, "It's strange not more has been written about this area."

"Folks that do write of it, exaggerate," my friend protested.

He told me about one of their young men who went up country for a haircut. When they discovered he was from Hatteras Island, they started questioning him. He told so many lies, he got tired of it and decided to tell them the facts. He explained about the high and low tides, and how the moon caused them.

Quickly his audience bristled, and a fellow finally told him he'd believed him up to now, but that he'd better stop lying!

Bud Rans told me about the grapes of long ago which grew in great profusion, especially from Kinnakeet to the Cape woods. These black grapes were here when the white man arrived. Grape vines so heavy they served as swings for the younguns, might be a hundred yards wide and five or six miles long, and loaded with grapes.

It was said sailors far out to sea could catch the delightful fragrance of ripened grapes when the wind was right, and if they were drying or rotting, the odor would resemble grape wine.

Bud Rans mentioned the great number of fowl flying in for the winter, and how they were slaughtered for their feathers which found a ready market in Elizabeth City.

There was another October evening with Bud Rans, which I remembered as especially delightful, but a night of quite different weather conditions!

The lumber from our old school building was used to construct the recreational center of the village. It always pleased me to think how the walls which had sheltered Kinnakeet's youth for generations, later served them recreationally!

It was called Pritchard's Place and was located right in the center of Cat Ridge. In fact, everybody on Dog Ridge used the expression, "Up to Pritchard's."

Despite the fact most of the Kinnakeeters thought recreation was the work of the devil, the place had two pool tables and many of the boys became experts at the game.

I decided that far more good was done here than harm, though I never played pool myself because of strong public opinion. There were music, soft drinks, candy bars, and Pritchard always saw that good behavior prevailed. Often, I went to spend an evening there, for I never neglected our comradeship, since the fine young folks invited me to join them. I was referred to by the boys as "Captain," while the girls addressed me, outside of school, as Señor Verde.

Thus, one warm October night, I sauntered over to Pritchard's Place, which was a dull place, tonight. Perhaps I just wasn't in the mood for it, but I left shortly afterwards, finding Sis Mitt and Bud Rans on Mrs. Keaton's porch, the three of them chatting together. They urged me to join them, and I welcomed the chance. I mentioned the balmy weather, and Bud Rans said it reminded him of October nights when he was a boy, "and there were trees on the beach, all the way from Kinnakeet to the Cape woods."

"Oh, come now," I protested.

He insisted the forest was dense, and the trees, huge. Live oaks, supposed to be over a thousand years old, were the prettiest things one ever saw.

But man began cutting down some of the trees, and shipped them away. The land became nothing but sand and shells, and it began to disappear into the ocean. Down at the Cape, a storm washed away half the sandhills, enabling one to walk along the ocean's edge at high tide, and pick grapes off the vines above.

The beautiful live oak lumber was sold to be used in shipbuilding. It brought a good price, and men were big enough fools to sell it.

Bud Rans said his father had been opposed to it, because nature spent a million years building this island and covering it with a vast forest, then along came stupid man, who undid it in a few years.

The three of them spoke of the elder Rans, who had preached endlessly about saving the trees he loved, and how he claimed cutting them down would be the ruination of the island.

"Back in them days, there was no such thing as a land tide," said Bud Rans. He remembered the first one occurring, though folks hadn't dreamt of such a happening. He had noticed the live oaks, their tops practically touching the ground, then his gaze went beyond, down the road toward Gibbs' store where he saw a great blanket of water racing toward his house.

"I bet you were scared,"

"I was frightened to death," said Bud Rans.

His wife yelled, and so had Mrs. Keaton, whom they always called Beck. By the time he turned around, the water was in the house.

"Seems silly, now that we're so used to land tides, but it was awful then." He laughed, remembering that the garden was ruined-all but the onions, which appeared to have benefited by the salt bath.

We sat quietly for a time, listening to the night sounds, when Bud Rans asked if I had ever noticed how close the lighthouse was to the sea.

"So close it seems as though the Atlantic might undermine it."

"Many people feel the same way, and when the tide's high, the breakers reach almost to its base."

I conjectured this was not the case when it was built originally.

He nodded. "Almost two miles away." He added just a short time ago, there was a baseball diamond just east of the lighthouse. At present, a good distance between field and the ocean remained.

"And the Cape used to be directly off the Cape Hatteras lighthouse. It's moved a mile southward; it's amazing the way things change around here."

He said vast acreages could change in one storm. A man could own several acres of land on the ocean side, and a storm would come along and the next morning all, or part of it would be gone.

"Then again, you might wake up and find you have many more acres than when you went to sleep!"

"A strange spot," I commented.

"And some strange folks, by and large. Take Ol' Bob. Did I ever tell you about him?"

Ol' Bob was a sailor, as tough as they came. He drank like a thirsty fish and the devil couldn't outcuss him. He apparently knew he was so mean nobody would bury him when he died, so he made himself a coffin. He took his own measurements and fitted it comfortably to the correct size.

When it was completed, he pushed it under his bed. However, as time passed, he formed the habit of sleeping in the coffin instead of his bed. He was probably worried folks wouldn't put him in the coffin, if he weren't already there.

"And what do you suppose he used the coffin for when he wasn't in it?"

I hadn't the slightest notion.

"He kept his homemade liquor there, and he had a supply that must have made him feel very secure."

Ol' Bob even went so far as to carve his own tombstone and epitaph.

"What did it say?" I was really curious now.

Sis Mitt said, "I can recite it, word for word.

"Poor Ol' Bob, here he lies
No one laughs and no one cries.
No one knows and no one cares
Where he goes and how he fares."

Mrs. Keaton stirred, wanting to add to the conversation. She said a new minister came here once to take over the Methodist pulpit, and he heard such wild tales of the storms that he departed, too frightened to remain.

"I never could understand such a man," she said simply. "Where was his faith? He should have known if he came here for a good purpose, the Lord would take care of him, just as he has for the rest of us for four hundred years."

CHAPTER 18

ICE CREAM

Once there was a time when the latter part of September would have made a better July, weatherwise. On Monday, which was uncomfortably hot, and without drinking water at school, the day seemed especially tedious.

I felt something secretive going on, a condition I prided myself on being able to detect unfailingly. Yet, with the thermometer reading as it did, maybe this time it was the heat rather than something being planned. I tried to tell myself this until school was dismissed, and four students remained. They loitered about, trying to look nonchalant, and I disregarded the fact they had not left with the others.

Going to the open east window, I gazed out on the Cape Hatteras Sea, acting indifferently, too. Finally, the students wandered over and stared at me until I had no choice but to turn and look at them directly.

One of the fellows said, "Mr. Green, wouldn't you like to make a lot of money for the school?"

There were certainly many small items which would do wonders for our studies and experiments, and to use for research references. "Like maybe a thousand dollars?" I teased him.

"We know a way," he said, soberly.

One of the girls broke in. "Big money, Mr. Green," She waved her hands over her head. "When we have an ice cream party, folks come from all over. Now with the weather so hot, they'll eat much more than usual."

First one would speak up, then another.

By "all over," they meant from other towns as Salvo, Waves, Chicamacomico, The Cape, Trent, and Hatteras.

Everybody came, from *younguns* to grandparents.

"Where, may I ask, would the ice cream come from?"

They groaned at me, surprised.

"We make it!"

"You are getting ahead of me," I said sternly. "We have nothing to work with-no ice cream freezers, no ingredients, nothing to serve it in, and nowhere to serve it. We need a place equipped to manufacture and serve it."

One of the fellows who had thus far remained silent spoke now; his tone was as restrained as mine had been.

"My dear man, Mr. Green, Captain, we don't have to have it at school. Kinnakeeters been having ice cream suppers since I was big enough to crawl, and I suppose long before that. We go all over town to procure what's needed."

"Beg, you mean?"

"We don't call it that. Almost everybody gives something and those that don't give outright, send us to the store for things we charge to their accounts."

Knowing Kinnakeeters as well as I now did, I supposed they were rational, yet, the whole thing sounded too wild. I finally yielded to their pleas, and when they had secured my consent, they left, all talking at once. I stood there bewildered, wondering if I had acted wisely. I was talked into something I knew absolutely nothing about, and it made me uneasy.

The date for the ice cream supper was set for a week from Friday night, and I could only hope the hot weather would hold until then.

The first of next week found them ready to explode with excitement. These isolated young people had so few social functions, I could understand why they anticipated so much. They were eager to get started on the project, although I protested it was only Monday.

Some items would be borrowed instead of donated outright, such as freezers, tables, lights, but I had to act the stern principal and hold them down.

"You don't need all week to get ready for this social," I warned them. "Your preparation must be done outside regular school hours."

The truth was, I had gotten a little excited about it myself, and because I was so near their ages, nothing would have suited me better than to lock the door and take off, helter-skelter to see how much we could collect.

One of the students said, "If it got to the point where needed time off from classes, we could have it, couldn't we?"

Purposefully, I remained vague, telling him we'd decide it later in the week.

But before they could settle down to their regular assignments, I had to appoint a committee to remain after school to plan the big event.

As soon as school was dismissed, I stood with the committee near the open window. If anything, this day was even hotter than the Monday when we first talked of this endeavor.

I still felt terribly uninformed and inadequate. "You mean everybody contributes something willingly?"

"You can depend on a Kinnakeeter; then they attend the party and buy it back!"

How many would be required to canvas the town?

They suggested all the high school boys.

I nodded, "All the boys, then."

The spokesman for the group said, "Bless your heart, Mr. Green, honey! When do we start?"

This strange habit of everyone calling each other "honey" still took me by surprise, but I ignored it, to formulate our plans.

"How about you two boys dividing the others into small groups, and giving each a definite territory? That'll make it orderly. Then Friday, we'll dismiss school early enough to accomplish everything and be ready to serve."

I waited for a reaction to this, but when none came, I decided their silence meant affirmation.

On Friday morning, the spokesman reported all was in order. They would bring the ingredients to school, make the ice cream here, and have it ready for sale when the crowds arrived.

My heart landed in my throat. "You call that good planning? For goodness sakes, boys can't make ice cream!"

"Why not?" retorted one of the girls stoutly. "They can make it better'n we can."

I thought of Bill Keaton and his potato salad that was the best I had ever tasted, but not being inclined toward cooking, I frowned dubiously.

One of the boys elucidated. "People from the mainland are kinda startled by the fact that the males in Kinnakeet are good cooks." I knew he referred to me.

School was dismissed early, and I went to my room, feeling a need to gird myself. I couldn't eat supper, so I returned at four o'clock to find that the boys had "gobs of stuff." A careful glance around appeared as though they had plenty of everything - eggs, milk, sugar, vanilla, and salt to pack with the ice into the freezers. And, certainly, there was plenty of boy-power to turn the freezers.

"What do you plan to serve it in?" I inquired.

They had attended to it; they liked cones, which the merchants donated. The older folks wanted theirs in dishes, and they'd bring their own. Some even took the ice cream back home to eat.

"You'll make enough to serve all of Dare County, including most of the Outer Banks." I frowned again. "You won't be able to sell all you're making."

A girl spoke up and said their big worry was they weren't going to have enough to satisfy the demand.

Just then, a scream sounded outside in the yard, which the Kinnakeeters referred to as the "pound." We all hurried outside. The slat fence enclosing it had a broken strip on it, and through this had come a huge black sow with six little pigs. The sow became frightened, and the terrified pigs set up a terrific squealing. The girl who screamed thought the sow, racing around to escape, was chasing her.

The boys ejected the live stock from the schoolyard, and we returned to the work at hand.

Suddenly, I shouted, "Ice! I bet nobody thought about ice to freeze all this," I turned an accusing glare on each of them. However, the boy who had been boss from the start took me in tow.

"Mr. Green, honey, come with me."

On the north side of the schoolhouse lay a block of ice which must have weighed two hundred pounds. It was wrapped in burlap.

"Make you feel better?"

I knew he was teasing me, but he had no idea just how much better I felt, being burdened with an awful sense of responsibility for the success of this function.

"Where'd you get it?" I asked weakly.

Uncle Clemy Gray had donated it, and if that was not enough, they were to go to his ice house for more.

It was a frustrating situation here at Kinnakeet-I had said it frequently, and I told myself again, as I stared at the tremendous block of ice. There was nothing these Kinnakeeters wouldn't donate willingly to their youngun; yet, they had let them suffer in that decrepit old schoolhouse until the hurricane made it impossible. And even then, I had to contrive obtaining seats before we could experience any comfort in the new building. It just didn't make sense!

By the time the sun set, ice was being pulverized; it went into the wooden freezers which the boys had meticulously scalded inside and out. First the ice went in, then the salt - more ice, more salt.

Next, some of the boys seated themselves atop the freezers to steady them, while others cranked.

It was a humid night and sweat poured from those turning the cranks. These young people worked enthusiastically, and it was a pleasure to see them so near the end of their project.

To my surprise, folks brought cake and pie to sell along with the cream. How they were arriving-from all directions! They came from the coast guard stations, and everything was fine at this point, except the building was not yet ready for night affairs and the lighting, inadequate, even though the girls brought extra lamps from home.

But folks were having fun; the schoolhouse was full, the "pound," too.

Suddenly, a strong wind came up, increasing in velocity, so no light remained burning.

What a predicament!

The cream was about half sold; plenty of cake and pie remained, but the place was plunged into darkness.

These inventive boys began to light matches, lining up around the refreshment tables. One boy would hold a match until it burned his fingers, at which point, the boy next to him would have one going.

Stolidly they kept at this continually, until every bit of ice cream was sold, every crumb cake, and every wedge of pie.

When we had everything ready to leave for the night, we went to Mrs. Keaton's and counted our money. I never would have believed it, the nice sum we had!

The whole project was so well managed and executed, the response so outstanding, that the next time those *younguns* asked to have an ice cream party I gave them full permission, without concern.

And that was where I made a mistake.

Ice cream was not sold on the island, and this, of course, was one reason for the eagerness of the citizens to attend such an event. Freezers were plentiful, and ice was imported from Elizabeth City and stored in the fish house out on the Sound, where it was needed to pack fish for exportation.

I was convinced now, whatever amount of ice cream was made, it was never enough to satisfy the demand.

Arriving later than I had previously, I found the ice cream already being frozen. There was a strong aroma permeating the room, but I gave it little thought.

The girls came with their beautiful cakes.

The ice cream had frozen and was set aside, heavily covered.

When they started serving, someone asked me, "What makes it so dark?"

Still unsuspecting, I shook my head. Finally, when I decided to purchase some ice cream, one of my girl students approached me, asking, "Mr. Green, honey, do you know what those crazy boys have done? They've spiked the ice cream."

"They *what?*"

"Everybody'll get some kinda drunk."

I was horrified, especially since most Kinnakeeters were strongly opposed to liquor. "You mean they put whiskey in it?"

She shook her head, no. It seemed the usual flavoring sold on the island had a high alcohol content, and the boys canvassed the town soliciting flavoring, so no one would realize the enormous amount they were using.

Hastily, I rushed to where the ice cream was being served. It was almost a chocolate color. Putting my hands behind my back, I stood watching, not certain what to do.

The sales were brisk! One freezer after another was quickly emptied, the purchasers spooning ice cream into their mouths in great quantities. They were laughing and talking with their neighbors, wonderfully animated. It appeared not to matter whether they rubbed elbows with someone from their own church, or from the church opposite one. It was inconsequential whether people went to church or not!

Perhaps this mild alcoholism was not so objectionable after all.

I became so entranced in watching the crowd milling about, many returning for seconds and thirds, that when I realized I hadn't had any, every bit was gone!

It was one time I pretended ignorance. The boys had spiked the ice cream, sold all of it, and listened to pleas for more. Everybody departed, happy, but the deception seemed better forgotten.

CHAPTER 19

MACK

Mack Gray was one of my first students at Kinnakeet. He was also a member of the first graduating class.

During the latter part of his junior year, we became quite well acquainted. He had then completed two years of high school under me, which meant I'd taught him every subject.

There was little age difference between us, contributing to the fact that we were able to become friends. It was from his written themes that I discovered this sixteen-year-old was a brilliant thinker. Gradually, we discussed subjects so often avoided by people.

Mack and I never claimed to have solved life's mysteries, but we did grope with subjects that had inconclusive answers.

Both of us were fond of strolling along the open beach of the Cape Hatteras Sea, deriving inspiration from the water. On one particular night, the moon was new, and stars twinkled with special brilliance.

Cape Hatteras lighthouse, six miles away, beckoned us, and we swung along, not talking for some distance. When we had gone about three miles, we each took an orange crate that was washed ashore, and sat down to rest.

"I'm used to the sea," he said, "but even though this is home, it's hard for me to realize we're sitting on the shores of the most destructive body in the world. However, it's responsible for every Kinnakeeter, living or dead."

I laughed, but he reminded me that all of them were descendants of shipwrecked people. They were from distant parts of the world who had no intention of being cast up on these wild shores. They were considered dead in their homelands. And cut off from their native lands forever. Many came from the homes of culture and wealth, and were forced to live on this isolated island, with only a small tribe of Hatteras Indians.

"The sea is a unique grave," I observed. "I am impressed by the lesson it can teach mankind."

I could not see my companion in the darkness, but I imagined him frowning. "You mean it teaches us to stay away from it?"

"No, nothing like that. Somehow all of mankind is represented. Many whom this sea has claimed were outstanding people. The sea is no respecter of race, financial status, culture, slave or freeman. Of course, some of Cape Hatteras Sea's dead were prejudiced against other races, religions, cultures or even places, but they all ended up in the same watery grave. They couldn't even live without prejudice, making earth a better place for all, but they sleep in death, side by side."

We rose from our orange crates and resumed walking on the sand, hard and damp in places, soft and yielding in others. Mack said he had never thought of it just like that, but he agreed.

I find that people like to discuss their problems, and aspirations with others, but mind you, not just anybody. Those who would serve as a confidant must be sympathetic, and never reveal any secrets.

Mack and I had many long walks in which we exchanged the intimate thoughts. It was a fast friendship, which we enjoyed, and did wonders for me in overcoming the loneliness I had known when first arriving in Kinnakeet.

I began to realize that more can be learned about people by such a friendship than all the psychology books can teach.

There are many people who live close physically, yet are worlds apart emotionally. They are strangers in a phase of existence which is all-important.

Like most teen-agers, Mack was unable to grasp the realities of life, and tried to rationalize them to his satisfaction, but always he found no adequate answer.

He was a tall, handsome chap with shocking blue eyes, and overflowed with dynamism. He had a good voice, and when he strummed a guitar and sang, it was something to remember! Often I wished that his abilities were fewer; he took them so for granted, and had never been challenged.

When we strolled together, or sat talking, we were pals, but I was still the principal, and Mack the student, in school. I never forgot my first duty as head of the Kinnakeet school system was to preserve law and order. If a decision had to be made, one must consider the welfare of the school as a whole, regardless of individuals.

Mack was seventeen in his senior year, and by then my fears became an actuality, life had become monotonous. He assumed an attitude of disgust with life. Although he was tops mentally and physically, there was no competition with other students, nothing to give him spirit, or make him fight to stay on top. He drifted, and the more he did, the greater was his disgust. Usually he was late, and classes he did attend were poorly prepared. Also, he took no interest in athletics connected with the school. But no phase of his schooling was as grossly neglected as was French. He disliked it, eventually reaching the point where he made no pretense of studying it. It was his first class of the day, and hence easily missed because he was late. When he was in the classroom, he was a disciplinary problem to his teacher.

Just six weeks before school was out for the year, a knock came on my classroom door. Before I could reach it, the knock sounded again, urgently.

The French teacher motioned me into the hall, clearly she was upset.

"I sent Mack away; he is not to come back, ever."

"What on earth did he do?"

She said it was not only what he had done, but what he hadn't. She had a long list of complaints about his disruptive attitude, generally. He couldn't understand why he was forced to study French.

I promised to see him after school. He was in my physics class and I told him I'd like to see him in the library after school. He said nothing, but of course he knew why.

The prospects of this conversation upset me. Why did it have to be him? His companionship meant so much-would he be lost to me now?

Mack was wrong, and I was the one who must set him straight. There was no way out, Graduation was close, and if he did not pass French, he wouldn't graduate.

After school, instead of going to the library, he came my classroom, saying he was in a hurry and could I see him now?

"No, Mack, go into the library and wait for me."

I knew him so well, I sensed he dreaded this private conference. So did I, for that matter. He probably believed the French teacher would be there, too. However, she had no more desire to be present than I did to have her. This was between

Mack and me. I waited until no one else was around. If I failed Mack now, he wouldn't finish high school, and he had such potentialities!

The library was a small pleasant room, with two large windows overlooking Pamlico Sound. It was a perfect day; sunbeams danced on the water, tinging it with specks of gold.

I shut the door noisily, but Mack, looking at the Sound, gave no indication he heard. I walked over to him and spoke his name. He turned and looked at me, his blue eyes conveying eloquently his dislike. He held a long stick in his right hand, which had been carved from an old broom handle. Without speaking, he handed it over.

"What is this for?"

"To beat the hell out me!"

I stared at him.

"You know I'd rather you did that than lecture. We're pals, do me a favor, beat me and get it over with, but don't preach."

I tossed the stick under the counter.

"Talking will only make things worse," he warned, as sweat trickled down his cheeks and down his collar.

I thought not only did I have to persuade Mack to return to his French class, but I had to convince his teacher to allow him back.

I looked at him without flinching; I meant business. "We're going to talk this through."

He continued glancing at me then out at the Sound.

"This is Friday and I'm free until Monday if need be, although, I can't say I want to spend the weekend here."

Another quick look at me.

"Let's get it over with."

He turned, saying, "If it's got to be, go ahead and preach your sermon. I'll listen."

I plunged in, trying to make him realize his imprudence, and give him initiative to accomplish something good.

"Everything here is between us, now, and I expect a proper answer to my questions. I expect the truth, and I mean business, so if you're not willing to take this seriously, we stay here until you do."

"Aren't you a little rigid?"

"If I am, I have good reason, but I'll give you all the chances necessary, to defend yourself."

He perked up, saying,

"Listen, Mr. Green, let me alone; forget about me. I'm no good; I ain't nothing and never will be. I don't like school and the French teacher doesn't like me because I'm a rascal!"

He pulled his right ear and rubbed his forehead, obviously waiting for my reaction. However, I stood unrelentingly, without speaking.

He conducted quite a monologue, his statements interspersed by pauses. "There's no use wastin' time on me, Mr. Principal. Tell me what she said about me. Oh, you wouldn't do that. I shoulda known, it wasn't anything good. She thinks I'm a skunk. Not just an ordinary one, but a dirty, low-down, stinking one."

He looked out over the Sound again, where flecks of sunlight danced on the waves. Moistening his lips, Mack stood for a while on his right foot, then shifted to his left one. Again, his hand rubber his forehead.

Finally, I asked, "You finished?"

"Ain't I said enough?"

"Are you through?"

"I'm through." He feigned boredom.

"There won't be ordinary questions, some will be very personal. Answer truthfully regardless of how they sound. Have I made myself clear?"

He said I was only too clear.

Ignoring his insolence, I said I wanted his honest opinion about a certain fellow. He was an unusual person, and Mack was to answer my questions with his first thought.

"Promise?"

"I promise."

Mack was anxious to get out of the library-so was I! We were both prisoners. He had been resisting my preaching-which was just what he wasn't going to get.

"The unfortunate thing about this fellow is that he's cruel without realizing the consequences. He is badly mistreating a certain person, or at least, that's how I see it. You might regard it in quite a different light, but don't forget, you have the privilege of interpreting the whole thing as you see fit."

I was rewarded by seeing the insolence on his young face change to an expression of mild curiosity.

"The strangest part is that he's cruel to only one person. And that person has many talents and abilities. The youngster he's so cruel to is in good health, and has an extraordinarily good mind. Besides all that, he is handsome."

"So, how was he mistreated?"

I took courage.

"That's the awful part of this kind of cruelty. It's not noticeable, yet it's cruelty of the worst kind. Despite the fact the world knows about this sort of cruelty, it ignores it, and it has held back man's progress more than any other thing.

"The young man being so mistreated had many wonderful characteristics, but he was rendered helpless when it came to developing his talents. He had very little opportunity.

"Besides, his growth was stifled, and he was so restrained, his most important qualities were dwarfed.

"In truth, his mental abilities, personality, and even his outlook on life is being warped. If this bondage is not ended, he will never be the man he was meant to be. As it looks now, the bondage still holds him. Alas, he will soon fade away, but he had such wonderful chances. What a pity he is denied the opportunity he so deserves!"

Mack appeared to have momentarily forgotten he was waiting for a *sermon*. He was intrigued by what I was telling him.

"What would you think of someone who hindered the growth of a young man, mentally, and from all appearances he'll never realize his potential?"

"If this fellow is keeping the youngun bound up like that, why don't somebody do something about it?" Mack pulled on his ear.

"How I wish I could answer that! Fact is, in spite of how this young man is being treated, no law affects the fellow who's treating him this way. Man never has learned how to control this. The fellow has the freedom to restrain the young man until his life is ruined."

Mack said he'd never heard of such a thing and couldn't understand how a feller could do it and get away with it.

"I suppose there are several reasons why. One is the guilty fellow is not aware of the awful damage he is doing to the fellow, and the sorrowful thing is, he might never know."

Mack stared at me, lips compressed, saying no more.

"Tell me the truth now-if you were the judge who meted out punishment, what would you do to this fellow who mistreated the talented young man?"

"I'll tell you what I'd do. I'd beat the livin' hell outa him."

"You would be that severe? You sound violent."

"He'd deserve the worst. Anybody that mean is crueler than the devil, and nothing'd be too bad for him."

"Slow down, Mack. He's human, you know."

"Perhaps, but he acts like a beast. I wouldn't treat anybody or anything like that-not even a dog."

"You sure about that?"

"Sure, I'm sure."

"You don't realize what you are saying."

He said he did, and might be good for nothin', but something like that was awful!

"That fellow doesn't realize what he's doing to the boy."

"I disagree. Anybody with sense would know if he were mistreating somebody."

I suggested we talk about the young man, even adding a few details previously unmentioned. Mack was to listen carefully, reaching his own conclusions.

The young man being abused was over six feet tall, with blue eyes. His physical and mental makeup was super, while his personality was outstanding, and he had a mind that was always inquisitive.

I paused, catching my breath.

"And, Mack, the astonishing thing is that the fellow being so maltreated is standing in this library, now. Mack Gray, you are mistreating yourself; you are the cruel master. Why don't you wake up? What's happened to you, anyway?"

He stared at me, saying nothing.

189

"You've described yourself this afternoon as a no-count, good-for-nothing rascal. If you are, and remember you said those things yourself-why? If what you said is true, the reason is because you have been abusing yourself through neglect. Why don't you stop it?"

I had caught him in a mental trap, and he knew it. Whether or not he wanted to admit it, he could see that he had wronged himself. I had Mack right where I wanted him.

The sun turned its usual brilliant red just before slipping below the Sound. I let Mack watch it for a while, then I reminded him we were going to finish this before leaving.

"You are well aware that you have an unusually good mind, aren't you?"

Silence confronted me.

"You know, you can speak to me confidentially. I repeat my question."

"Since you insist, I believe I have."

"When you try, you have a good personality, people like you!"

"Yes sir!"

"Then why in the name of common sense, do you want to cheat the world? Why are you letting so talented a youth turn into a no-count skunk? Why don't you see that you become an upright, intelligent citizen?"

The silence seemed to go beyond the little library, encompassing the entire building. Mack was not looking at me but studied his left hand, rubbing it with the thumb and forefinger of his right.

There was no red ball of sun now, dusk was gathering rapidly. The annoyance that was in my heart turned to pity, when I noticed an expression on the boy's face that I hadn't seen before. He was lost in thought; he was the old Mack before succumbing to this madness.

Had I suggested, I dared not guess, but I had done all I could. I suggested, "Let's go home."

We walked out together, and as I was locking the door, he relieved me of the stack of books I carried. We walked along the beach, going through Cat Ridge, toward Dog Ridge, talking easily, of things other than school.

I decided to say nothing to the French teacher. It was up to Mack now, but I was anxious about Monday morning, would he show up?

Mack was at school early, which meant he intended to attend French class. I did a lot of checking that first period, to see if he came out or remained. What a relief when he appeared along with the others at the close of the period. I would say nothing more to him or the teacher!

When the seniors marched across the stage to receive their high school diplomas, Mack was there to get his. Tears filled my eyes; I couldn't have endured that graduation, otherwise.

And the important thing was becoming friends again. Mack was out of school now, and there were no more restrictions. We took our walks together, whenever his work allowed us to do so.

Mack Gray would make his contribution to the world!

CHAPTER 20

PLAYING DOCTOR

Early during my stay at Kinnakeet, there were many situations which amazed me. Not the least of these was there was no doctor on the island-not even a nurse!

When I became better acquainted with Mrs. Keaton, I mentioned it. She agreed, it was not good, but so far, they had managed rather well. Babies came into the world aided by midwives, and home remedies were used for treating various ailments. They thought themselves healthier than folks in the up-country areas.

Since the citizens appeared to feel their lack of medical help was not serious, I learned to accept it, too.

The necessity of getting a doctor quickly occurred one day when a small boy, playing baseball, stumbled against a piece of driftwood as he tried for a home run. He threw his shoulder out of place, and I lifted him, starting into the school building, frantic because no doctor was available-when it snapped back into place.

This, I told myself, was pure luck. It could have failed to correct itself, or it could have been a broken arm or leg, and I knew little about first aid.

Again, I mentioned it to Mrs. Keaton.

"The coast guard will call for a plane," she informed me. "It comes from Norfolk, and takes the patient to a hospital there." The service was available to anyone on the island.

This was a relief, until I pursued the conversation, asking what if during a storm the plane couldn't make it, and the boats, too.

She frowned at me for a moment. "Lets hope that never happens."

These people! They had the same attitude about having no doctor as they did about living on shifting sands where the rising sea entered their homes and threatened their lives.

A few weeks later, I awoke on a Saturday morning with an excruciatingly severe pain in my neck. In no position could I get comfortable.

"Just be patient," said Mrs. Keaton when I had gone downstairs, refusing breakfast. "I know just the person who'll fix you up. She's as good as any doctor when it comes to a crick."

The woman was Miss Omie, the kind lady who had urged us to take drinking water from her home to school.

Another convenience missing in Kinnakeet was telephone. Mrs. Keaton had to leave her morning chores to fetch Miss Omie.

"If you're willing to let me use an ol' remedy, I can make you feel better," promised Miss Omie.

I told her to go right ahead.

She asked for a kettle of boiling water, a hand towel, a bath towel, and a wash pan. "You got plenty of turpentine, Beck?"

These requisites lined up in the kitchen, I was called down and seated on a straight chair, my shirt away from my neck. Miss Omie dipped one hand towel into the pan of hot water; after shaking out most of the water, she wrapped it around my neck. Quickly, the dry bath towel towel was wrapped around it, and I remained like this five minutes. When the towels were removed, my neck was massaged with turpentine.

In a while, I couldn't have told that I ever had a crick! Home remedies were familiar enough to me from childhood, but I couldn't remember results like Miss Omie's.

As the school terms progressed, year after year, and no serious accidents occurred, I was inclined to forget our handicap at Kinnakeet. However, the biggest danger we faced in the new school building was from slamming doors. Since the school was built right on the open beach, there was nothing to break the force of the wind. Therefore, it was not long until two doors slammed shut with such force, they were severely damaged.

One spring we had endured strong winds from all directions, and usually a sou'wester was never destructive, but one kept the open doors slamming constantly. The outside door on the north blew shut with such force, breaking the glass and cracking the door. After that, we were doubly careful. All outside doors, except the western double front doors were closed and locked. Orders were issued that the front door was to be used exclusively.

There had been a long, dry spell and the loose sand made it impossible to go by car to Oregon Inlet for a ferry to travel to a doctor. Tides were rough and high, eliminating the wash as a highway, and we couldn't send to Norfolk for a plane, because it couldn't possibly land or take off on the open beach in this wind.

All my old misgivings about no doctor depressed me that spring day, and it was a relief when the school was dismissed and the youngsters hurried out of the building.

The few of us who remained got ready to leave.

Then it happened! A girl was leaving by the heavy front door, when the 2x4 used to hold one of the double doors open, collapsed and the door slammed, catching her left wrist at the base of her hand, cutting the main artery in her arm!

When she rushed over to me, crying, "Oh, Mr. Green, honey, do something!" I was ready to faint. The sight of blood always made me sick, but I fought violently against it.

Gulping, I turned to a teacher who had hurried over, hearing the commotion. "Bring the first aid kit!" I demanded.

Aside from the loss of blood, I thought of infection.

With the kit open before me, I stared at it helplessly. How I wish I had taken courses in first aid! The role of doctor repelled me, and I refused to watch when someone else aided an injured person.

I pulled the leaders and muscles together; then with plain tape, I bound them thoroughly. When I finally finished, I had used a whole roll of tape. In my excitement, I had neglected to disinfect the wound first. I decided to say nothing about my oversight.

"It's all I can do," I said weakly. "If the wind will just die down, we'll get you to a doctor tomorrow."

Luck was with us, then. A doctor was flown in the next day. He removed my clumsy bandages, examining the arm. "Who fixed you up?"

When she told him, he nodded. "Couldn't have done better myself."

He probably disinfected the wound before he bandaged it again, and I was sure he spoke so well of my efforts, more to soothe his patient than as a genuine compliment. I could have assured him I would never try to compete with him. As far as I was concerned, he had the field of medicine to himself.

CHAPTER 21

THE DOG AND THE CHEESE

Creative writing did not always come easy to Kinnakeet high school boys, so accustomed to action, working around the fishing boats, and doing a man's job after school. Yet, like other things, they were ready to try, and because of their efforts, I now possess a treasured paper, especially interesting and well written.

It was about a ten-year-old boy and his dog named Seawee. No doubt the tale was handed down, and it may have been fiction, but it does show the nature of a Kinnakeeter. Thus, I have recounted it here as I remember it. Kinnakeeters were ready to care for another's pets as well as dig someone out of the sand when his car stalled.

My Dog Seawee

A severe storm had just passed off the coast of Kinnakeet, and it was Saturday morning. I strolled along the beach seeking flotsam and jetsam. A small lifeboat was beached just north of town, but no one was in it.

As it was low tide, I rolled up my trousers and waded out to where the boat was stuck fast in the sand. Low tide had left only shallow water surrounding it, and all that appeared to be in the boat was an old tin bucket on one end, and a pile of seaweed on the other. Being accustomed to finding various things along the shores of the Cape Hatteras Sea, my first glance satisfied my curiosity. But a second glance aroused even more curiosity. A

197

portion of the seaweed moved! At first I thought that it was my imagination, but after a few moments, I knew positively.

A living creature had to be underneath it. But what? Perhaps it was a strange sea creature that jumped into the boat as it drifted landward. Even though I was afraid, I jumped into the boat. Suddenly, a black, curly-haired puppy feebly raised its head, looking at me. He seemed as if he was about to breathe his last, and my heart went out to him because I always loved dogs. He made a feeble attempt to come to me, but couldn't because he was too weak.

Quickly, I lifted him out of the seaweed; he was so frightened, his little heart beat as though it would explode. The pup's eyes expressed fear, but at the same time, his tail wagged hopefully. His hair clung to his body.

When I picked him up, he was just about frozen. Water was under the seaweed, and being partially submerged he was chilled to the bone.

My mother was very discouraging, saying he would surely die. I thought so, too, but I was determined to save him.

Milk and bread were offered to him, but he wouldn't drink or eat, but just lay there with a look on his face which said, *I am going to die.*

I took one of my old coats and wrapped him in it, placing him on the back porch. My mother did not like this one bit, but she didn't make me unwrap him. Next, I got some old planks and made a box for him, lining it with tow sacks. Just before night, I took him, coat and all, and put him in the box, leaving him on the porch.

Several times before bedtime, I tried to get him to eat and drink, but he refused. Just before leaving him for the night, I looked at him once more, sure I wouldn't see him alive again.

My first look at him next morning found him still breathing, but too weak to stand. I tried everything by way of food-milk, ham, eggs and bread, but he turned away.

Mid-morning, my mother came from shopping with the week's groceries. I managed to rummage through her purchases when she wasn't looking, and she hadn't forgotten to buy my favorite food, cheese! I cut a slice, and went to the porch, when the puppy began crying pitifully.

This was the end - he was dying! I ran to him, and in my excitement, dropped part of my cheese, which fell into the box. He tried to get on his feet but failed. Trying again, he managed to propel himself to where the cheese lay. Instantly he swallowed it!

My hopes soared. Maybe, if I were to name him, it would be good luck. The name Seawee intrigued me, since I found him in seaweed.

I gave him the rest of the cheese, never tasting it myself. He lay down, went to sleep and I covered him. He slept all day, and when I looked at him before going to bed, he was still asleep.

Before daybreak the next morning, Seawee awakened me with a long whine. I rushed to him, taking care not to awaken mother. Seawee was standing up, and when he saw me, he wagged his tail, trying to bark, but did not utter a sound.

I slid into the pantry and whacked off a hunk of cheese, offering it to him. He ate it so fast he almost choked, but now he did not lie down but started walking around.

He finished off the cheese, with a big bowl of milk that night, after a day of slumber again.

Now I knew my sea dog would surely live.

I went to bed joyfully, and was awakened early next morning by Seawee's barking. I rushed to him, and what a surprise to find him standing at the back door, waiting to come into the house.

My parents could hardly believe their eyes when they saw him, active and hungry. It was like the dead coming to life.

For breakfast, he ate bacon and part of an egg. It wasn't nearly enough to fill him, but he refused more. Cheese! That was what Seawee wanted. He liked it better than I did, if that was possible. I rushed to the store and bought some cheese, and no sooner had I reached the front gate, when he probably smelled it, and began to jump around. When I gave him a piece, he was the happiest dog I had ever seen.

Soon Seawee was the beloved pet of the family. He was so smart, we thought of him as human. My father always said I gave him the wrong name-he should have been called Cheesie instead of Seawee. My mother claimed it was bad luck to change a name, and we never did.

Seawee grew into a beautiful dog with a wonderful personality. Everyone loved him, and no one made a truer Kinnakeeter. He never visited town without getting a piece of cheese. Children brought cheese to school just for Seawee.

He had a perfect school attendance record. Every day he would accompany me to school, lying beside the teacher's desk. He never failed to do as she asked, and she often said she wished all her students were as obedient as Seawee; she loved him very much.

It was well known that Seawee craved cheese as a drunkard, whiskey. If Seawee failed to get cheese from people, he was always sure of it at any store in town. Merchants never hesitated to cut off a generous portion, giving it to him.

One late September, a terrible hurricane played havoc with Kinnakeet. The freight boat, *Missouri*, had just arrived the night before, loaded down with supplies. Only part of the groceries had been unloaded before the storm broke, and none of the cheese hoops had been taken from the boat. All the merchants had a big supply of cheese aboard because Kinnakeeters were great cheese eaters; one reason why Seawee endeared himself to everyone.

The hurricane destroyed the boat, and all the cheese, too.

Due to the storm, all transportation was cut off for a week from Hatteras Island. There was enough food available, so none went hungry, but it was not long before there was no cheese.

From the first day without cheese, Seawee became increasingly nervous. At times he acted ill and frustrated; by midweek, he was frantic. No alcoholic ever craved liquor more than he craved cheese. It was clear something horrible would happen to him if he did not get cheese.

I went all over the community begging for cheese, hoping somebody had a stale piece he had forgotten about, but there just was no cheese to be had!

Every time I came home from my search, Seawee seemed to appreciate my efforts.

"Poor Seawee," I told him. "Please try to endure it a little longer; a boat of supplies is due any day now."

The look on his little face was awful.

Supper time came; we ate and I prepared food for my dog. He had refused it for the last three days. I decided to give him a treat tonight, and I cooked a steak. Next to cheese, beef was his second choice. But he was so sick from lack of cheese, he merely turned away.

As was our custom, we went upstairs afterwards, and I always read before going to bed, while Seawee lay beside me.

Finally I went to the window and looked out over the Cape Hatteras Sea, where a full moon was rising in a dark, clear sky. That moon looked as big as a yellow wagon wheel!

"What a sight," I exclaimed. "It looks like a big ball of cheese!"

Seawee stood on his hind legs at the window, peering about him. He must have heard me, and looking at the yellow moon must have convinced him that it was cheese, even though he couldn't smell it.

Before I know what was happening, he jumped out the open window, trying to catch the moon hanging there in the sky.

I ran down the stairs as fast as I could; common sense told me he'd be badly injured.

He lay there in the yard, his neck broken.

My grief was awful, and when the Kinnakeeters learned of the tragedy, there were many to share my mourning. Tenderly I buried my Seawee the next day. Then, just as I had promised him, it was announced that a freight boat was coming in. I ran down to the Sound, just as she docked.

Late in the evening, I was able to purchase cheese, and I put a big portion of it on Seawee's grave. He could not eat it, but it helped ease my grief, knowing it was there for him.

CHAPTER 22

GIFT FROM THE SEA!

The Canadian geese which migrated every autumn never ceased to attract my attention and admiration. One fall evening as I walked home from school, I heard their raucous honking, and looking up, saw a large flock of them headed southward. Scarcely had they disappeared from sight, when there was another flock on the horizon, flying in the same triangular formation as the first.

After the second flock had passed, I started to leave the open beach, entering Dog Ridge.

I could scarcely believe it when I saw the third flock-they were flying in no particular formation, and I was not able to see their leader. Had some hunter made them leaderless? There was another difference, too-the flock was much smaller than the others.

This was not the first time I had watched them flying over, and I had also seen many after they were shot. I had seen others that the natives kept in pounds, but never before had I observed three flocks flying so close together.

How wonderful it would be to own some Canadian geese! The idea possessed me as I trudged home, to Mrs. Keaton's. What a treat it would be to care for them, tame them, and be able to reach out, touching those gorgeous creatures.

In front of Gibb's store, one of my students hailed me, "Captain Green, did you see all those geese that just flew over?"

I told him it was the most I ever saw at once, and asked him how many he guessed there were.

"No tellin', but they're coming south, kinda fast. Remember, soon as the hunting season opens, you're goin' huntin' with me."

I had already told him repeatedly that I couldn't hit an elephant, much less a bird flying. Again I reminded him, but he shrugged it off. He'd soon have me shooting geese all over the place!

I much more preferred live geese, but I hurried on home, realizing I was unusually hungry.

As I washed up before supper, I heard Mrs. Keaton calling me. Towel in hand, I went to my bedroom door where Mrs. Keaton said, "Supper won't be ready yet, but come down soon's you can. Bill has a surprise for you."

"What is it?"

She laughed. "Just come down and see for yourself."

This really aroused my curiosity and I hurried down to where Bill and his mother were. She was serenely rolling out the dough for a chicken pot pie, while Bill stood in the outer kitchen doorway, a cigarette between thumb and forefinger. I watched the smoke curl lazily around his face.

At that moment, Bud Rans and Sis Mitt arrived at the door, apparently they had come just for this occasion. They both had conspiring looks on their faces.

Mrs. Keaton was putting the dough into the chicken pot, while Bill wriggled restlessly, telling her to hurry so they could show me what they had.

After finishing, she stood wiping the flour from her hands, while Bill said grandly, "Mr. Green, I have something for you that every male in Kinnakeet desired. Of course, they all couldn't have them, so they voted them for you; the vote was one hundred percent."

"Bill, what *are* you talking about? You really have me excited."

Bud Rans laughed happily, saying Bill really did have *sumpin!*

"And they're kinda pretty, too; prettiest I eve did see," Sis Mitt contributed.

Bill led the way out into the back yard, and over to the chicken pound which was only a few yards away from the house. I glanced from one end of the pound to the other, noticing nothing unusual. A big red rooster and a dozen hens approached us looking for food.

We continued until reaching the west side of the pound where there was a large water bush. In front of it was an old wooden box, with a dirty strip of canvas thrown over it. Bill said, "Mr. Green, pull back the cover and see what it is."

I hesitated, were they playing a joke on me? No, it was not like them to do that!

Finally, I went over, and took the canvas by one corner, giving it a quick jerk.

Well, no more than an hour ago, I longed for a pair of Canadian geese, now here was a pair of them, beautiful but frightened! They stuck out their necks and hissed at me. Maybe they didn't like my looks, but I liked theirs.

Carefully covering them, I turned to see the foursome studying me, their smiles saying how glad they were that I was pleased.

"Bill, are they really for me?"

"Feathers and all!"

"But you don't want them?"

"You just better bet I do; I'd pay a fancy price for them."

"Then you must take them." I said I had no idea how to care for them.

"Couldn't take them, even if I was to buy them."

"Nonsense, they're mine, aren't they? If I want to give them to you, what's to stop you from accepting?"

"You forgot, I said we voted to give them to you."

He told me then, how he had acquired them. The goose had gotten ensnared in a fisherman's net and couldn't free herself. Her mate, the gander, came to her side, refusing to leave her, apparently choosing death, if such was to be their fate.

I shook my head; as I said before, they were superior to humans.

Bud Rans said, "No doubt about that!"

I knew the males of Kinnakeet well enough to recognize Bill's feelings, the pair was mine, and he'd feel bad if he owned the birds instead of me.

It was during supper that I told Bill and Mrs. Keaton what happened on my way from school that same night; how a desire for some Canadian geese overwhelmed me. It was unbelievable that I now owned a pair.

The goose in her struggle to free herself had broken a wing, I learned, but they'd be easily tamed, and would soon eat out of my hand.

I lost no time in starting to work with them, and I came home with a large sack of grain from Mr. Gibb's store. However, the geese would have nothing to do with me; the gander always got between me and his mate. However, gradually they became less excitable.

Since the goose was unable to fly, I felt certain the gander would never leave her, so I soon gave them the run of the pound.

In two weeks, they started greeting me when I brought their food. Slowly, they got the idea I was their friend.

One night during supper, I expressed the wish that my family back home could see this beautiful pair. They, and the entire countryside, would get very excited about my geese.

"Why don't you send them there? They're tame now, and surely your folks have a chicken pound?"

I said that would be the least of their problems-but how could I get them home?

Mrs. Keaton shrugged, "Send them to Elizabeth City by boat." She reminded me that the *Missouri*, a freight sailboat, went from Kinnakeet to Elizabeth City every week. From there they could go by train, which was not a great distance.

Bill volunteered to make a sturdy crate so they travel in comfort.

Thus, I wrote to my family immediately, giving all the details, and telling my sisters they were to continue petting them, although I was sure they'd do that without being told!

At the beginning of the next week, the *Missouri* took my geese, headed for Boiling Springs, North Carolina. They were leaving the world of water they knew, for the foothills of the Blue Ridge Mountains of western North Carolina. But since, they no longer flew, I knew they would be happy there.

A letter from home came unbelievably fast; the geese arrived in good shape, and talk about excitement! When word got about that two wild, Canadian geese were actually coming to live in Boiling Springs, the neighbors gathered with my family awaiting their arrival. Nobody had ever seen a dead Canadian goose, much less a live one.

They even enclosed a newspaper clipping, and from it, I learned the excitement was not just Boiling Springs, but in all of

Cleveland County. The news of their arrival was spread in headlines across the front page.

From then on, until school was out the next spring, every letter from home carried details on the geese. On arrival, they were upset, but in the chicken pound, they soon adapted themselves to their new environment.

By the time I arrived home the next year, to spend the summer with my family, they birds were cherished pets. They had complete freedom of the back yard, which was unfenced, and one of my sisters had trained them, so that when night came, they followed her into the chicken house, where she locked them in for the night.

They followed her, but if a stranger appeared, they were hostile. If the stranger remained, they would flee from him.

I wondered if they had forgotten me, and I went into the back yard. They did not run away, and shortly they began coming toward me, nodding their heads and hissing. What a reunion! It was like being welcomed by old friends. I gave them their grain, and while they ate, they stared at me, heads bobbing as though they were thanking me.

Occasionally, my sister forgot to put them in the chicken house, making the gander worry about the goose because she couldn't fly. He knew she needed the protection of indoors. Thus, they would commence honking until my sister put them to bed.

One summer, when I was home, five years after the geese came to live at Boiling Springs, we were awakened early one morning by the gander's peculiar sounds. My first thought was that something had fallen on him, trapping him. We all rushed to his aid, but instead found his mate lying dead!

Examination convinced us that she died of natural causes, but his mourning was an awful thing to see. He would look at her, then at us. But how powerless we were to lessen his grief, and explain to him about death, without understanding it ourselves.

Tenderly, we buried the goose with the broken wing, while her mate moped around, dazedly. We tried to get him to eat, but he touched nothing.

A few days brought a slight change where he ate a little, and drank some water, but he was never lively again. Occasionally in the middle of the night, we would be awakened by his lonely call for his departed mate.

One morning, a few weeks later, we found him dead in almost the same place where his mate had lain.

With equal tenderness, we buried him beside the goose, placing their coffins close in the cool earth, firmly convinced their devotion would surely find its reward.

CHAPTER 23

OSCAR

After my arrival in Kinnakeet, I amazed my students by acting in the first school play. The same boys who vividly made ice ream for a social, flatly refused to be in any public program-whether it was a play, making a speech, or even singing in a glee club. Previously, when plays were put on at school, the girls had to play the male roles.

I decided if they could take pride in their culinary talents, they could find pleasure in their ability to entertain or instruct.

The fact that each of the nine students forming the first Kinnakeet graduating class, delivered an oration spoke of my success. I decided that if they could cook, they could orate, too!

They did a good job, and thereafter, speech making was an exciting adventure which frequently took the place of sports.

For a community of seven hundred people, the new school building had a large auditorium. But it soon became apparent that people must arrive early to find a seat during commencement week festivities. Those who were not fortunate, had to stand in the hall back of the auditorium, and if the weather was warm enough, windows were left open so people could stand outside and listen.

This custom of each graduate delivering a speech was unique, and we were justly proud that no student received a diploma until he had orated.

These youngsters had more than ordinary ability, and once they were introduced to it, they loved public speaking.

An extremely appreciative audience contributed greatly toward their success. The adults were interested, and these young men and women influenced education in Kinnakeet, as nothing else could. Their speeches caused as much excitement as sports would have done. In fact, public speaking became the most poplar event in Kinnakeet. The youngsters learned the feeling of power through oratory.

I tried constantly to teach them that oratory could be used for good or evil, and their speeches were to be used for the good of mankind.

Each year, two prizes were given for the two best orations-one for a young woman, the other, a young man. This caused even more planning: they worked hard on their speeches, arranging them to fit their personalities. They practiced their delivery endlessly, and with high hopes, came to know every sentence, clause, and meaning. Their speeches became a living thing to them and they experienced every emotion expressed. And because this was so, the audience shared their experience.

There was much research involved. The student would take famous speeches, varying them with certain ideas of his own. The speech must be his, setting forth his own beliefs. If he thoroughly believed every word he said, he could say it more convincingly.

The seniors soon formed the habit of preparing their graduation speech as soon at school started in September. They were interested in the prize, naturally, but I never felt this was the main motivation; they wanted to hold their audience through their oratory!

They even began to frequent the open beach of the Cape Hatteras Sea to practice speech making. Many preferred the calmer Sound, while some orated in the privacy of their rooms.

To see a speech making youngster along the beach was as accepted in Kinnakeet as it would have been elsewhere to see an athlete working out.

It became a way of life, and youngsters starting school looked forward to becoming seniors, when they could orate.

People came from far away to hear the speeches in this isolated village, declaring they had never heard better, not even in college and universities.

One Monday morning during the second school week of the year I got to school especially early. I noticed a freshman standing in the room, and I asked if there was something he wanted.

Oscar attempted to speak but couldn't. Then I remembered that the elementary teachers had spoken about his stuttering. He had been like this since early childhood, so they didn't call on him to read in class.

I looked at him, and he stared back with troubled eyes. His face showed that something was troubling him, but not a word passed his lips.

Moving closer, I asked what was wrong. He struggled mightily, finally managing, "I-I'"

"Take your time, " I suggested.

With great effort, he wanted to know what he'd do when he became a senior.

I took a deep breath. "Oscar, my boy, you've got three years to figure it out. After all, you're only a freshman, now."

He appeared to have relaxed slightly, as though he really wasn't pressured by time. Oscar was a sensitive looking youngster, endowed with an alertness which added to his general good looks, as did the freckles that spread across his face. For a fourteen-year-old he had a good physique, but because of his stuttering, I could see that he was most unhappy.

"There's nobody here but the two of us, so pull yourself together, take your time, and tell me what's on your mind."

I could actually see the effort he put forth to become calm, and he spoke more coherently.

"What I'm--talking about is--my stuttering. If I get the least bit excited I stu-stutter, I--I always have. Teachers won't call on me to read."

The way he got out the last statement without stuttering was encouraging.

I told him it was a rather common ailment, but since he always stuttered, why was he so concerned about it now? Had someone teased him about it.

"How--how--can I ever make my speech when I--when I--get to be a senior?"

My heart went out to him. Although he was loved by everybody in town, nobody expected him to make a speech when he graduated. What could I say to him? Surely it was not right to encourage him, yet I felt it would be cruel to exclude him.

I put my hand on his shoulder. "As I said before, it's a long while before you'll be a senior. There is one thing we all must learn, that is we can't cross our bridges until we get to them. Wait until you get to the bridge, then we'll cross it."

He said nothing, and I felt as though he was not quite satisfied.

"The day you become a senior, we will work on this problem. Come to me then, and we'll thrash it out together."

He gave me a broad grin, and turned, leaving the room.

I gave him no further thought, but Oscar hadn't forgotten.

Three years later, on the second day of school, I was at the blackboard when I sensed someone near me. I turned to find Oscar there, his facial expression, distressingly serious.

The whole conversation came back to me vividly.

I had no reason to presume his stuttering improved, but I realized that a decision had to be made. There was only one answer, which was for him to forget all about orating. All he would have to do was finish some project, which would get him graduated. Thus, forgoing the speech which entitled him to a diploma. Why not a research paper? That should be sufficient.

Yet I found myself putting him off. "Oscar, the students are arriving. Let's talk after school."

He went away, and I felt relieved because I did not have to discuss it then. As soon as school was dismissed, Oscar returned. We sat down, and I felt it would not be necessary to discuss this very long, because the solution was obvious.

Out of kindness, I asked, "Tell me what's on your mind, and what conclusions you've reached?"

"You--you said when I started to high school we--we would talk about--about the speech in my senior year."

I said time sure did fly, and that I thought about it, and was delighted to tell him he had absolutely nothing to worry about.

He waited, so I continued, "You see, Oscar, there's no law that says you must make a public speech before being awarded a high school diploma. The custom has become popular here but nobody is obligated. So, if it will make you feel better, you can do something else, such as writing an extra paper."

Never have I seen more disappointment on anybody's face. Tears came to Oscar's eyes, and he certainly was beyond

215

expression. As I stared at him, I realized how blunt I was. In fact, without intending it, I was downright inhuman. Apparently Oscar had yearned to recite during his school days. He had wanted to be encouraged being ambitious, and what a disappointment I must be.

Oscar was not looking for excuses, but he wanted to know if he could do the impossible.

I did some fast thinking.

"You really want to make this speech?"

"Yes sir!" Then he became excited, stuttering terribly as he admitted he didn't know how he could manage it. However, he did not want to be the one to ruin the school's perfect record.

There was school loyalty, of course, but also the personal need to succeed, too, especially since a brother and sister had already graduated and delivered especially inspiring orations.

"Oscar, you have reached a point in your life when you must make your own decisions. I cannot do it for you, but I will do anything I can to help you. Take a few days to study the situation, then let me know."

I still believed there was only one decision he could make. Oscar must not attempt the impossible.

"Don't--need--time, I--I--want-to-to-make that speech." His face was blood red, and inwardly I groaned.

There was determination in every fiber of him. What would the other teachers say? What would the students do about this? What would be the reaction of the Kinnakeeters?

Oscar, standing before an audience, delivering an oration! Oh, the pity of it! Surely he wouldn't go through with it. If nobody knew his intentions, he could change his mind at the last minute, with no embarrassment. I said, "Let's make a bargain. Keep our decision between the two of us. Don't let anybody, unless it's your family, know that you are preparing an oration."

This appealed to him, and I took his hand. "If you are determined to go through with it, I promise to help you all I can. I have never failed to help anyone, but I only help those who request it. Do you want me to help you?"

He wanted it very much.

I suggested he start on it without delay. He was to select what he wanted, obtain the speech, and reword it to suit him, then I would assist him.

I assumed the quicker he got started, the sooner he'd decide against it. Also, the quicker he made that decision, the more time it would give him to adjust to the fact that he was incapable of delivering an oration, and he could still write the extra theme.

In a few weeks, Oscar received by mail his copy of a famous oration. He rewrote it to suit himself, fitting it into his beliefs, and then memorized it. Several times after school, he attempted to read it to me, but he couldn't get through one paragraph without stuttering.

How I wanted to shout at the boy to forget the whole business!

But the more Oscar stuttered, the harder he worked. Winter passed and spring found all the seniors working on their orations. The school record would be broken this year, but nobody blamed Oscar because he stuttered. It hadn't leaked out that he was working on a speech! I was grateful for this.

Six weeks before the end of school, brave Oscar had me convinced that he was going to stand before an audience, regardless if he said anything. He hadn't the slightest notion of not doing so. He might go down in defeat, but he'd go down fighting.

Faithfully I worked with him in secret. At night he practiced at home, and when I thought him ready to practice in the auditorium, the two of us would slip back to school after dark, and he would stand on the stage while I remained a spectator. On moonless nights, the place was so dark we couldn't see each other.

It was painful at first, but he finally was able to go through the entire speech without stuttering. Even this was not encouraging, because he was in a darkened auditorium, and knowing I was out there didn't bother him. He still uttered each word as though it were a separate unit. What would happen in a lighted auditorium full of people, with his astonished classmates seated behind him? I was increasingly pessimistic as the time drew closer.

It was impossible not to admire his dogged persistence; he never despaired, or failed to put forth the best he had, and made slight progress.

Twenty students would graduate this year, evenly divided between boys and girls. So it was that the speaking contests were to be held in two night sessions, prior to the graduating exercises.

As was the custom, cards with numbers on them were placed in a box and each speaker drew a card. The number he chose indicated the place he would assume in the contest.

Oscar drew number ten, which meant he would be the last speaker. Now, if he failed, the program would be over, and his failure less conspicuous. Only then did his classmates suspect he was going to make a speech. But they did not take it seriously and soon forgot it.

When only a week remained, I was walking home after school, when I met his mother on the bridge, spanning the swamp between Dog Ridge and Cat Ridge.

"Mr. Green," she greeted me, "I don't know whether I can live through this speech-making; seems like I can't endure it. Why won't Oscar just forget it?"

How I wanted to agree with her, but I felt a deep loyalty to Oscar. "Oh, it's not that bad, is it?" I asked, lightly.

"You know that if he gets the least bit excited, he stutters kinda bad. His daddy hasn't said much, but I can tell he's worrying himself sick about the outcome."

"We must just wait and hope."

She was in an emotional state; Oscar's room was above hers, and often she awoke during the night to hear him reciting the speech. "And Mr. Green, honey, just one word at a time. That's no way to deliver a speech."

"Whether he succeeds or not, you are to be proud of him. If he gets up there and doesn't utter a word, the fact that he has tried so hard is a credit to him, his family, and his school. Please, stop worrying."

I knew very well that she wouldn't, and neither would I!

Finally, the crucial day arrived, warm and sunny with a calm sea. It was a day of unusual stillness, as though everything was in abeyance, waiting for Oscar's speech.

Long before sundown folks began to enter the auditorium. It filled, and still they came, jamming the hall. The windows were opened and still they gathered outside.

When it was time for the program to commence the tide was low, and scarcely a sound from the sea was heard.

I felt as though it was an unreal night, as I took my usual place on the stage. I listened to the glee club sing out with "Oh,

219

That We Two Were Maying," and saw the first speaker take his place. He did a magnificent job, as did the eight who followed. They brought honor to their school and community. All of them were dressed alike-white shirts and black ties, black coats with white trousers, white shoes and socks. Pride swelled my heart. Now if only it were over!

When it became known that Oscar was going to speak, folks had come in even greater numbers. They were kind people, filled with sympathy for one who might be "on a spot," but basically they came because they couldn't believe that Oscar would attempt such a thing.

Butterflies had fluttered inside of me for weeks now, but as I saw the boy rise, they did not stir.

Oscar stood for a moment, then turned acknowledging, "Mr. President," and walked to the center of the stage. I looked out over the audience; the ones who had been sitting with bowed heads lifted them; all but one, Oscar's mother, who sat with bowed head praying for her son.

During rehearsals, I had coached him to take three deep breaths before starting to talk, no matter how long it took. He did this when we practiced, would he now?

He took his time, and nobody knew why he stood there without saying a word. Oscar's father wiped his forehead while his mother continued praying.

Seconds seemed like minutes, and people squirmed. But I was relieved that he took time to compose himself.

When he started, he spoke softly, and deliberately, but his words were clear, well enunciated, and there was emotion! People sat back, eyes focused on him. His mother lifted her head, and his father put away his handkerchief.

Every paragraph saw an improvement as he talked with vigor and emotional appeal.

Oscar, just like every other graduate, was now feeling the power of oratory. He knew that he had the audience's attention, and for the first time in his life, he knew power over man. Oscar became lost in his speech, forgetting himself. He spoke louder, gestured, and dramatized. He thoroughly sold himself, through deep conviction, on every word he was saying, and he was convincing the audience.

I had never been aware before that he had a good speaking voice. Now, the nerves and muscles in his throat were coordinating satisfactorily, and I hadn't suggested that he gesture, presuming it would distract him. But he seemed unaware he was gesturing. Natural, eloquent, and convincing, Oscar brought his speech to a mighty climax.

I have never known such complete stillness as permeated the auditorium, followed by applause that was like an explosion.

The three judges walked outside, talked together briefly, and returned to the stage.

I was not surprised when they announced Oscar the winner, but what amazed me was talking with a judge later, who informed me that all the students were strangers to him. He had known nothing of Oscar's handicap-he won the prize simply because his oratory was the best.

CHAPTER 24

MEALY MOUTH

From the time I first came to Kinnakeet, I kept hearing stories of a certain bull which had been something of a character around town. However, I never learned enough about him to complete a story.

One weekend evening , I had gone to Pritchard's for a while, and was headed home, racing a threatening storm, when I was hailed by Gibb, who was locking up unusually early.

"Business ain't good," he explained laconically. "What's your hurry?"

"The weather," I responded, equally brief.

"Come and sit a spell."

Just then, the heavens opened up and the rain poured down, as it did only in Kinnakeet; together we dashed into his house.

"Good night to listen to some of my bull," he stated. That gave me the idea of finding out the details about the bull, called Mealy Mouth.

I sat in a small rocker by the south window, and for a time we made no attempt to converse because of the roar of the storm outside. Gibb quietly chewed his tobacco, reminding me of a hungry rabbit in a cabbage patch. At the same time, he kept scratching his head.

As soon as the rain assumed a steady beat and the thunder did not sound with such frequency, I prompted him by declaring that I thought Mealy Mouth was a fable, and not a real creature. Although, my students declared that they had often heard their parents and grandparents mention him.

"Knew him from a calf until the day he died, he was very much a part of Kinnakeet. The stories about him are contradictory and all I really know was that he lived some fifty years ago."

My host appeared reluctant to forgo his plug of tobacco, so I prodded him with, "I've thought he was a combination of the devil and an angel; he could have been a super being of some sort."

Gibb disposed of the tobacco. "The truth about him does sound more like fiction." He meditated. "Hard to believe, though, that such a lovable bull could have existed."

"I've heard he gored folks to death," I contradicted.

He did not commit himself.

"If he was that dangerous, why was he allowed to roam around? Why wasn't he shot?"

"Green, you're like all outsiders. I've been asked that same question so many times because nobody outside Kinnakeet knows the whole story."

He took his time, seeming to have difficulty deciding just how to tell his tale. Finally, he said, "He attracted more attention the day he was born than a whale coming ashore. Everybody said he was the prettiest calf they had ever seen, black as tar, except white around his mouth and over his nose. Made him look like he'd stuck his head in a meal barrel. That's how he got his name, Mealy Mouth."

The calf's mother died shortly after he was born, thus, the Kinnakeeters gave him a great deal of attention. Everybody mothered him, and even though he occasionally roamed with the wild herds of cattle on the beach, he was more at home in the village, with people.

"Not after he was grown?" I interrupted.

"My boy, when he grew to be a bull, they petted him more'n ever. The attachment to Mealy Mouth grew slowly but surely, and with all the affection showered on him, he became very lovable."

Gibb said there was no stock law at the time, and the bull went everywhere. To meet Mealy Mouth along a path or road was like seeing an old and dear friend. He was fed candy, and scraps from the tables.

"Was he big?" I wanted to know.

"Green, he was tremendous! In appearance, he was sleek, and black as a crow, with long, sharp horns pointing straight out from his head. Now let me tell you why he left such a lasting impression on the town."

"Do!"

"I remember everything that occurred on Mealy Mouth's last day on earth. It was brilliantly sunny, and Cape Hatteras Sea was boisterous because of a freak storm the day before. But that morning, Kinnakeet was quiet as a bushel of potatoes."

He had opened the store as usual, when all hell broke loose. Women and children began to scream, "They're after Mealy Mouth!"

"Who?"

"Dogs! Two fierce cattle dogs."

And Mealy Mouth, changed from the town's lovable pet into a stampeding, bellowing bull. He was so mad he could have killed everybody."

"Just because the dogs chased him?"

Gibb said the whole thing was crazy, especially when Mealy Mouth was universally loved, and men serving in the Coast Guard all over the world would ask about him whenever they wrote home.

"And if it hadn't been for one thing, he wouldn't have turned into a man-killing beast."

"What was that?"

"The Kinnakeeters didn't own him-this made all the difference."

It seemed like the bull's mother belonged to some outsiders, and so, according to law, the bull belonged to them.

"Why didn't the Kinnakeeters buy him?"

Gibb frowned impatiently; all this happened without warning. Why should they, when he was already so much a part of them?

The owners came to claim him because he would fetch a handsome price up-country at the beef market. The owners needed quick money, so they planned to catch Mealy Mouth and ship him out. They knew better than to sell him for beef around Kinnakeet. To eat him would have been like dining on an old friend.

All that was necessary, had the owners gone about it correctly, would have been to coax the bull aboard a freighter with a few kind words, a pat on the nose, and a treat.

But instead, they brought in two vicious dogs, relying on them to chase their prize bull into a pen, then onto the boat.

The dogs appeared without warning and attacked. The bull never had to protect himself, knowing only kindness and love. There was nothing in his background to prepare him for this.

Dog Ridge and Cat Ridge were infuriated over this incident. One dog was on the bull's right, the other on his left. As each grabbed at his head, he thrust them to the ground; they kept attacking with more force, sinking their sharp teeth into his bleeding tongue.

"It was a terrible sight," said Gibb, sighing. "The barking, wounded dogs trying to do their duty, and the bellowing Mealy Mouth with blood streaming from him."

I sympathized, "Poor Mealy Mouth!"

Finally, the bull was backed against the yeopon-covered sandhills, and nobody dared approach the combatants, nor could they have helped.

"I tell you, this town was in an uproar. The dogs were getting weaker, with Mealy Mouth throwing them farther each time he gave them a toss."

The bull took refuge between two sandhills in central Dog Ridge, as one of the owners attempted to stop such sadism. He called the dogs away, planning to rope Mealy Mouth, bringing him out into the open.

Gibb raised his voice.

"Then the excitement really began. Mealy Mouth's fear turned into hate and revenge. He stared at the stranger approaching with a rope; again it was a new experience."

"That fool didn't try to lasso him?"

"He did just that, and Mealy Mouth lunged. His beautiful long horns tore away the man's clothing, and gouged a hole in him."

"He's killed the man," the people yelled.

Then Mealy Mouth snorted, and lowered his head, while those nearest, fled. Women and children ran toward shelter; Mealy Mouth was nobody's friend now! Some of the men grabbed planks, and others, axes. They even broke limbs from trees, and a few procured bricks. Many followed the women and the children to places they hoped would be safe.

It was not long before the populace realized the only effective weapon would be guns, and shouts rang out for them.

Soon rifles appeared-pistols, automatics, and double barreled shotguns. Something had to be done quickly. Mealy Mouth had been forced into this fight, and he was going to make the most of it!

With bullets flying thick and fast, the bull sensed his time was limited. He turned and headed toward Pamlico Sound, taking refuge behind a sandhill, as bullets kept tearing into his beautiful body.

Gibb lowered his voice.

"He struggled to leave the sandhill, but he was too weak; besides, the bullets blinded him. Thus, on top of the sandhill in the middle of the village he breathed his last, falling to his knees, sprawled out on the ground. Everyone knew his beloved pet had left for good."

"Man's greed again," I philosophized. "Animals have so much to give in love and companionship. It would be marvelous if man deserved their trust."

Gibb sat quietly, as the rain continued. The oil lamp flickered, causing long shadows to dip and sway on the wall. Thunder no longer sounded, but the Cape Hatteras Sea was very noisy.

I sat there, reluctant to leave, thinking about Mealy Mouth. I had the feeling his spirit lingered about, perhaps among the nearby sandhills, where the yeopon trees clustered.

CHAPTER 25

A UNIQUE BANQUET

I found myself unusually tired one March evening, because it had been examination day at school-a difficult time for teachers as well as students. Depressed, I sat down to Mrs. Keaton's delicious pone bread and cabbage, topped by a huge portion of lemon pie. Invariably, my spirits soared!

By the time I set out for Pritchard's to keep a seven o'clock appointment, I was my old self again, and grateful for it, since the air was crisp, and the stars, brilliant.

Just as I passed Gibb's store, one of my students who was a junior came dashing out. She made me stop, and immediately I was surrounded by most of the other junior girls, and we stood together under a live oak tree.

"Mr. Stanley Everette Green," began the spokesman of the group, "the girls of Avon High School want very much to have a consultation with you."

In a more considerate tone, she said she realized I was in a hurry, but they did have something of great importance to discuss with me.

"We have a request which you've probably never heard before."

"I'm ten minutes late for my appointment," I protested. "Can't this wait until tomorrow?"

Reluctantly they acquiesced, "But you've got the surprise of your life coming,' they foretold, strolling off, and I hastened toward Pritchard's.

Students were always requesting something, but the expressions of these young ladies showed they were extremely enthusiastic. Usually I gave something of this sort no further thought, but tonight I was curious.

The leader did not arrive the next morning until the bell sounded, so there was no time to discuss the matter before school. However, during the first period, she came to the front of the room ostensibly to ask me a question from her English textbook, but actually saying they'd meet me on the road that night and tell me their plans.

"But where?" I thought of the long road connecting one Ridge with the other.

"In front of Gibb's store."

It seemed like a rather odd place to meet, but I acquiesced. There was no doubt every girl in the class knew very well that Hazel hadn't asked about the book she had open. Every boy did too, but they were obviously as ignorant as I was.

What in the world were the juniors up to-and why had they kept the boys in the dark?

The fact that nothing more was said about it that day only whetted my curiosity. I pretended to have forgotten it, but when school was dismissed, I went to my room faster than usual. Then, since time passed too slowly, I forced myself to grade papers until suppertime.

Having eaten, I lost no time in starting out. The sun was partially hidden when I set forth, vaguely aware of the crisp and azure sky, and the happy shouts of children.

Before I reached Gibb's, the junior girls hurried forth to meet me; we regrouped again under the huge live oak, then started toward Pritchard's. At the Methodist Church, they said they wanted to go to the beach instead of their usual place.

Protesting that it was too cold, my argument fell on deaf ears. It was never too cold for a Kinnakeeter!

They broke into joyous song as we headed for the beach and I thought I had it now! They were doing everything to put me in a good mood, so I'd consent to whatever they wanted.

I gathered my coat around me, and noticed that the girls did likewise. However, it was not long afterwards, that a gentle breeze blew up from the southeast. Having experienced this before, I knew this was a characteristic of the Cape Hatteras Sea. For weeks the wind had come from a northerly direction. Now in a matter of minutes, the temperature reversed itself. Suddenly, winter turned into summer-no longer was the air icy, but, blowing from the Gulf Stream, it was balmy.

Even the wind conspires with these girls, I told myself.

Removing our coats, we found a lifeboat which had recently washed ashore, and sat around it on piles of dried seaweed.

For amateurs, these junior girls were marvelous psychologists. They hadn't mentioned what brought them here, they only wanted me to ask them. I pretended I was disinterested.

They sang a while, popular songs and older ones, well aware that I never tired of hearing them.

Finally, I was the loser, knowing we couldn't sit here half the night engaged in a songfest, and I suggested they reveal their plans. They stopped singing and Hazel took over, standing before us, the Cape Hatteras Lighthouse causing its beams to shine on her face.

She addressed me by that endearing title they had conjured up some terms ago.

"Señor Verde, we have something important to tell you, but first promise you won't tell a living soul. You must also swear that you'll consent to let us carry out our plans."

"Oh come now, I can keep a secret, but don't expect me to buy a pig in a poke. Until your secret is revealed, I cannot promise!"

I had spoken very emphatically, but the girls began to beg, assuring me I'd be so proud of them I'd never regret it.

"If it's so great, why not tell me?"

"You've told us our class is one of the most intelligent you've ever had."

I waited, silently.

"Please give us a chance to prove it."

Each took a turn convincing me. It would be the greatest thing that had ever happened in Kinnakeet. It would make history and be an unforgettable event. Future generations would read about it. I planned to write a book, didn't I? Well, it would be worth a whole chapter!

Just then we were surprised by a car coming down the beach on the wash of the sea; it was low tide. It moved rapidly, since after a northerly wind the beach was as good as a highway, except one had to keep a sharp lookout for obstructions.

We climbed atop the lifeboat, waiting for the car to pass between us and the wild Atlantic. It was heading toward Kinnakeet, but suddenly it left the wash, it's lights flashing full on us. It seemed for a moment as though it were coming right at us, and the squealing girls clung to me as though I could protect them. Finally, the driver maneuvered away from us, and it appeared as if he were dashing into the sea.

We learned he was a traveling salesman who traversed this road frequently, and having gained control again, he continued towards Kinnakeet.

"Quiet!" I admonished the girls. "What do you think he thought when he saw all of you clinging to me on top of the lifeboat? You were jabbering and screaming worse than a flock of wild geese!"

I insisted that we get serious, and the quicker the better.

Hazel took over.

"We juniors have planned thoroughly the junior-senior banquet."

I jumped down from the lifeboat.

"Is *that* it? Really, I thought I was going to hear something. Are you implying that you are planning to put on this event by yourselves?"

They said it was so.

"Why did you bring me here?"

"Oh, Señor Verde, we think it's a wonderful secret. Did you ever hear of a junior class doing everything themselves? Don't you think we're an extraordinary group to assume all the responsibility?"

They were crestfallen over my disappointment as was I over their inconsequential revelation.

Lamely, I assured them I did appreciate their willingness to do something worthwhile, but admitted I couldn't understand why it was so secretive.

"It's more fun that way," said one, with customary female logic.

They said they realized I had work to do, but they wanted to relieve me of all the responsibility concerning the banquet.

"Without the aid of a teacher, parents, or anybody?"

"Right!" they chorused.

I pretended to take a cynical view, when actually, it was the best news I had heard in weeks. The very thought of having the responsibility lifted from my shoulders filled me with delight.

Proceeding cautiously, I told them they must realize they couldn't do everything by themselves. "Your task of putting on a first class banquet is much more difficult here than up country. We don't have equipment like they do in other schools, nor do we have a lunchroom. We lack so much, and this is a big job you've assumed."

"We want to prove we're as smart as you claim we are. All we're asking is permission."

"All right, I'll give my consent, but this banquet better be perfect. Don't forget there will be important guests, and Kinnakeet has to look good."

"Bless your heart, Señor Verde. This will be one banquet you'll never forget," said one.

"And you, as principal will be the honored guest," another reminded me. "We want you to be the last to arrive, at exactly one minute to eight. Everything is going to be a surprise for you. Doesn't that make you feel good?"

I could not honestly say it was reassuring, but before I committed myself, Hazel was being urged to tell me their plans, which I was not to reveal to anyone.

I promised.

Again she emphasized I would be the honored guest, and all details of the banquet were secret, but there was one item which must be discussed with me.

"You know, of course, there's and English lord and his wife living down on the Cape. You're aware also that we have invited him to be our commencement speaker. Therefore, don't you think the least we could do is invite the lord and lady to the banquet?"

"Girls!"

"We have already done that," they chorused, gaining strength in unity.

"Do you realize what you've done?"

They said it was merely difficult to imagine a real lord and his lady as banquet guests.

"I wish you had told me this before I gave my permission for you to assume all responsibility." Even as I reproached them, I was well aware I was tricked! They had planned well the order in which information would be doled out to me.

Again Hazel emphasized the banquet would be so unique it would take up an entire chapter in my book, and how proud they'd all be.

Since a pact had been made between the girls and myself, we started back to Kinnakeet. They resumed singing, exultantly, rejoicing in victory, and as always, I was crowded right in the middle.

I left them at Gibb's store sauntering in to sit awhile on the counter, my legs dangling.

They lost no time, using the money they had raised to order decorations, food, souvenirs, and programs. By then, the girls revealed their intentions to the boys, swearing them to secrecy.

A new classroom in the rear of the auditorium was under construction and would be partially completed, so that the banquet could be held there. The fact that the banquet would be its first, added to the excitement. Three coats of white paint had been used there, and four high windows looked out onto the Atlantic. It was a cheerful room, and I was proud of it.

Since Kinnakeet was so isolated, this was to be the juniors first formal occasion. It was the highlight of their young lives, therefore, I let them have considerable time to prepare for the exciting affair. Their enthusiasm was contagious, and it did seem, as the days passed, that all Kinnakeet was excited!

By the time the last week arrived, the students spent every spare minute in the new room working on the affair. Both boys and girls worked as though their very lives depended on it. From the club houses near Kinnakeet and from private homes, they borrowed fine tables and chairs, working incessantly on decorations.

Not once did I break my agreement with them. I did not so much as peek into the would-be banquet hall, and as to exactly what was going on in there, I hadn't the least idea.

The week flew by, and I must admit that they were not concentrating on their lessons, but it was easy to understand why, and forgive them.

On the day of the banquet, the sky was a gay blue, and a gentle breeze swept in from the southwest. We went through the class routines, but all of us were thinking of the banquet.

As quickly as school was dismissed this Friday that would make Kinnakeet history, the juniors and seniors left in a special rush.

I had purchased a new suit especially for the occasion, and I bathed and dressed with considerable care. Even so, I was ready at six-thirty, which left me about ninety minutes before the time specified me to enter the banquet hall, precisely one minute to eight.

This would be the first time I was an honored guest, and I wasn't exactly calm, myself. I tried to read but it was no good; I turned on the radio, but it only upset me.

What if everything hadn't been well planned?

What if the colors of the decorations clashed?

Why had I ever given my consent for the girls to assume this responsibility without an adult to advise and counsel them?

This had to be an occasion of which all Kinnakeet could be proud, and I wanted the guests to praise it enthusiastically.

One bad blunder could ruin it!

We had many influential guests, who had accepted the invitation, and it was necessary that they depart from the event feeling that we were cultured people, with an eye to the niceties of life.

A terrible thought popped into my head causing me to jump from my seat. The school had four gas mantle lanterns. Under good conditions, they would emit plenty of light, but if they hadn't been cleaned and new mantles put on them, they would be very dim.

What if the girls forgot about this?

It worried me to such an extent, I left the house immediately. As I hurried along, I tried to analyze this sudden worry. Up to now, I had given the gas lanterns no thought; why had they become so important to me now?

I was almost running as I approached Gibb's store. Gibb stood in the doorway, shouting, "Now don't ye feel important?"

I went into the store, vaguely aware of his comments that I was to be the honored guest. He even knew the time of my arrival.

Once inside the store, I tried to calm myself. I took a Coke from the ice box and sipped it. Finally I said, "I have a feeling I should have checked on this banquet. There'll be many important guests, and if anything goes wrong, folks will blame me."

Gibb thought I was ridiculous; the younguns had worked too hard not to have done everything perfect. He invited me to sit down and relax; there was a whole hour yet to wait.

He chewed his tobacco as swiftly as a rabbit nibbling a carrot, and I was gulping my Coke so rapidly, I felt like a thirsty cow.

A great compulsion drove me toward the schoolhouse, though I had promised to keep away. A great struggle occurred within me, but I knew my promise would triumph over my insecurity. I agreed to arrive at one minute to eight, and that's when I'd come! I returned to my room - thirty minutes yet! At a quarter of eight, I departed, even though I could walk it in seven or eight minutes, I stopped again at Gibb's store.

An oppressive silence dominated the town from one end to the other. It was so quiet it hurt! Apparently all who'd be at the banquet were already there. I had the road to myself, and with each step, the dread of reaching that familiar front door increased.

I had timed it perfectly, at two minutes of eight, I walked through the front gate surrounding the building, and at one minute to eight, I entered the front door.

Well! All the seniors and guests were in the hall instead of the banquet room. To get into the banquet room, it was necessary to pass through the auditorium. However, this was not what was delaying matters-of this I was sure.

But what was?

To add to my perplexity, there were no lights in the hall and none in the auditorium. Darkness had already begun to make itself felt.

The understanding between the junior girls and myself was that the guests would be seated in the banquet room, and upon my arrival, the banquet would start.

I dashed through the darkening auditorium toward the banquet room, and just before I reached it, a great commotion broke loose. As I jerked open the door, I saw a banquet room fit for a king!

Tables were spread, and laden with home-cooked Kinnakeet food, but not a light shone. The junior girls were running around frantically.

"Where are the lights?" I managed to squeak.

Hazel came over to me, distressed. "Every mantle on the gas lanterns has come apart and we don't have any light."

I turned to the boys. "Go to the store for some mantles."

"We've been and there's none to be found."

I made the understatement of the year when I said quietly, "This is awful."

Glancing over the tables loaded with fried chicken, hot biscuits, salads, mashed potatoes, and tall glasses filled with iced tea, it seemed that nothing more could happen to make this banquet a bigger failure.

But just then another girl rushed up, They had borrowed knives and forks from the south clubhouse, but someone had stolen them.

"Well, we have spoons," I stated monotonously.

Slowly a soft light fell across the room, it caused me to turn and look. A full moon was coming right out of the Cape Hatteras Sea, and its beams spread over sea and land, making it a golden world. Our white walls, so freshly painted caught the gleams and our banquet room became a veritable fairyland.

"Calm yourselves, everybody," I cried in stentorian tones. "You've said it right from the beginning I was in for a surprise, and you were right! We shall eat by moonlight, and to add to the uniqueness, with spoons!"

The guests were great sports and the program went off perfectly. Instead of misfortune handicapping the success of our junior-senior banquet, it added to the enjoyment of the occasion. I was sure none of us would ever attend another dinner which would stand out in our memories, as this one.

No apologies were made, not by me to our important guests, not by my students to me, for the simple reason that we had all enjoyed it so much.

CHAPTER 26

ADULT EDUCATION COMES TO KINNAKEET

For four years, Kinnakeet had an accredited high school in our proud new building. It was then we realized a terrible truth-Kinnakeet was hopelessly doomed; there would be no more high school here! At first none of us was able to grasp this fact, yet the undeniable truth was there. The likelihood of such a catastrophe had confronted us before, but it was overcome. This time, hope faded. Due to a large graduating class, and a very small freshman one, the school's enrollment dropped so low that the average daily attendance wouldn't be great enough to keep the school accreditation for the ensuing year.

Kinnakeet would lose its high school!

Oh, there were enough young people to overcrowd the building, easily requiring another teacher, but for years, there was no high school. In fact, many of the youngsters never attended high school. By now, many of them would be several years older than the present high school students. Trying to interest them in returning now was out of the question.

I felt the teen-agers as a whole, in school and out, largely possessed brilliant minds. Thus, it was merely indifference in the past that had deprived not only Kinnakeet, but North Carolina and the nation, of much brain power. It was too late to do anything about it, now, that is, under the prevailing conditions.

But regardless, the whole town was greatly perturbed about losing its only high school. The people as a whole evinced great interest in the school, and there was real pride in their hearts and minds. By now, many students had graduated from the local high school, and folks took it for granted that many others would follow. The townspeople had ceased to be concerned about Kinnakeet boys being incapable of entering the only occupation offered them, the United States Coast Guard. The mere existence of a high school stopped them from worrying about being uneducated.

The sudden word that there would be no high school next year was like thunder from a clear sky. The cause of this tragedy was simple; last year the senior class was unusually large for the school, but the freshman class, strangely, consisted of only five students. These figures made it impossible for the required attendance to maintain accreditation.

This definitely meant the demise of the school after this year, for at least a term, which would complicate matters greatly.

The youngest teen-age boys were the most affected; at least they gave this impression. They knew when they became old enough to enlist into the coast guard, they would be ineligible without a high school diploma.

Everyone awakened to just how much their school meant to them. Most Kinnakeeters were not financially able to send children off to a boarding school; thus, the more folks talked about it, the more depressed they became.

As for myself, I gave up. There seemed no way of overcoming this situation. If there weren't students, there was nothing I could do. I failed to interest those in their late teens and early twenties in reentering school.

I spent the entire third week of school trying to think if a solution, but there appeared to be none. This defeat was not good for me; it was my greatest failure up to now, and I tried to accept it.

The fact that I was extremely busy helped-there was so little time left to worry. Not so, on the weekend; late Friday afternoon, the teachers and students left the building while I sat alone, discouraged; the world looked very dark and dreary.

Uncle George Meekins, out dearly-loved janitor, could be heard cleaning in the next room, but I was so deeply engrossed in my thoughts, I was scarcely aware of him.

Suddenly, he stood in the doorway. Glancing at him, he was obviously excited about something.

He greeted me, saying, "I'm some kinda surprised! Was jus' thinkin' about ye. Got something mighty important to discuss with you."

I waited.

"Have ye found any way to save the high school?"

I told him no. "Uncle George, you know how stubborn I am, but this time I'm licked. It's literally making me sick!"

"Same here, Brother Green! Haven't slept all week. Keep waking up every night, thinking, and praying. I've experienced many hard and bitter days, but the loss of our high school has hit me the hardest."

What could I say? I felt sorry for the old man, but I was depressed myself. He resumed cleaning, while I went home.

Walking rapidly along the beach, I did not turn into Gibb's store as usual, wanting only to be alone. At Mrs. Keaton's, the house was empty, which pleased me. In my room, I forced myself to stretch out on my bed, but my nerves were jumpy.

I went downstairs, pacing back and forth across the comfortable living room. When Mrs. Keaton arrived from her errands, she greeted me with, "You know, I've never seen

Kinnakeet so concerned about anything as it is now. We never had a high school before, but you'd think we never knew anything else, the way folks are agitated. The children are so hurt they don't mention it, but that's all the older folks do talk about."

Just as with Uncle George, I assured Mrs. Keaton that I had scrutinized it from every angle and if I saw a speck of hope, I would certainly put up a fight. It was out of our hands-if there weren't enough students, there was nothing we could do.

"That's what I say, but this is something Kinnakeet will never live down."

Saturday morning, I set out unusually early to hang some maps on my schoolroom wall. How quiet the village was! A few light clouds hugged the horizon, and the only noise was a gas truck rumbling by. The wind was from the northeast, and the sea sounded louder than usual. Gibb had already opened his store and stood leaning against the counter, busily chewing tobacco.

A stranger would have assumed this village by the open sea was perfectly peaceful, but I knew there was turmoil in the hearts of the people.

Repeatedly, I asked myself why Kinnakeet had to be deprived of the same educational advantages enjoyed upstate. I understood the problems, but why couldn't special provisions be made? As always, I respected the facts. Consolidation of schools on the island was impossible-there were no highways and school buses could not travel in the soft sand. Thus, the majority of Kinnakeet's youth would never be able to finish high school.

The more I mulled this over in my weary mind, the faster I walked. Now I was out on the beach where the breakers crashed louder than in the village. Even so, I faintly heard someone calling me, waving his hat high above his head. As he came nearer, I recognized Uncle George Meekins. He appeared to be very upset and it frightened me. I wondered if some great tragedy occurred during the night.

As he got closer, I could tell by his face that he was *happily* excited.

"Got something important to tell you."

He was panting from his run, and I waited for him to breathe normally. "My prayers may be answered; I think I have the solution!"

Incredulously, I asked, "You mean there's a way to keep the high school intact next year?" I wished heartily that I felt as optimistic as he did. Poor Uncle George, a dear old man, but senile. Patiently, I said, "Let's have it; What's the solution?"

"Does age have anything to do with going to school?"

I shook my head. "Not as far as I know. Why do you ask?"

"Well, if a person's age don't matter, us old folks can attend school. You know without being told, we never had much chance to go to school. All my life, I've wondered what it would be like to attend high school. You got no idea how I've envied the younguns. So what's wrong if I still want to go to high school?"

I thought his idea too fantastic, and I was very unimpressed. He began to substantiate his arguments; in performing his janitorial duties, he overheard me telling a student never to stop learning. I said that life was one big school-from birth to death.

"Yes, but-"

"You said it, di'n't you? Then why are you stalling now?"

The old man was so intense, I had no choice but to listen to him.

"You want to get adults to return to school? Also, you want to know whether or not they'd be accepted as regular students."

Uncle George replied, "Exactly!"

I promised him I would contact the proper authorities and make sure about ages. However, it was merely to humor this janitor of whom I was so fond. Everybody in Kinnakeet loved Uncle George, but this morning he was not to be put off. At his insistence, we both walked back to Gibb's store where I put through a telephone call to headquarters.

"Is there any age limit for a person attending high school in North Carolina?" I queried simply.

The reply was equally direct and uncomplicated.

"There is no age limit."

What else was there to do other than tell Uncle George? His elation was something to see. We fell in step and were soon back on the open beach, neither of us speaking until we reached the school.

He must have sensed my indifference, for he said, "If you don't like the idea, we can call off the whole thing."

There was such disappointment in his tone, and I felt ashamed for being unable to act enthusiastically. I said casually, "Let's give it a try and see what happens."

"You don't go for the idea, and it does sound crazy, but nobody's come up with a better one."

"Nobody's come up with any," I elaborated.

"Now you won't have to take the responsibility of getting folks here and keeping 'em. You won't have to do anything but teach."

"You get 'em here and I'll teach 'em," I mimicked him.

Uncle George got busy with this chores while I started putting up the maps.

Kinnakeet's philosopher hummed loudly; Kinnakeet's principal did not. Uncle George was obviously happy, while I had considerable misgivings.

The truth was that many of my scientific ideas were contrary to those of the adults. I hadn't forgotten the several times we had heated discussions regarding them. My theories would be far too radical for them. Try as I would, the old axiom that you couldn't teach an old dog new tricks kept running through my mind. If Uncle George Meekins succeeded in interesting the adults, which I doubted, my troubles would be multiplied. I could see no bright future, whichever way the idea worked itself out.

As usual, I wanted to walk. Nothing soothed my nerves more. Thus, after an early lunch, I went along the shores of the peaceful water of the Pamlico Sound. Below the "landing," I sauntered among the myrtles, yeopon, and bullrushes.

It was a time for deep and logical thought. Uncle George would recruit mostly older folks, many of them past working age. The books I had read, the lectures I had attended, and the people with whom I had discussed education-none had given me any inkling of how to teach grandpa and grandma, pa and ma, along with their children, simultaneously. I was even sure that no such training was available. Where could I turn for advice in this unique situation?

It could only happen in Kinnakeet, I told myself, and I must solve it myself. I began to wonder what the adults would think of my teaching methods, and ideas.

If they criticized me too much, the school was still doomed! In fact, the downfall would come this year if Uncle George recruited his friends, instead of next year.

Kinnakeet had problems, but as I paced, my hands locked behind me, I felt they didn't compare to this one. It was like being used to a mouse, and all at once, confronted by an elephant.

The tempting aroma of greens cooking on the stove welcomed me as I entered Mrs. Keaton's. Going into her kitchen, I asked, "What would you think about adults going back to school in order to save it?"

"That would be something to go down in history!" She laughed heartily. Clearly, she didn't take me seriously, and I decided to change the subject.

The boiled cornbread, succulent greens, and Bill's unexcelled potato salad combined to put me in a better mood. After supper, I went to the various stores and meeting places to mix with the older folks. It was Saturday night and everybody seemed happy. I kept waiting for someone to mention Uncle George's idea, but there was no hint of it.

Again that night, I courted sleep in vain. My common sense told me it was an impossible and unworkable idea, better left alone.

There was great pity in my heart for Uncle George, but I was relieved that I had reached a decision. Upon awakening Sunday morning, I told myself that probably Uncle George had seen the folly of this, too. He had left it up to me from the start, and all I'd have to do was to say that after much thought, the idea simply was not workable.

His solution upset me much more than the original situation, and, by comparison, I was fairly calm now, since it was something with which I wouldn't have to cope.

However, I hadn't reckoned with Uncle George Meekins, fisherman, janitor, village philosopher and lover of youth. He came to me that Sunday, the most radiant old man I've ever seen.

"I've not only completed the plans, but I've worked out every detail. The folks have promised, and they're bound to carry it out."

Faintly, I queried, "What do you mean by details?"

"I mean my work has been finished. All you have to do is teach 'em."

I swallowed. "You think these people will come to school and stay there as long as they're needed?"

"They'll stay 'til they graduate," he bristled. "When a Kinnakeeter tells you he'll do a thing, it's so! He may have all kinds of faults, but he'll never break a promise."

I knew better than to doubt it. "How did you manage?"

The previous afternoon and evening, Uncle George had canvassed Kinnakeet with great care. He would go into a home, saying, "You know, it's too bad if we lose our high school. Would you do *anything* to save it?"

Invariably, they acquiesced, then he returned with, "This family is to send one of its members back to school, somebody who does not work, if possible, somebody in his late sixties or seventies. With everybody's cooperation, we'll keep our high school for our younguns. It's up to you."

A bargain had been made, and he had requested they say nothing until he had contacted everybody.

I nodded, understanding why I had heard nothing the night before.

Uncle George had his list of new students, too. He certainly did take car of every detail! Thirty-five new students would report for school the next morning. They were the folks all the way from their early twenties, to great-grandparents.

I left for Sunday school at the Methodist Church, and now there was plenty excitement, especially among the youngsters.

I hadn't reached Gibb's store before a crowd of them came hurrying toward me, their faces reflecting delight. Had I heard the news? Wasn't it simply wonderful?

"*Folks in this world,*" I murmured. "*Oh, folks in this world!*"

Fortunately it was almost time for Sunday school, so we all hurried along silently.

Slowly, I crawled out of bed on Monday morning. There was not enough breeze to rustle the leaves outside my window. It felt like the quiet before the storm. My heart was heavy, but I was determined to be there early, ready to meet the enemy. Hastily, I ate breakfast and hurried off. How was I going to get through this day? How would I get though all the other days stretching before me? A Kinnakeeter kept his promise, I reminded myself. These new students were committed to school, and come they would. I just couldn't reconcile myself to this fact.

The retired folks went to bed with the chickens, and I suspected they arose at the first hint of dawn, and I was determined to beat every last one of them to school this morning.

I had not been there long when one of my freshmen arrived, looking restless. Saying nothing, he moved about, glancing out the window. As for myself, I could find nothing to do, so I cleaned the spotless blackboards, and sorted the textbooks on my desk, putting them in their proper place. It was not warm, but I raised the windows, anyway.

Arthur had left the room, then suddenly I heard him dashing back, yelling for me to come out in front.

What I saw made me want to jump in the Atlantic Ocean. Coming up through Cat Ridge was a group of thirty-five elderly people. They huddled together and moved like a plague, heading straight for the school building. And school wasn't due to start for another hour yet. They were eager as kindergartners starting school.

Uncle George and his wife, Aunt Liza Ann led the others; obviously, he had rounded them all up. I wished they could have drifted in singly! I was rooted to the front door, shaking each one's hand as he entered.

Gradually, I realized they hadn't come grudgingly, but were a happy group of people, with much curiosity. Probably, I told myself, they recalled experiences of their childhood. By the time I finished shaking hands, my spirits had risen, slightly.

Every extra seat and chair available was placed in my classroom. Even so, there were not enough, whereupon my regular boys insisted on sitting on the floor, or leaning against the back walls of the room, just as they did when the building was new, and we were without seats.

When I stood before them, the warmth radiating from them enveloped me. I smiled, thinking I would challenge anyone in the teaching profession to cite a similar situation.

How much I had to learn! By the end of the first week, one of the older students expressed it, saying, "I already feel twenty years younger."

251

Youth was rubbing off on age!

And how about the younger students? They were benefiting, I had no doubt about it. Wisdom acquired through experience rubbed off on them.

But none had profited by these first few days as much as I had, for now I realized that our modern education lacked something of great value, when it didn't provide more opportunity for youth and age to come together.

It was not that I didn't believe people shouldn't have the opportunity to relate with others of the same age, but to have no positive programs for youth and age to mix distressed me! It was lack of sound judgement whether in the home, the church, or the community. The mixture at my school pointed this out to me.

A great democratic society grew out of an agricultural culture where youth and age worked together, played together and worshipped together. Thus, the youngsters were closely associated with older people, and I was satisfied that this was responsible for making a great country.

Thanks be to God for people like this!

One Tuesday in sociology, I remarked that it was a pity we had so few books on the subject in our school library. An adult student interrupted my lecture to ask how much it would take to buy a good collection of books on the subject, for a small high school library?

"Three hundred dollars would buy a wonderful collection for a large high school library, to say nothing of a small one like ours," I replied. In the late 1930's, the amount would easily buy one hundred topnotch sociology books.

We continued our assignment, and I thought no more about the discussion. The next Saturday morning, as I was going from Dog Ridge to Cat Ridge, I met the adult walking along, grinning broadly.

"You can go ahead and get the sociology books for the library," he greeted me. "I can't wait till I can start reading 'em."

He reached into his trousers pocket, coming forth with a roll of money which he handed me, adding forty-five cents in change. Bewildered, I began counting: these was a total of three hundred fifteen dollars and forty-five cents.

"Folks in this world! Where did all this money come from?"

"Your old students got together, went down into their pockets and raised it," he said proudly.

I stood there, speechless. If these people hadn't attended school, but had been asked to contribute to such a fund, probably not over ten or fifteen dollars would have been raised. Now they had a new interest in life. They were on the inside looking out, and didn't have to be sold on the idea.

I was overwhelmed; I held the money in my hand, staring at it, and all I could manage was, "Thank you all very much." This seemed appropriate, and I felt the man who made the presentation sensed the depth of my emotions.

We started to work on a play, and the young students were thrilled some of the older ones were going to be in it. At first, this would have been the worst thing we could have done, but now it was a matter of maturity and youth learning to understand each other.

As preparations got under way for the play, the women teachers dared me to assign the role of the comedian to the most dignified man in Kinnakeet.

By this time, I was ready to attempt anything, and I took the challenge. He was a member of the Board of Education, our

Mr. Fields Meekins, who accepted eagerly, and put on an outstanding performance. The youngsters loved him, and he became one of them.

Gradually I began to analyze my reactions, and the results of the program. Teaching the adults along with the "younguns" in the same classroom was one of the most wonderful experiences I could ever hope to have. It was also one of the greatest innovations that ever occurred in Kinnakeet, with a value to both young and old which was immeasurable.

The devil never made a more invidious statement than the one about not being able to teach an old dog new tricks. Bless the old dogs who were able to teach us more than a few!

And our deepest thanks went to kind old Uncle George Meekins who ambitiously solved the problem of saving our Kinnakeet high school.

CHAPTER 27

WAR COMES TO KINNAKEET

It had been a strange autumn in Kinnakeet, the year, 1941. For as long as any Kinnakeeter could remember, fall brought mosquitoes in such vast numbers, they seemed like a rising dark cloud.

This was the hurricane season, yet the weather remained placid and Hatteras Island assumed a look of unusual beauty-the water bushes were dressed in white blossoms, and between these, were long, broad strips of yellow goldenrod. Branches of the live oaks were covered with acorns, ripe and brown; even the yeopons were lovely with their thick green leaves and scarlet berries.

Natives marveled at the perfection of nature, but even more, they spoke in hushed voiced about an unusual situation. For a number of years there had been no death in town, and the demise of Kinnakeeters in other parts of the world, had not been reported, either.

Thus passed September, October and November, and when December arrived, the usual Christmas celebration among the teen-agers commenced with the three o'clock rising; the jolly sound of carols, ringing bells, and the blatant beating of pots and pans.

It seemed that they embarked upon this custom with more than the usual fervor, as soon as December arrived. And on that awful Sunday when news came of Pearl Harbor, despite the inspiring church service, the calm beauty of the day, and the general air of peace, I was depressed. Alone with the radio on, I heard news of war's imminence.

Dazedly, I walked out of the house; along the road, I met others looking incredulous, too.

Most every Kinnakeet man was in the coast guard.

"Some of our own are in Pearl Harbor, " murmured one after another. They were on ships that had been bombed.

Kinnakeet, gay with Christmas celebrations, changed in the twinkling of an eye and mourned. And just as with every other situation, war dealt differently with Kinnakeet, for several reasons.

The fact that so many of our men were in the coast guard brought war closer, and because we were on a strip of land standing precariously on the Atlantic, we became more involved. We saw the battles, and our school building, out on the beach, made it possible to look out our windows and see the conflict!

As though angered by man's destructive intentions, the weather changed, becoming rough with sea gales and heavy rains. Children no longer romped and played, and teen-agers did not gather at Pritchard's to laugh and sing. Also, the older people were stolid and uncommunicative.

Yet, those who had not been snatched into service shouldered the added burdens of the ones who had. The holidays came, but how different from any I had enjoyed in Kinnakeet.

During peace time, the off-limit shoreline at sea was three miles, but now at war, the line was increased. Since the United States had declared war on Germany and Japan, the off-shoreline was extended to ten miles on the Atlantic and Pacific; thus, the boundaries of North Carolina extended ten miles out to sea. Not that the line would deter the enemy, but for other reasons, we felt reasonably secure. There was the protection of quicksand beds-what wonderful traps they'd make; besides, coast guardsmen were on duty!

While one of the world's greatest highways passed Kinnakeet's east front door, her treacherous shores kept traffic from entering. The quicksand was one reason; the mysterious Gulf Stream another; here the north ocean currents met those of the south. The area immediately east of the quicksand beds was better for sea transportation than farther out, thus, for generations, all civilized countries followed this time-saving route east of the treacherous waters off of Cape Hatteras.

Through the aid of the Panama Canal, ocean traffic from every part of the world used this route. Early America was greatly influenced by it, but, because of it, now war was at Kinnakeet's front door. Hitler seized the advantage it offered by sending his submarine fleet to lie in wait, then blowing up ships as they headed toward their destination.

It happened in mid-January, at an hour of night when Kinnakeeters were all asleep. Suddenly, the whole sea appeared lighted by fire. Jumping from my bed, I saw the town was still intact, but the outer world appeared to be an inferno.

The German fleet of submarines was the biggest and best the world had ever known, and now the line of ships that sailed east of us was a lifeline of the United States and her allies. For the first half of that year, commercial ships in our area were helpless. To go west was to meet a quicksand grave, to go east was to be blown up by sub torpedoes. There was no choice at all except to risk going west, and in their attempt, they were caught within the water limits of North Carolina and blown up.

Some of the worst battles were fought in North Carolina, in the United States of America. The North Carolina Outer Banks of which Cape Hatteras was the outermost past, was cut off from transportation to the mainland of the United States. In fact, we were cut off from the rest of the world!

Thus, school children looked out the windows to see bombed ships going up in smoke. Once, the concussion was so great from an exploding tanker filled with millions of gallons of high test gasoline, a pane was broken in an auditorium window.

The German subs had practically all the advantages, and the toll was tremendous. Yet school continued, students and teachers giving evident of calm and determination.

Tankers were their favorite victims; they carried material vital to the war; besides, they made an awful sound and were a terrifying spectacle to behold.

When the first such night was over, the sea was a burning hell. A mild easterly wind enshrouded Kinnakeet with stifling fumes. The next day we witnessed a terrible sight-the beach, composed of white and brown sand, had become as black as tar. The winds brought residue from the burned fuel oil to the shores at low tide, and a band of sticky, tar-like substance bordered the seashore.

For months untold loss of ships, cargo and lives continued in the sea battles, and we were to discover that these were largely kept secret from the public. News reports mentioned only of the number of ships sunk in the Atlantic. Yes, Kinnakeeters were truly on their own, and the town functioned as nearly as normal as possible.

Our beautiful shores became increasingly tragic. A partially-burned empty lifeboat-spoke eloquently of the fact that its occupants had burned to death. And soon the beach was strewn with dead sea life. Fowl by the thousands had been caught in the sticky tar and could no longer fly, many could only creep along the beach. There was a Canadian goose so saturated with tar she could scarcely move; but the gander stood with her, although he could have flown away.

High tide was coming in fast, so I picked up the goose and set her far from the sea so she wouldn't drown. The gander kept near, bobbing his head, as though he were trying to tell me of the awful tragedy which had overtaken them.

All of them faced a slow, painful death, and in the distance could be heard the cries of seagulls, the honks of more Canadian geese, and the pitiful quacking of wild ducks.

War was merciless, not even sparing an innocent bird.

Mrs. Keaton's home was on the west side of town, near the shore of the Pamlico Sound, but one early Monday morning, I continued east instead of going through the village. When I reached the open beach, I turned north towards the schoolhouse. No sooner had I come in sight of it when I saw a group of little girls running around, excitedly. Usually they played in the schoolyard, while the little boys romped on the beach.

Today there were no small boys on the beach!

When I saw the girls coming to meet me, I was sure that something was wrong and walked faster. When we met, they were too excited to talk clearly-all I could make out was, "they're buried alive."

My first reaction was the enemy had slipped ashore and buried the little boys alive. Just then, I saw some of them peeping around the north end of the building. At the sight of me, they disappeared.

"They done it!" the girls accused.

High school students were arriving now, and when we questioned the boys, they admitted they had buried some of the tarred birds on the east side of the building.

We grabbed shovels or whatever was available and started digging frantically. At least they had used sticks for tombstones, and broken branches for flowers, thus aiding us in locating their victims.

Finally the head of a Canadian goose stuck up through the loose sand, and I grabbed one of his wings and jerked him free. With a great flapping of wings, he ran down to the beach, honking his protests.

We all worked quickly, freeing many birds from their graves. Because they hadn't been buried long, and because the sand was loose, not a single one died. However, it wouldn't have taken much longer for them to suffocate.

Most of them were too tarred to fly when the boys found them. They felt sorry for them, thinking they were doing them a favor. Strangely, we discovered they had, for the struggle the birds put up to get out of their graves caused much of the oil to be rubbed off their feathers, and they were almost normal.

Just as everywhere else in America, complete blackouts were important. However, here we were in greater danger should a light show. Kinnakeeters felt the children were safe at school, or as safe as they would be at home.

One clear, cool morning in February, a nor-easter had recently blown itself out, but the sea remained unusually rough. There was not even the whisper of a breeze; it was high tide, and the ocean spray shot into the air as I walked to school.

I was conducting my first morning class, when throughout the building sounded hysterical screaming and crying. I rushed into the hall, location the commotion in the first-and-second grade room at the far end of the building.

My students had left their work and stood with me, then we all rushed to see what caused the disturbance.

Everyone in town was well aware of our location here and how easily we could be blown from the face of the earth.

The door down the hall opened and children piled through it, struggling and screaming. The teacher stood white with fear, trying vainly to silence the children.

The south window sash had suddenly exploded, throwing broken glass over that part of the room. The children, of course, thought a German submarine had bombed the building.

"What did hit the window?" I wanted to know.

No one knew; everything was quiet, when suddenly the sash popped and glass flew about.

All of us checked the room, but couldn't find the cause. We went outside, and looked under the building; there was nothing extraordinary.

Some of my bigger boys climbed on top of the building and reported no ships in sight.

There was nothing else to do about the mystery, so we cleaned up the broken glass and the children returned to their seats, nervously.

We pretended to get to our routine, but my calmness was all pretense. I felt as though bugs were crawling over me; that sash did not disintegrate on its own.

As I conjectured, and my students pretended to be doing their written assignment, there came a loud banging on the door. I dreaded opening it, but when I did, there stood the teacher. I closed the door, going out into the hall.

With a peculiar expression on her face, she put a baseball in my hand.

"What's the meaning of this?"

She said that after we left, she was so nervous she walked around the room to keep the children from guessing.

She noticed on the coat rack that some of the white paint had been knocked off. Searching further, she found the baseball which had dropped into the wastebasket in the corner.

I nodded slowly and, with the ball in my hand, returned to my classroom, placing the ball on top of my desk. The students noticed it, but said nothing. I, too, was silent, and walked back to the window where I had been standing, and glanced over the room.

There were two boys apparently working intently on their English lessons, but this was not as surprising as the fact that they hadn't arrived until after the episode occurred.

They were the only two who really seemed to be concentrating on the lesson-what an act they put on, I thought!

I walked casually over and looked straight at them, but they pretended to be working so hard, neither looked up. I put on an act, too, making believe nobody was a suspect.

The rest of the day, the boys were perfect students. Finally, I asked them to remain after school; they had nothing to say to me as both looked out the window.

"Why were you late for school this morning?"

Joe said he overslept.

Jack said he did, too.

"Joe, you live on Dog Ridge, and Jack, you live on Cat Ridge. How much difference was there in the time you both arrived this morning?"

They said they came in about the same time.

"Odd," I said. "Did both of you enter from the front door together?"

They nodded.

"Quite a coincidence," I told them. "Or *was* it?"

Joe said, "No sir. We first met at Farrow's store." This was a general store on Cat Ridge.

I turned to Jack. "What were you doing there during school hours? Didn't you know it was school time?"

Jack stepped nearer, looking straight at me for a moment. "Mr. Green," he said, "you know everything, don't you? Why are you bothering to ask us all the questions when you know we broke the window?"

"So you admit it?"

"Yes," they chorused.

"I guess you know it could have been serious. Our nerves are on edge during such times as these."

Joe confessed, "You don't know how it scared us. What we did was unintentional; it was an accident. We're sorry about it."

"Why didn't you speak up?"

They looked at each other. They were too scared when all the screaming began, and felt like criminals. They were so excited they couldn't speak.

"If it wasn't an accident, maybe you'd better tell what did happen."

They seemed relieved at the chance. Jack said that actually both of them had overslept. He found Joe on the store steps as fidgety as a worm in hot ashes, afraid to go to school late.

Jack suggested, "Let's be late together."

He had his ball and glove, and since they were already late, it seemed logical that being tardier wouldn't matter much.

As they approached from the south side of the building, they began to throw the ball to each other. Jack pitched it too high, and Joe missed it, and the ball hit the sash so hard it blew to pieces.

"Just like a bomb hit it," they agreed.

Thus, Kinnakeet lived in a constant state of suspense. Americans read of the ravages of war in Europe, but few realized that actual battles were being fought within the limits of the United States.

Week after week, the German subs kept sinking ships in North Carolina waters, and as the battles on the coast raged, fears of an invasion of Hatteras Island worried several naval authorities.

As the war worsened in Europe and Asia, and millions of Americans were being drafted, I was placed in Class 1-A; this meant I might get drafted any day.

My students began to beg me to join the Coast Guard before it happened.

"You are a true Kinnakeeter now, and we are coast guardsmen, not soldiers," they argued.

I agreed, after being there for twelve years, my interests were here in the town and its people.

Thus, I went to Norfolk, Virginia, and signed up for the coast guard on October 1, 1942. However, I could not be placed on active duty until November 5, so said nothing to my students until the last minute.

That I was leaving my beloved school seemed beyond comprehension. But these were days of unreal happenings, which were brutally real!

At the end of school on Friday, I called my high school students together, telling them I had come to the end of twelve years and one month of teaching at Kinnakeet. On Monday morning, they would have a new principal, because I'd become a member of the United States Coast Guard.

"Wherever I am, my thoughts will be with you," I said nostalgically.

CHAPTER 28

THE HORSE PATROL

I left my cherished school with the conviction that my work at Kinnakeet was over, that I would never return.

On the third day after taking my oath, I was sent to Big Kinnakeet Coast Guard Station, only our miles south of Kinnakeet. We had come down from Norfolk via Oregon Inlet, reaching our destination at night fall. What an overwhelming desire I had to rush over to my beloved village, but I was too exhausted to do anything but tumble into my bunk.

The next morning at dawn, I could see the school through the north window, and my deep love for it and its people was never greater than at that moment.

The second night at the Coast Guard Station found me on my first war assignment, patrolling the shores of the Cape Hatteras Sea. There was still danger of invasion, and our patrol was on actual war duty, not merely training exercises. And to think that a week ago, I was an educator; now I was a seafaring man!

Four miles down the beach-four miles back. My shipmate was from Brooklyn and as we paced the beach together through the familiar soft sand, we talked of many things, but never of war. We carried walkie-talkies and loaded pistols, all of it so unreal.

There was no heavy artillery on the island, but our walkie-talkies kept us in touch with the Station, which in turn had contact with military forces in Norfolk, as well as Elizabeth City. Our pistols were supposed to protect us long enough to report a landing party, and I was careful to conceal the fact that I was the world's worst shot. My knowledge consisted of loading a pistol and pulling the trigger.

Soon after my arrival at Big Kinnakeet Coast Guard Station, men poured in from Chicago and New York; later, they began coming from Texas. There were Texans and still more, until the station was filled with them, however, the Texans kept coming. Even the attic was cleaned out, to make room for them. At first, I paid no attention to them, but as I got to know them better, I saw they all had one outstanding characteristic, which was a thorough knowledge of horses. They were expert riders, and I admired this, since it was the one thing in the world I would never do. I liked horses, but a bad scare from seeing a man thrown when I was little had left its mark on me.

I should have been prepared when I heard a boatload of horses had arrived, but even then, I supposed the Texans would ride them to patrol the beach, while my duties would be around the station.

But how wrong I was! We were instructed to build a pound, which was fine with me. We would take good care of those Texas horses for our Texans!

The O.D. further announced that during the day, patrols could walk or ride as they saw fit, while night patrols must be on horseback.

"Sir," I questioned, "That doesn't mean all of us? Some don't know how to ride."

"Green, I mean you and everybody else." He studied me sharply, then explained horses could see and hear at night better than men. If the enemy were hiding behind a bush, a walking patrol might be ambushed before they could whirl around. Besides, a horse could run much faster than a man.

It made sense, of course, but I was more fearful of riding a horse than I was of being stabbed with a dagger. How I wished I were on the high seas where there were no horses.

A tall Texan, nicknamed Tex, of course, had charge of the horses, as well as the responsibility of teaching us to ride. I regarded him as the enemy. That night I had the dead man's tower watch from midnight to four, yet I was grateful because no horses were involved.

The watch tower was south of Big Kinnakeet Station, and from it one could observe the whole island, as well as the Cape Hatteras Sea and Pamlico Sound. It was my duty to be alert at all times, and if I saw anything extraordinary, I reported it to the O.D. by telephoning him at the station.

In the later afternoon, the sky turned dark and a strong gale blew out of the northeast. After supper, I went to bed hoping to get some sleep before midnight, but it wouldn't come because I kept thinking of horseback riding. Finally, I slept only to dream about horses. I was out on the plains when a horse standing nearby looked at me with glassy eyes. Suddenly, he opened his mouth and neighed, "Come on boys, let's get him!"

I started running, but behind me thundered a herd of wild horses. When they were about to overtake me, I was shaken awake by the O.D. who said it was ten to twelve.

As I hastily dressed, the rain, beating against the window, combined with the howling wind to make my dream more vivid. As I started to leave for the tower, the O.D. asked if I were ill.

I shook my head and dashed out into the storm. I was sick all night, but I had no intention of telling anybody why.

The storm enveloped me alone in the tower. There was only the roar of the sea and wind, and the darkness at this late hour.

I had too much time to think. My duty was only to keep my eyes open and, if I sensed danger, report it immediately. My thoughts all focused on the fact that I'd have to patrol on horseback. The more I fought against thinking about it, the stronger my thoughts came, and always the nightmare was before me.

By the end of my watch, I was sick with fear. What would my Texas shipmates think of me? And there was no way out, I would have to patrol the wash of our world's roughest sea on horseback, if it killed me-and I was convinced it would!

My relief was a chap from New York. We spoke of the weather, and I couldn't refrain from mentioning the poor fellows on horseback riding up and down the beach.

"Did you ever ride a horse?"

He nodded; he had an uncle living on a farm, and he enjoyed riding horses whenever he went to visit.

So even a city boy could ride a horse!

The next morning, I tried to talk with Tex alone, and it was almost lunch time when I succeeded. I told him of my fear, and said he'd never make a rider of me.

"That's all you wanted to see me about?"

"All? It's enough!"

He tossed his head back and roared, "Listen, Green, I'm going to teach you to ride, so let me do the worrying. It's my job, so forget about it, eh?"

"You don't understand; I'm not worried about you being able to teach me. My trouble is that I'm afraid of a horse." I explained about the episode when I was little, and how the fright remained with me.

He put a broad hand on my shoulder, comfortingly. "I can teach you to overcome your fear; I have dealt with it before."

The horses had arrived by then, and due to the shallow water near the shore, the boat anchored near a sandbar about two hundred feet away and the animals waded in. The Texans herded them into a pound, and from a safe distance, I surveyed them. They were young and frisky, and a beautiful sight to see. But when I thought of having to mount one, my fears rose up within me.

The rest of the afternoon was devoted to the horses by Tex and the others, who saddled and rode them. They were excited about the odd situation they were in, and needed exercise after the long boat ride. They were handled carefully, and gradually grew calm. I knew this was largely due to the expert hands they were in.

Shortly before sundown, all the horses had been checked.

Soon after supper, Tex called the crew together.

"Men, we have an extraordinary herd of horses, with one exception. Somebody gypped Uncle Sam, because we've got us a killer. I've ridden horses all my life, but I wouldn't think of touching that one. I don't want any of you to, either. I'm asking that every man obey my order because manpower is too valuable for us to lose one of you because of that horse."

Just as he finished, he glanced at me. He did not suppose I'd try it, did he? If that killer so much as looked at me, I would take to the open sea.

"You'll know him," Tex continued. "He's the only horse with a black spot over his right eye."

The horses would accustom themselves to their new home tonight, and tomorrow night they'd be pressed into service. As for those of us who must learn to ride, they would be given three days.

The unmanageable horse became known immediately as Wildie, and he was a real beauty. But there was a look in his eyes which spoke clearly of his hatred of man.

I had no patrol the next night, and soon after dark, I heard Tex calling me outside. It was a clear night, with a new moon shedding faint light.

"What do you want?" I queried suspiciously.

"Come on over to the Sound side, I want to talk to you."

My eyes were becoming used to the night and I could see he was on a horse. He rode it down the shore while I walked beside it. We had not gone far when he slid down ordering, "Get aboard, Green."

The horse seemed like a monster, and when I tried to mount, I froze in my tracks.

Tex said, "I chose him just for you; he's a good horse, steady and dependable. I'll hold the reins and you mount. Repeat three times, 'I can ride a horse!' then up you go."

I mounted him, sure that Tex would lead the beast, but as soon as I was settled on his back, Tex thrust the reins into my hands and told me to hold them lightly, because the horse would trot slowly.

Down that shore we went, and I was too frightened to do more than hang on. Tex ran after us, yelling at me to pull hard on the reins with my left hand. I did this and the horse returned to Tex. He commanded it to stop, and it obeyed.

"Now who said you can't ride a horse? Turn him around and do the same thing without me."

My heart beat wildly in exhilaration, I was trembling, but I was proud.

Tex said I could take my second lesson the next day before the others. Suddenly, I realized that he had been very considerate to let me have this first one privately. He was a kind, gentle man, and an understanding teacher.

By the end of the third day, I could saddle up, mount and dismount-it was a miracle!

On the third night of my training, my first patrol was to take place. Tex approached me, "Just a few words mate, a horse is a sensitive, affectionate creature. Make him love you, and realize you're his friend, and the rest will be simple. Of all the horses here, this one is the best; he's young and frisky, but affectionate. Make him your pal."

I thanked him, sincerely.

"What are you gonna call him?"

"Jim," I said. That name came quickly to mind.

"Always call him that. Pet him, feed him, and talk to him, and he'll love you."

Thus, the next three nights I patrolled on horseback, and to my amazement, Jim and I got along better than I dreamed possible. The first nigh was routine, but being on horseback for four hours made me unusually tired, but the fact that I managed a horse made me quite a different man.

On the second night, when I reached the south patrol where I halted the night before, Jim stopped, turned around and started north again. As we approached the station, he turned west and went straight to the pound, without being told.

After my third patrol, a whole new world opened up. I was proud-my fears had been conquered.

But I had grown confident too soon.

For several days after my third patrol, I had watches in the tower instead of beach patrols. During this time, I was able to relax the soreness in my muscles. I never missed a chance, either, of seeing Jim. I wanted him to love me; we were fast becoming devoted friends, and this made me feel like quite a horse trainer!

It was the night of my fourth patrol, when one of the Meekins boys from Kinnakeet and I were to patrol together. We were surprised when we dashed out into the darkness to see heavy clouds and no moon. There was not a stir of wind, but the roar of the sea was thunderous.

My eyes would adjust to this piceous blackness, I told myself, after awhile. But such was not the case, the blackness of the night was too intense. We groped our way to the pound, got bridles and saddles, while I wondered how I was going to find Jim out of all those horses.

My companion for the night was an expert horseman who saddled the first horse he touched, mounted him and waited for me at the open gate.

"Hurry up, Green," he called. "It'll soon be midnight."

"I can't see a thing, What should I do? I can't find Jim."

"Call him."

I hadn't thought of that.

However, Jim did not come when I called. I walked around the corral, hearing an occasional whinny, and feeling breath on my neck. I kept talking, hoping Jim would recognize me, but every horse I touched moved away.

I was in trouble. We had to patrol under orders, and I couldn't find Jim!

My shipmate grew impatient. "Saddle up any horse, or we'll both land in the brig."

At the moment I was rubbing a horse's head and he remained still, standing solid as a rock. Relief flooded over me.

"Meekins, I've found Jim!"

Hastily, I slapped on the saddle and put on the bridle. How simple! Why was I so afraid all these years? Now I had a new skill, and it felt wonderful.

My right foot went into the stirrup, while my left foot followed. I was going to show my buddy from Kinnakeet horsemanship that matched his own. I began to yell, "Stand aside, mate, I'm coming out," but the words never left my lips.

Suddenly, I felt myself rising into the air as though I were shot out of a gun.

The truth dawned on me; I had mounted Wildie!

I never knew any living creature, without wings, could rise so far off the ground. There was no need for Meekins to move from the open gate, because Wildie didn't pass through it. He jumped over the fence of the pound.

At that point we separated-he went in one direction, while I took another.

In retrospect, all I could brag about was that I probably was the world's fastest man *off* a horse.

CHAPTER 29

COAST GUARDSMAN GREEN

One morning, I gazed delightedly at myself in the mirror, and a clear-eyed chap stared back at me. That fellow wore a crew cut, and his skin was tanned by the sun and open sea. He was rugged, with muscles that bulged across shoulders and arms. By then, besides the riding patrol, we had been taught boat rowing and life saving, and all of it had added up to physical fitness. It was incredible that a short time ago, I was in a classroom, explaining the difference between a conjunction and a preposition, or how to solve a problem in algebra.

Stanley Green was now a man of the sea!

Our immediate concern at this point was with the air force. It was rumored that an instructor was coming to give a selected group a course in airplane recognition. This course normally took three months, but because of the immediate pressures, he'd remain with us a week.

The rumor proved very upsetting; men with considerable experience vowed it was not possible. Even they, with a knowledge of planes wouldn't presume to be able to learn it all in one week.

It became our main subject of conversation, and I understood the requirements to pass consisted of learning to recognize at any distance and height, all makes of planes, especially the military ones in the United States, Germany, Japan, and England.

Casually, a shipmate asked, "Green, what would you do if you were selected to do twelve weeks work in one?"

I shrugged because I didn't think it concerned me.

"And what makes you think you're immune?"

The answer struck me as obvious, but I explained I knew nothing of aircraft, nor was I mechanical. I simply would be no good. There was nothing in my past records that would indicate I'd be an asset in such a source.

However, soon afterwards, I was summoned to the commanding officer on the double. As I broke into a run, my thoughts raced even more rapidly. What did he want?

He was on the telephone as I arrived, and I heard him say, "You mean there's no way to get someone down here? Well, I've already made that decision, and I hope it works out. Yes, I'll have a man there tonight, and with luck we can get him across Oregon Inlet on the last ferry."

Before he could talk to me, there was another telephone call. I couldn't hear this one, because I was too upset over the possibility of having been chosen for that impossible course.

The commanding officer turned abruptly from the phone, saying, "Green, there is an important and urgent duty awaiting you. Because of the manpower shortage in the air force, it's impossible for anyone to come to Big Kinnakeet Station to give the course in Airplane Recognition. Yet it must be taught at all costs; it's very important while our ships are in this area."

Why was he telling me this? He was commanding officer while I was a seaman first class. Could this mean I was one of those chosen for the course? But no, there'd be no reason why he'd tell me, and not the rest of the group.

"You see that army car out front with a chauffeur in the driver's seat? You are due in Norfolk tonight, and he's waiting to get you across Oregon Inlet on the last ferry. The tide is low now, and he should be able to ride along the wash. Headquarters wants you in Norfolk tonight, at all costs. I'm giving you twenty minutes to pack your bag and be off."

I stared stupidly, rooted to the floor.

"I'm sending you to the Monticello Hotel in Norfolk, where Air Force Headquarters are temporarily located. Due to the shortage of teachers, it is impossible for one to come here. You will finish the three month airplane recognition course given by an air force instructor in one week."

But where were the other boys who'd accompany me? I blinked, but said nothing.

"Get this straight, Green. This is an important mission. You are not going as a regular recruit, or to simply take a course. You must attain a score high enough to obtain an airplane recognition officer's certificate, which will qualify you as an instructor. You will then return to Big Kinnakeet Coast Guard Station and teach the men who have been chosen to take the course. From Big Kinnakeet, you will give this same course to all the other stations in the area. What comes after that, I can't say."

"But, sir, I know nothing about planes. There are men here who are more qualified."

I was irritating him. "Did I ask what you know?" Patiently, he reviewed the situation. There was the five-day course in airplane recognition, and I was to score sufficiently high to secure an officer's certificate, return to Hatteras Island and teach groups at various stations.

"Do you clearly understand the order, Green?"

"Aye aye, sir."

As I reached the door, he commanded me to wait. He had a few more words to say. Perspiration was oozing from my body, and I was breathing hard. When I stood before him again, I was surprised to see a sympathetic look.

"Relax! I know this is a difficult order, but these are extraordinary times. Our lives are at stake; some of us have to assume more responsibility than others." He said he supposed I'd been selected because I was a teacher. "Of all the men stationed at Big Kinnakeet, you are the only teacher. You have been trained to teach and you've had the experience. Your mission is important, being able to recognize friendly planes from enemy ones, is vital to our ships and cities. You cannot fail!"

He shifted in his chair, "If I ask you to do something which you can do, will you do it?"

I assured him I would.

"Then I have your word of honor on that?"

I nodded.

"I am asking you to carry out your assignment in Norfolk, take the course, and do your best. Whether you fail or pass, all I'm asking is that you do your best."

My mates queried me as I packed my seabag. I said I was being sent to Norfolk to take the course, but I didn't reveal that I'd be teaching it in another week.

There were twenty-nine men taking this course besides myself, and they were from all parts of the country. I soon discovered that I was the only one who knew nothing of planes or mechanics. It was not reassuring.

I lost no time in informing my instructor that I knew nothing, but he apparently thought I was exaggerating. He would soon discover I was not!

With all my powers, I concentrated on whatever the instructor said, every picture he showed, and every remark my classmates made.

Each night, I studied the sketches of planes, and read the same books repeatedly until sleep possessed me. The course consisted of body form, engines, size, power speed and other details about the Americans, English, German and Japanese planes. It was easy to see why it usually took three months for the course.

It was a week I shall never forget. The final examinations would be on Saturday morning.

After supper on Friday, I sat on my bed reviewing, but I was so exhausted I fell asleep and knew no more until breakfast call.

Nothing had ever seemed as futile to me as going down to take that test. However, I had promised to do my best, vowing to see it through, and at least I would go down fighting. I wanted to look at my commanding officer directly, saying I had tried. This should teach him not to send a man so ignorant of mechanics the next time.

I began to write, and was greatly relieved that my mind functioned clearly. Pictures of planes stood vividly before me. It was a long affair, but it did seem much easier than I had anticipated.

Having finished, I waited with calmness to learn my fate. When the paper was checked, *I had passed.* Not with flying colors, to be sure, but high enough to secure an officer's certificate.

I returned to Big Kinnakeet Coast Guard Station in an army car, so relieved that I felt mischievous. I would go to the commanding officer with a dejected look in my face; I'd let him suffer for a while.

Thus, I put on a downcast look, slumping over as though I were exhausted. The door was opened by the officer himself, and before I had time to say anything, he grabbed my hand. "Congratulations! You made it! You don't know how glad I am."

Disappointed, I mumbled, "Who told you I passed?"

"Nobody."

"Then what made you think I got the certificate?"

He said he'd been watching for me over an hour concerned, until he saw me leave the car, pick up my seabag and head for his office. "I could tell by your actions you made it, so don't put on an act now!"

I handed him the official papers and was instructed to start teaching on Monday morning.

There were thirty-two in the class, and at the beginning I treated them as the C.O. had told me, outlining the importance of the course. But I added that I expected those who knew about planes to aid me with some explanations.

I really enjoyed my teaching job, and it was rewarding that many men in the various stations where I taught were issued certificates.

I really felt I had done my best, perhaps for the last time. Soon after fulfilling the instructions in that general area, I was back on beach patrols, awaiting further orders.

The United States was rapidly becoming better prepared and the chances of invasion of the Outer Banks was proportionately less. Therefore men were being transferred from Cape Hatteras Island to other theaters of war.

These transfers affected Kinnakeet, which returned to the sort of place it was before the war.

Those of us remaining at Big Kinnakeet began to relax because no ships had been blown up recently. One night a frigid mass of air from the north brought freezing temperatures and boisterous December winds. A storm would really make invasion impossible, I reasoned, and the harder the wind blew, the lower the temperature dropped, and the safer we were.

After the duty list was checked with my name missing, I felt like a boy on vacation. We dined that evening on roast Canadian goose with oyster dressing, hot bread, and coffee. There was potato salad, too, though not as good as Bill Keaton made, but tonight it satisfied me completely.

It was an evening of joking, laughter, and letter writing. I retired at ten o'clock, and by then my window was coated with ice. My bunk was warm and cozy, and I fell into a deep sleep.

I knew no more until I heard, "Men on the double! Invasion coming ashore!"

Men on patrol with their walkie-talkies were calling in.

"What kind of men?" somebody asked, as though it mattered.

The more I tried to dress, the less time I made. I did observe the wind blowing at a terrific rate. My window was completely coated now, and it was obvious that sleet was mixed with rain, the way it beat against the station.

There had to be some mistake, under these conditions, the Cape Hatteras Sea would smash a small boat to bits.

When we had put on all the clothes available, we grabbed our walkie-talkies, and loaded pistols, dashing out into the awful night. Orders were to march to the sea in single file, so more area would be covered. We were to report everything we saw, which the O.D. would relay to headquarters at Norfolk.

I wondered what good it would do if Norfolk were notified. No plane or ship could come. No outside help would reach us at all.

And what could a few men do against an invasion? We had only had our pistols-we were as good as dead!

An order was to be obeyed, so on we pushed. Rain and sleet struck our faces like tiny slivers of glass. The darkness was intense, and the heavy clothing I wore slowed me greatly.

Each man had struck out by himself, adding to my own sense of loneliness. I struggled along until I reached the open sea where spray from the breakers covered me.

This was my destination, and where were the invaders? Anger consumed me. Somebody played a cruel joke! If ever we learned who had conjured this, without a doubt he'd suffer.

But as daylight spread over land and sea, we found that men *had* come ashore. They lay sprawled on the sand, and at first we couldn't decide whether they were friend or foe, for they wore either working clothes or pajamas.

They were rushed to the station, and all were dead except two. We learned they were from the *SS Louise* which was blown up while passing abreast Kinnakeet. It was a merchant ship, and probably a more seaworthy crew never sailed the high seas. The captain and his men escaped on rafts, and everyone made it ashore to Hatteras Island, or at least, their *bodies* did.

Most of the sailors were Greek, and what a handsome crew they were! In fact, there was a look about them which attested to vibrant health. I asked a doctor, "Why don't these men look dead?"

"They didn't drown; they froze to death. It'll take several hours before death begins to show on their faces."

The two survivors knew the others well, I found out. They appeared greatly devoted to each other, and were able to give the necessary details concerning their deceased shipmates.

When this sad duty was finished, they broke down and cried, as they were rushed to the marine hospital in Norfolk.

CHAPTER 30

FAREWELL TO KINNAKEET

I had served at Big Kinnakeet for about a year when my transfer came. I would go to Elizabeth City Coast Guard Air Station, and from there would be transferred to the D.E. 383 *U.S.S. Mills*, which would be heading for the war-torn Mediterranean.

For twelve wonderful years, I had served Kinnakeet, and it was here my interest lay. However, one more night would be the climax of service in this little village, in peace and in war.

As a rule, a transferred man has no duty on his last night, so I was disappointed when I looked over the duty list and found my name on the midnight to four shift, and I had a beach patrol all to myself.

Jim and I were such pals by now, he seemed actually human. I was glad he'd be with me, although I wondered why another man was not assigned to accompany me. Men were scarce, but not that much!

I was unhappy about being treated differently on my last night. If I had to patrol alone, why this one, known as the dead man's?

At midnight, when we set out for the beach, I thought sadly, this was my last time with Jim. When we reached the open beach, I dismounted.

"Jim, the weather's fine. The visibility is perfect, and we've plenty of time. You and I will patrol the beach together like pals."

Accordingly, we started out, and then I discovered my assignment was the beach section abreast of Kinnakeet.

Whether this was intentional or pure chance, made no difference. I was thankful it happened. I loved these people and felt truly one of them. My last active duty was to be for Kinnakeet, and nothing pleased me more.

That four-hour patrol offered an opportunity for some of the most profound thinking I've ever done. The night was pleasantly cool with a crescent moon in the western sky, and I could see far out to sea. Jim and I couldn't have chosen a better time for our stroll along the open beach by the Cape Hatteras Sea.

In the distance was a clear outline of the village, which I liked to remind myself that I was guarding. It was though I were dazedly reliving the fascinating twelve years I had spent in Kinnakeet. I even recalled Uncle Tom carrying me ashore upon my first arrival.

There had been much living here, joys, grief and rough weather; all of it contributing to my present need to ably serve my country.

Now in the late stillness, the village lay in deep sleep, while Jim and I patrolled dutifully. How often I strolled this beach when school was over, and how eagerly I sought it, when there were insoluble problems.

Tonight my imagination took over-instead of my own trivial concerns, I envisioned all the ships which had been lost at sea for four hundred years, naming the waters the graveyard of the Atlantic. In fantasy, they surfaced now, moving proudly over the waters, their crews splendid in their devotion and energy.

And somehow, a peace came to my soul, a sense of well-being that dispelled the uncertainties which lay ahead. I felt myself a part of all mankind. The free world was fighting for its existence, yet, for the first time in my life, I was cleaned of prejudice toward any people.

Jim rubbed his nose against my face, reminding me that our patrol was almost over. By the light of the stars now, and the slit of moon, I looked again at Kinnakeet. I saw the school building outlined dimly, in fact, it was no more than a few hundred yards from where I stood.

Suddenly I called, "Come on, Jim, let's go!" I broke into a run and he trotted happily beside me. Soon I was on the front steps, and to my joy, the door was unlocked. Tying Jim's rein to the knob, I entered.

Down the familiar hall was my classroom! There I stood, letting its atmosphere envelop me. For a few brief moments, I relived twelve years. Then I was satisfied, and I closed the door gently behind me, as if I shut out that part of my life.

Standing there, I faced the village, "God bless you, Kinnakeet. I love you more than you'll ever know. I am thankful for my years as one of you."

Jim whinnied softly. I think he understood how important this last patrol was to me.

AFTERWORD

The beginnings of getting this book republished, where I had to find the rights to the book and Stanley Green's estate, certainly took time and energy, but they were well worth it. Just as daunting were the mechanical aspects. The book had to be transcribed into a new format. Since there was no digital copy of the book, it meant I had to type in the entirety of the memoir, which was no easy task. I sat at my desk, with an original copy of *Kinnakeet Adventure* propped open and held down by whatever I had to keep the pages from flipping on their own. It was both an easy task and a difficult one. I had no real thought in the creative process, since the book was already written. That meant that I could type for hours, sometimes not paying attention to the words written, as long as I put them down. It was certainly time consuming. I worked for hours at a time under a self imposed deadline for each day and each chapter.

The new version is as near the old as possible. I kept the basic layout of the title pages and Table of Contents. There were very few typos and misspellings to fix, and if there was a word that used a more classic spelling, I kept it in the book. These are almost exactly the words that Stanley originally wrote, with nothing left out. A few layout changes include a slightly different font, size, and margin, as well as placing all the chapters to start on the right hand side.

Addition comes in some added photos, maps, and the appendixes. I originally wanted to do something similar to what I did with *Nag's Head*, a book written in the 1850s. I annotated that book extensively, explaining a lot of what was said, translations of quotes and sayings, that sort. I found with *Kinnakeet Adventure*, Stanley did a great job of at least touching on most any thing that needed explanation. Early on, he quotes many Kinnakeeters as using the affectionate term "honey" for everyone. While he never explained it, he did later on admit that it happened regularly, and that he wasn't used to it. I felt like having Stanley address it was good enough, and I didn't have to dive any deeper. The book works on its own without any help from me to steer the tiller, let's just say.

What I did discover was a lot more about my own family, in a way. I was thinking about how my mother knew about Stanley Green, if I had only thought to ask. After writing the book, I considered how Stanley moved from the relative comfort of Chapel Hill and Boiling Springs to the isolated splendor of the Outer Banks. It reminded me of my own move as a baby, when my family moved to the coast. We stayed in my great uncle's beach house, a wonderful old sprawling wood home, right on the beach. Within a year, my father had built a new home on the sound, complete with central air conditioning, trees to climb, a yard to play in, all that was wanted for a family. The air conditioning was especially important. My mother had spent the summer suffering in the beach house and had demanded that my father build a new home for us.

I always liked that story. Mom is kind of like Stanley, brought to an island from the comforts of the city, with little in the way of comfort, and having to give up her old life and fit in with strange new people.

When I mentioned this to her, she said that wasn't entirely true.

All this time I remembered this version of my family story, and in reality, well, it was a little different. She was agreeable to move, but they had already planned to build a house, and we moved out of the beach house into a rental not because it got too hot, but because the beach house had no heat for the winter.

It was a little thing, but I liked how even now after all these years, I still get to learn new things about my family.

Like Stanley, we all quickly began to fit in to life on the coast. For me it was easy. I often joke that I learned to talk on the Outer Banks; I learned English soon after. While I don't have a typical brogue like the true natives, I can easily bring it up and sound like the other kids I went to school with. Looking back, I see how well we all did, my parents and older brothers. We found our places on the shore, fitting in just like all the others did, either by shipwreck or mailboat or Dad driving us in the station wagon as we arrived. And while we have also been pulled away, the coast still calls us. I still think of Kill Devil Hills as home, even though I have traveled and lived across the country. I was surprised that Stanley didn't end up back on the islands after his service in the Coast Guard. You have to pry me away from the beach whenever I am home on the Outer Banks.

At the beginning of this book, Stanley dedicated it to all Kinnakeeters, past, present, and future. As I said, I changed nothing, including the dedication. It's his book. The little bit that I have done is here in the back. It's the color I discovered, both in research and in growing up on the beach. I am part of that land, the very bits of sand are comfortable to me, and I wanted to share that part with the readers.

So for this part, my little part here, I want to dedicate to my Mom, Joyce Sledge. She is a lot like Stanley in many ways. She came to the islands, almost out of necessity, and made it a home for her and her family, along with all the work and volunteer contributions she did as soon as she arrived, to become a part of the community and the land. She still looks back fondly on our home, and loves to go back when she gets a chance. And I completely understand her feeling that way.

Because I do, too.

J.S. - Feb. 2023

MAP LOCATIONS

Many of the places mentioned in *Kinnakeet Adventure* have disappeared over time. Certainly Avon, along with much of the Outer Banks, have been developed and redeveloped over the years since 1930. This map shows a basic location of several places mentioned in the book. Locations are approximate.

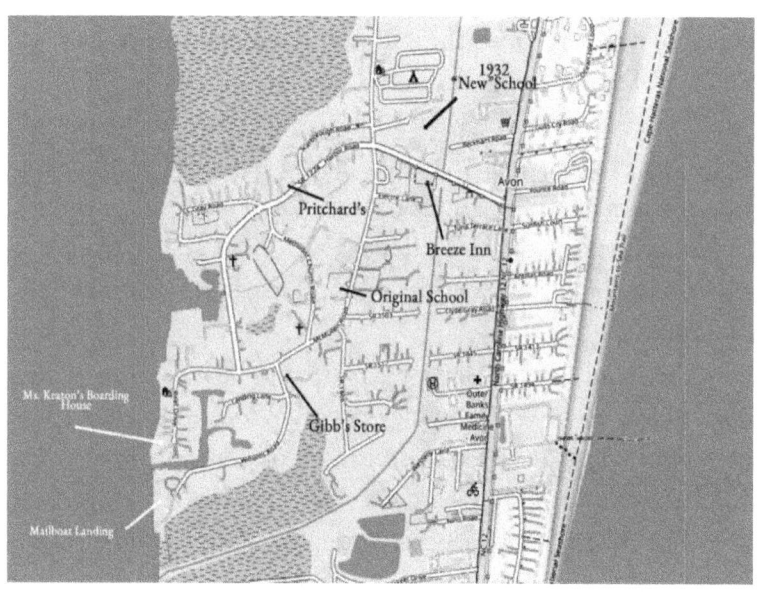

Stanley would have arrived at the south end of Kinnakeet, below a large creek known as Uncle Bate's Ditch. The larger marina to the north was not cut until later.

Just north but on the other side of the ditch was Ms. Keaton's. Rebecca "Beck" Keaton ran not only the boarding house, but a farm and dairy, where she sold milk, ice cream, hand cranked just like the students did in the book, and sour cream, among other dairy items.

Gibb's Store was owned by Gibb Gray, and the building is still there, but used as a private residence now. Gibb would have lived across the street.

The original school from the book was just up McMullen Rd. There is nothing left of the school. Stanley mentions the wood was used to build another place, the Breeze Inn.

The 1932 school was located just inside the Kinnakeet Dike, somewhere near the current fire department and the Sands of Time Campground. At the time, as mentioned in the book, there was no Highway 12, nor were there the man-made dunes, so even though the shore might have been half a mile away, it was all open land, probably sand, with no protective barrier or dyke at the time. This is why Stanley describes it as right on the beach even though it seems like it is in the middle of the island.

Pritchard's is on Harbor Road, west of where the school would have been. While Stanley describes it as a place for teens, with pool tables, it was also later more of a men's place, not as much for teens or girls to gather.

The Breeze Inn was located near the entrance to the village, where the electrical station and water tower are now. It too, was a bar meant more for adult men. When the CCC came to the coast to build the dunes, many places like these became rough gathering places for the men to hang out when not working.

PLACE NAMES

As is addressed in the book, Kinnakeet is the original name used by the locals to the area. In 1883, the village of Kinnakeet was renamed Avon by the U.S. Post Office. It was done so like many towns on the coast because of the length and difficulty of writing and saying the longer aboriginal names. Kinnakeet may come from an Algonquin word meaning "That which is mixed." The village has been described as a mixture of smaller villages and settlements. It could also have been derived from the aboriginal native tribes that lived there along with early settlers, or a meeting place of different tribes. There are old histories telling of a ruler of the native tribes named Kinnakeet, as well, which may likely be the source of the name. After hundreds of years, it is difficult to impossible to actually determine the true history of the name. Avon was probably chosen at random, though it is possibly from the English river of the same name.

Many places along the Outer Banks coast have seen their names change over the years. Some have clung close to their original name, while others have been changed completely, with little reasoning. Ocracoke was rumored to be named so by Blackbeard's last cry, "O cry, cock!" in hopes that the sun would rise and a rooster would crow, providing his severed head the light it needed to find his body so that he could continue fighting. But Ocracoke was long known by that name, coming from the name Woccocon, or a derivative of the word, such as Occacock, which either is a name of a local tribe, or a word from the Algonquin as well, meaning stockade or pen.

Hatteras is ripe with name changes. The area itself is named for the small tribe of Hatterask natives. And Frisco, the wooded area to the south on the island, is known by many as Trent Woods, a hiding place for mystery and ghosts from long ago.

The three connected villages between Hatteras and Oregon Inlet are known as Rodanthe, Waves, and Salvo. This area was originally known as Chicamacomico, with north or south used to distinguish the different areas. Again, the towns were renamed by the post office. Rodanthe was chosen for one, with it being the name of a non-native flower. Waves was chosen to describe the ocean and beach for tourism. Salvo has a more interesting history. Originally called Clarks or Clarksville, during the Civil War, a Union fleet went south to attack the forts around Hatteras. A crewman noted the tiny village, but it was on no map. The captain ordered a volley of gunfire, a salvo, and the crewman dutifully noted the attack on his charts. When later maps were made, the name was applied.

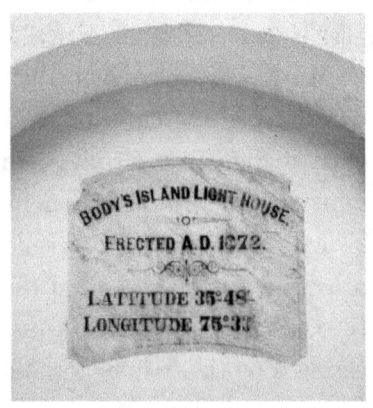

Farther north still there is the lighthouse on Bodie Island. Rumors and legends say it was named after the many bodies that washed ashore from the shipwrecks of the Graveyard of the Atlantic. In reality it has just gone through respellings of the island name. Originally Boddy's Island, and later Body's Island, it finally arrived at Bodie Island, with a soft 'o' sound.

Bodie Island is currently connected, but there were many inlets cut through the Outer Banks, including at Nags Head. This area was probably named after a place in Britain, a head of land. Legend tells of land pirates walking an old horse or nag with a candle lamp around its neck across the low hills to simulate a ship bobbing at anchor, in order to lure in unsuspecting ships to a false safe harbor. The story has lead to many sales of novelty horses with lamps tied to them, but it is completely untrue. Nags Head even was known as Griffiths for a short time, another post office change.

Kill Devil Hills also gets its name through legend. This time it is from the shipwrecks bringing rum from the Caribbean. It was said the rum was so potent and harsh that it would kill the devil. Those facts maybe true, but the name likely was originally Killdeer Hill, named after the shore bird.

Kitty Hawk, famous for being branded with the Wright Brothers, was, again, an Algonquin name, Chickehauk, and it probably referred to the area's good hunting grounds for geese.

Duck however was a planned community, built beginning in 1910, and the post office asked for a name. Considering the number of waterfowl around, it was an obvious choice.

Corolla even had a different name. It was originally Jones Hill, which was oddly rejected by the US Postal Service. Corolla is the name of the outer petals of a flower.

COASTAL GEOGRAPHY

In Chapter 17, *My Friend Bud Rans Gray*, Green records a tale told by Gray which includes the description of large trees growing right upon the shore of Kinnakeet. It seems like an unbelievable occurrence, having tall trees growing up right on the shore, but this was actually commonplace.

Live oaks were an established old growth forest all across the Outer Banks for a long time. Gray mentions his father was opposed to cutting the trees, saying "nature spent a million years building this island and covering it with a vast forest, then along came stupid man, who undid it in a few years." While some of that might be hyperbole, the meaning behind the statement is accurate. Live oaks are giant, twisted hardwood trees, capable and comfortable of growing in the harsh conditions of the coast. The wood was popular for shipbuilding, due to those same traits. In earlier years, during colonial times especially, buyers would find the giant trees and pay the property owners an exorbitant sum to cut the trees down for ship materials. As seen in the book, it would have been hard pressed for a person living on the ragged edge of existence on the Outer Banks to turn down such a bounty. They would not realize just what they gave up until the tree was cut and removed from the land, forever altering their view to their detriment, while temporarily changing their purse to their benefit. Most people regretted the choice.

But were there really trees stretching across the beaches at the time? Gray mentions this happening when he was a boy, which could be somewhere between the 1870s and turn of the century. While there are no photos of the land like this, there is ample evidence of much of what he says taking place. We already know of the commercial aspects of clearcutting the valuable oak trees that were going on for even centuries before. At a different beach farther north, there is also proof emerging that there were huge forests of these trees growing along the coast.

Along the Corolla shore in Currituck county, the remains of a coastal forest is emerging from the sand and dunes. Bare tree stumps and trunks have appeared on the beach and in the tide. The trees are the leftovers of the forests that used to sit behind the dunes, when the shoreline was much farther out to the east. As time passed, the dunes pushed back over the land, covering the trees. Additionally, the homes that were there were also covered. Some houses were set on rollers to be pulled west as the sand started creeping in. An entire town was abandoned and covered by the drifting dune line.

Additionally, even later on, there is some written evidence of the trees and their remnants being on the coastal shore. In the book *Taffy of Torpedo Junction,* by Nell Wise Wechter, the hero, Taffy, leans out into the breakers to grab a piece of wood with a dog tied to it. The dog was a victim of a U-boat attack during the early days of World War II, and its owner tied the poor dog to debris so it might float to shore. In the chapter, Wechter describes Taffy as holding on to a tree to reach out to get the dog.

Further evidence comes from an even more unlikely, and mysterious, source. The coast is ripe with legends and tales, including the ghost ship *Carroll A. Deering.* The tale of the *Deering* involves a mystery of it washing ashore in 1921 along the Hatteras shore. It was completely abandoned, but entirely shipshape. It was still capable of sailing, yet the entire crew had abandoned her, and they were never found. Only the ship's cat was rescued.

The Carroll A. Deering at sea

The legend is an intriguing one, but for this subject, its construction is of more vital importance. It was built within two years of its wreck, in 1919, and at the time it was considered one of the finest wooden ships on the Atlantic. It was the end times for wooden ships, with new metal hulls just beginning to go into service. But at that time, and before its construction, wood was the material of choice for shipbuilding. The demand for oak, especially coastal live oak, would have been high, as much of the trade that happened at this time still was taken by large wooden sailing vessels.

This was not the only major change that would happen along the coast at this time. At the beginning of his book, Stanley mentions his desperation of needing a job, as the country was in the midst of a depression, and work was scarce. Jobs programs from the Civilian Conservation Corps and the Works Progress Administration would soon come along to provide jobs to hard working young single men on the beach. There was worry that the shorelines were moving slowly west. In the book, there are multiple examples of this. Stanley mentions early on taking a walk to see old graves from a cemetery where it is mentioned that the bones from the buried dead are being uncovered along the shore, and that the cemeteries are now only on the more protected sound side. In his chapter that describes the hurricane flooding the village, he describes the town as being flooded over, as if the homes and small hills are islands in the ocean that has washed over the land. Both of these were likely accurate descriptions of the time. There was worry that the continual overwash might destroy the western forests and woodland, or that an entire island would be washed away. The CCC and WPA brought in young men to build protective dunes across the entire shore. Dunes were built from the northern parts of Dare County in Kitty Hawk all the way down toward Hatteras, in hopes of protecting the beaches and the land behind the shore.

The dunes would do their work well, but at the same time the dynamics of the moving shore were not fully understood in the 1930s. While the storm overwash was stopped in several places, the continual pounding of storm surge would damage the dune lines, and create weak points where blowout inlets would occur. These are still evident today, and still occurring. New Inlet, near Rodanthe, opened at a weak point where other inlets had occurred for decades and centuries before. Northern Rodanthe has been susceptible to flooding over its roadway, and recently has seen breaches in the dunes as the area is left to go back to a more natural state with the completion of a new bridge leading into the town, bypassing much of Pea Island.

The dunes also have a negative effect on the soundsides of the islands. When the blowout inlets occur, they create washover fans, where the fast moving water pushes silt and sand into the western side of the barrier islands. This allowed the west side of the Outer Banks to grow as the ocean side was worn away, keeping the islands about the same width while moving slowly westward. Additionally, the more dangerous hurricanes that bring soundside flooding now pile in water which is trapped by the low land, with no escape into the sea as it blows across the islands. In the book Stanley mentions how quickly the flooding dissipates, which does not happen as easily now.

Vestiges of the more natural areas can still be seen in some areas. The entrance to the Cape Hatteras National Seashore has some leftover live oaks. The large preserve of Nags Head Woods shows what the native land would have looked like as far back as 150-200 years, where the first settlers and shipwreck survivors in Nags Head would have lived. Coquina Beach is a popular natural beach setting for swimmers, but it also offers a glance at how the coast would have looked before the big dunes. There, the dunes roll in low hills. They were probably started by shrubs or beach grass taking hold, then gathering sand until a mound was created. Now the area is a patchwork of hills instead of one dune line. The hills worked as speedbumps of sorts during storms. The waves were allowed to pass through the dunes, while being slowed and broken by the many small impediments. As the waves washed through, they would dump first the heavy shells and debris, then smaller pebbles and sand, and finally the lightest silt would be carried over to the western sound side.

The entirety of the Outer Banks as a living geological formation, along with the changes made by human intervention. It is a very complex and interwoven system that is seeing changes almost season by season now.

HURRICANES AND STORMS

There are multiple chapters that deal with the hurricanes and storms that have continually graced the Outer Banks with their presence. Stanley seems to deal with them with a mix of utter dread and nonchalance. He discusses his fear and apprehension, but then realizes there is little to nothing he can do to hold back the tide. His descriptions and reaction are curiously close to the way many locals have handled storms through the ages.

In Chapter 12, *The Night Of The Storm*, he describes what it was like for him to ride out a hurricane, his first on the coast. I find no need to reiterate much of it. His description of the village being flooded, and how the winds shift to cause that flooding, are accurate. And to a certain extent, the stoic helplessness of standing in the flooded kitchen drinking coffee is probably not atypical of your typical Outer Banker, though it would be as likely that we would be outside as soon as the wind stopped, even if the water was deep.

The hurricane he described passes by in a few pages. A night of storm and flooding, followed by a flooded morning, simplifies the tale. This was likely a famous hurricane, though. He mentions it occurs eight weeks into the school year, which would be the very late summer or early fall of 1930. Later chapters refer to events in 1931 and 32, so this was likely 1930. The only hurricane to pass by was known as the Dominican Republic Hurricane, or Hurricane San Zenón. It crossed over the island of Hispaniola, dumping most of its rain and damage on the Dominican Republic. The damage was extensive, with total loss of power and communications. It is estimated that between 2,000 and 8,000 people died as a result of the hurricane and its aftermath. It entered the Gulf of Mexico, crossed Florida, and restrengthened in the Atlantic. It grazed the coast of North Carolina around September 12, 1930. His short description is just one of the many that were made of the storm. It is one of the few accounts written of the event at Avon in a somewhat contemporary account.

The Ash Wednesday Storm occurred three decades later, but photos of the damage and flooding in Nags Head would be similar to the earlier hurricanes that Stanley would experience.

In Chapter 14, *Second Year*, Stanley quickly describes a storm on March 6th, 1932, where he travels to Manteo for a school district meeting, and the weather turns from warm to a horrific storm within the evening. While he describes both the wind speed and direction changes as hurricane strength, it is likely that this was more typical of the cold Nor'easters that blow through the coast in springtime. Again, he does a perfunctory job of describing the event, and his fear of the aftermath of the town being "washed off the map." What is important from that bit of the chapter is also important in a later chapter.

In Chapter 17, *My Friend Bud Rans Gray*, Stanley recounts a tale from Gray, where the creation of both the Oregon Inlet and Hatteras Inlet were formed by the same storm in the same day, September 7th, 1846. Gray describes more of how the people gathered at the north end of Hatteras village to ride out the storm, which through happenstance or higher power left the southern part empty. This is where Hatteras Inlet formed, wiping out the entire village, but sparing the lives of all the villagers.

First, the story comes from an oral history, told to Bud Rans Gray, who passed it on to Stanley to print the events for the first time, an important document in itself.

What is more telling is that Gray reports how the entire island, including the southern part which is now a two mile strip of inlet under water, was occupied at the time. Not only that, he describes the long grape vines that stretched across the land. There are also mentions of peach trees growing in the area. These little historical curiosities paint a very different picture than the current day open seagrass covered lands of the Outer Banks.

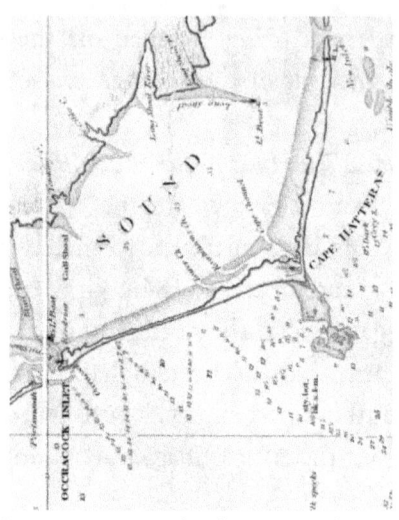

This early map shows Hatteras Island connected to Ocracoke down to the inlet by Portsmouth Island. Note the "New Inlet" at the top of the map.

Coastal residents and visitors will attest to the generally pleasant nature of the weather and waters. The Gulf Stream can provide a mediating heat to the cool winters, keeping the Outer Banks warm even in early spring, as Stanley attested in his trip to Manteo. And the warm weather generally kept freezing winds away. Most wouldn't know that for a long time, great peach and orange groves grew along the coast. Lemons were probably grown as well. Stanley often mentioned in the book of how Mrs. Keaton would make lemon pies. The orchards of Cape Hatteras were documented years later in a popular decorative map of the Outer Banks. Along with the other additions of stylized shipwrecks, jumping fish, monuments and lighthouses was the incongruous addition of a large orange tree on the inner side of Cape Hatteras point.

310

If you have been swimming at different spots along the North Carolina coast, you can attest to the significant change in temperature. The Outer Banks generally has warm water in the summer, with temperatures in the low to mid 70s, perfectly refreshing on a hot day, but not overly warm. The southern tip of Hatteras and down toward Ocracoke, with the curve of the Gulf Stream coming close to land, can see water up to ten degrees warmer, along with warmer air. And further south, along the east west facing beaches as far down as Oak Island, the water can be downright hot. Or, as your editor once described, "Like swimming in soup."

BEACH TRANSPORTATION

Stanley Green makes mention of the transports used during his time living in Kinnakeet, especially the freight boats that sailed between Elizabeth City and Hatteras. In addition to the *Missouri*, mentioned in the book, there were the *Cathleen*, the *Virginia Dare*, the *E.H. Brown*, and the *Julia W. Bell*. The schooners carried more than the basic necessities of flour and meal, but canned foods grown as far away as California, and more exotic and wanted products. In the chapter *Kinnakeet Christmas*, he mentions how the students buy up the crepe paper ribbons from the local stores for use in Christmas decorations at the school. The schooners, the *Missouri* especially, were well suited for the travel along the sound waters. It was purely a sailing vessel until 1939, and would draw only three feet of water even fully loaded, which allowed it to traverse the shallow waters, and get fairly close to the shore for unloading.

In other parts of the Outer Banks, Nags Head specifically, houses and piers were built out over the shallow water, sometimes reaching out hundreds of feet so that the big mailboats could dock and deliver their goods.

They delivered passengers, too. Stanley describes his travel from Manteo to Kinnakeet in one way, by showing how much time he had to converse with the others on the boat. These boats, powered by sail, were great at covering the distances without much issue, but speed was not their talent. They hauled large amounts of goods. Passengers were secondary, and there were generally no amenities, which meant no chairs to sit, nor a head for a bathroom. On rough travels, the passengers took their risks sitting with the shifting cargo in the hold.

Sharpie schooner Iowa, the sister ship to the Missouri.

Of course, car travel was a regular occurrence, as noted in the book. The vehicles drove down the shore on packed sand. There were no roads at the time from Nags Head southward. It wasn't until 1924 that Oregon Inlet was even passable by car, when a ferry service was offered by Toby Tillett. This allowed cars, again, mostly salesmen, to drive down the beach if the tides were right, into the towns all the way to Hatteras. Most people didn't even own cars, since they would serve little to no purpose on an island where sand would catch a car's tires and hold on with a death grip. This was another regular occurrence, where inexperienced drivers would find their cars caught in the sand, and have to abandon the vehicles to rising tides. The cars would get buried and rust away over years, sometimes over decades.

Current day still mimics this, as many a traveler on the Hatteras shore has not aired down their tires and found themselves stuck.

The Midgett family bus line takes one of the many Route 101 roads, here covered in rainwater, up and down the coast.

An intrepid but unfortunate man saw the need for travel on the coast around the same time as Stanley Green's tenure. In 1938, Theodore Stockton Midgett saw the value in a bus route from Hatteras to Manteo, which he knew would serve him and his three sons well as a business venture. He had purchased a new Ford station wagon and the franchise to transport people on the route. Sadly, the very day he signed the papers, he passed away from a heart attack. With the need to care for family always on the forefront, his three sons, Harold, Anderson, and Stocky Jr., all mourned their loss and then went to work. They took passengers on a wild ride in the back of station wagons, trucks, and buses, anything they could use over the years they served the islands as the only passenger service available. The riders were probably a mixture of amazed and terrified. The bumpy sand roads had to seem daunting for any driver, but when they saw Stocky Jr. driving, they may have wondered if

they should just walk. Stocky was the youngest of the three brothers, and began his driving at the age of 10. He was too short to even sit in the seat. He had to stand in order to see and work the pedals.

The family of brothers ran the bus line successfully until the 1960s, when the Herbert Bonner Bridge opened and freed cars from the ferry ride over Oregon Inlet.

The "roads" they used were more paths cut in the sand. The beach was preferred, but if there was a high tide or storm, the bus took the "inside route", which was on the western side of the dune lines. The soft sand, flooded roads, and myriad paths led the Midgett boys to term the path 'Route 101', because there were a hundred and one different ways to go. Vehicles would find the easiest, sometimes highest or firmest, path, drive that direction, while others would follow their tire tracks, until that path was too beaten and untrustworthy. After which they would begin to make another road. Visitors were often told to follow the freshest set of tire tracks they could find.

The difficulty of driving didn't mean that the people looked at travel as a chance to suffer, however. Many of the longer dunes would have wooden bridges built over them to accommodate the cars, trucks, and buses to roll over the steep hills without either destroying the dunes or getting a vehicle stuck or flipped over in the middle of the path. The small bridges also brought out a bit of terror as some of the Midgett bus line vehicles took them with more vigor than was sometimes necessary.

Other bridges were more resolute, though maybe not as needed. Visible today still are the remains of an old wooden bridge crossing over the marshy wetlands on the sound side of the islands. The bridge was built after a hurricane created an inlet nearby. With the open inlet and water flowing freely to and from sound and Atlantic Ocean, the entire southern part of the Outer Banks was cut off from vehicles. Two bridges were built on the sound side to accommodate vehicles to pass over the open area, but by the time the bridges were completed, the inlet had closed back up and beach travel was available again.

The remains of one of two bridges built to cross the inlet.

Even today, these same events occur regularly, and can be seen by the results they cause. A new bridge has taken the place of the old Bonner Bridge. The New Inlet opened up, necessitating a temporary Mabey bridge, later to be nicknamed the Lego Bridge for its many pieces of steel plate. The bridge was replaced with a permanent bridge named after Captain Richard Etheridge of the Pea Island Lifesaving Station. Further south still has the more recent Jug Handle Bridge, which bypasses the more fragile area of the S-Turns leading into Rodanthe from the north, as well as the preserve area around Pea Island.

The 1930s of Stanley's time would be the end of the Outer Banks as an inaccessible barrier island. Events would put in place both the needs and wants to have roads and access to the the coast. By the late 1920s, a plan was put in place to build the Wright Brothers Monument. But part of the plan included building and updating roads. Even during the Recession, the coast saw the upcoming demand for tourism far beyond the lone sportsman coming down from the north to shoot ducks. Highway 12 in its current form would begin in 1953, along with the state ferry system creating links between islands and the mainland. In 1957, Hatteras and Ocracoke would be connected by ferry. The road would be considered complete in 1963 when the Herbert Bonner Bridge spanned the wide Oregon Inlet. With free access all the way to the end of Hatteras, it also meant that the next year, in 1964, the last mailboat would make its delivery to Ocracoke village, ending an era of water borne deliveries that had lasted for generations before.

OLD CHRISTMAS

Stanley goes into detail about how the students celebrate Christmas in Kinnakeet, with the daily early morning parades, as well as decorating the school and the traditional gift giving to the teachers. This is one of the few places where the traditions are documented.

Much of the Christmas celebration tales of the Outer Banks are dominated by the stories of Old Christmas in nearby Rodanthe. Stanley notes the students referring to it in passing at the end of Chapter 16, *Kinnakeet Christmas*. The Christmas break had been shortened that year, and right after the holiday was celebrated school began again. The students mention going up to Chicamacomico for that celebration. While Stanley mentions he enjoys it, he does not describe the events, with is too bad, because the celebration of Old Christmas at Rodanthe would benefit from as many first hand depictions as possible.

Old Christmas is generally celebrated on the last day of Epiphany. It comes from the changing of the calendar from the old Julian calendar to the Gregorian calendar, starting in 1582, by Pope Gregory XIII. The Julian calendar had become out of date with too many leap days added to keep up with the solar year, which was important to the Catholic church, because it determined the date of Easter based on the spring equinox. It would take until 1752 for the British Empire to adjust to the new calendar, which removed eleven days. Christmas was moved to the current date of December 25, with Old Christmas, in many places called Little Christmas, falling on January 5.

With another leap year coming forth for the Julian calendar, Old Christmas moved to January 6, which fell in with the day of Epiphany, and the day for Old Christmas locked itself in with that date.

Why the people of Rodanthe still celebrate Old Christmas seems to have two origins, both similar. One is that being on an isolated island, they simply didn't receive the news of the calendar change for so long, the holiday had become built in to tradition. The other more colorful version is essentially the same reason, but adds that the locals were being stubborn with their holiday and simply refused to change.

Old Christmas in Rodanthe has changed over time, though.

There are some similarities in the history of events. Both Kinnakeet and Chicamacomico had local parades or marches, as well as pageants and plays done around the Christmas season. Stanley mentions with delight in passing how the students, who were supposed to be so rowdy and challenging, also were very spiritual and religious, and had a great deal of respect for the holiday. In early Chicamacomico, predating the name change to Rodanthe, the villagers would also meet for parades and antics. One of the earliest events passed down through oral traditions first was how people would go to the Lifesaving Station to see the chief, Captain Ban Midgett, shoot apples off the head of crew member Thomas Payne with a .22 rifle. Afterwards, the captain was known to take a pole with a steer skull on it and parade through the towns.

This early parading with a cow's skull is sometimes described as just happenstance, but there are lots of historical tie-ins to this type of event. Going from door to door with a cow or horse skull on a pole has roots far back into the early

1800s in South Wales. Called Mari Lwyd, it is a wassailing tradition where men carrying the horse or cattle head would march from house to house at Christmastime, singing carols. When they arrived, they would sing a song demanding entrance, often with the skull singing along via a wire attached to the jawbone. The homeowner would then be forced, goodnaturedly, to sing back why they just couldn't let the men inside to drink all their alcohol. Then the men would take another turn, and when one side or the other ran out of excuses, they would either leave for the next house, or more likely, come in, barge around, knock over stuff, and drink.

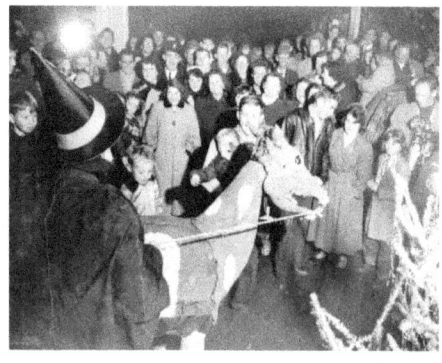

In Rodanthe, the story has more local roots. And curiously, it overlaps lightly with a tale that Stanley tells in his book. A big part of the Rodanthe Old Chrismas celebration is the visit from Old Buck. The beginnings of this tale start with a bull arriving from a shipwreck, or possibly thrown overboard to save a ship from foundering. The bull likes the sweet grass and plentiful cows on the land. Indeed, the locals let loose their many cows to the beach so that the bull can help sire calves. Soon named Old Buck, he becomes well liked on the islands, and is considered a gentle and kind animal. He was free to roam around the land, finding comfort in the woods. Sadly, he was seen as a prize for a hunter, and shot and killed.

Even though the locals were saddened, they remained affectionate toward the bull, and began telling stories of how

Old Buck still would come out of his hidden land, once a year, on Old Christmas. A bull's skull, with a brace adorned with cow hide, was attached to a wheelbarrow, or sometimes walked like a pantomime horse, with two people under a cloth, into the celebrations. He would occasionally chase some children, if they had been naughty over the year, or be chased out by the good kids. The traditions changed over time, but Old Buck always made an appearance before disappearing back into the woods for another year.

In Chapter 24, *Mealy Mouth*, Stanley tells a story quite similar to the Old Buck legend, but with a different name, and a more public and sanguine outcome. While it may be that both stories share a common root, it is more likely that both tales are separate but similar. For hundreds of years, cattle roamed freely

 on the islands, with no need to fence them in. Rodanthe actually had a fence around the village specifically to keep the cattle out of the streets and yards. It is much more likely that the two events both happened, and the similarities just overlap.

An addition to the parades and celebrations is a marching drum, which has been used at Old Christmas. The legend tells that a young Scottish man, Donald McDonald, who had been wounded in battle in 1746. Later, he took a ship to the New World. Heading to the coast, was caught up in the great Autumn Storm of 1757 and shipwrecked off the shore. In his effort to save himself, he used his drum as a lifesaver, floating to shore on it. The local Payne family found him, saving his life. He saw the value in his drum helping him get to shore, so, he kept it as he grew up in the village. It was passed down in the Payne family, and used every Old Christmas as part of the parades. Later it was brought out in the community center for its traditional playing. The drum currently is on display at the Chicamacomico Lifesaving Station in their museum.

There are other tales told of the drum, and this story may be an embellishment of history, but it is the most popular and retold of all the tales. The drum really did belong with the local

Payne family until they donated it, and it still is used for Old Christmas.

Rodanthe's Old Christmas in recent years has carried on with similar traditions, while passing over others. The original marksmanship demonstration has changed to an oyster shoot, where people take turns shooting at shells to win a bushel of oysters. Old Buck still makes his appearance, and people have continued to do early morning parades in some years past. But the current celebration is much more family oriented. A band plays for dancing, while oysters are steamed outside. The mix of steam and fire balances with the sometimes freezing cold, but everyone looks forward to the result. Inside the community building, a long held tradition of chicken and pastry continues.

Community donations and lots of helping hands cook chickens and roll out dough for a food that can serve large numbers of people, even if it may not be as easy as hot dogs and chips.

ABOUT THE AUTHOR

Stanley Everette Green was born in 1905 in Boiling Springs, North Carolina. The story of his winning his A.B. in Education at his state university is told in his book. (Later he was to earn a master's degree in the same field at New York University.)

Interested in music, drama, reading, writing, travel, lecturing, gardening, he has recently retired as a school counselor.

-from Kinnakeet Adventure, original biography on back dust cover.

Stanley Everett Green was born on March 27th, 1905, in Boiling Springs, NC. This book chronicles most of his life from the time of his graduation from the University of North Carolina Chapel Hill until his continued service in the Coast Guard at the end of World War II. After being reassigned to a new post at the end of this book, Stanley served on the *U.S.S. Mills*, a destroyer escort that performed convoy duties across the

Atlantic. On her second voyage, the *Mills* rescued several sailors from a liberty ship during an attack by the Germans in the Mediterranean, as well as saving the crippled boat. Stanley was awarded a Good Conduct Medal, American Campaign Medal, EAME (European Asian Middle East) Campaign Medal, and a World War II Victory Medal.

There is little to describe Stanley's life after his service in World War II. He later gained his Master's Degree at New York University. Stanley returned to his home town and worked at Garner Webb College as a student counselor.

Stanley penned *Kinnakeet Adventure*, his memoir, for publishing in 1971, soon after retirement. He lived a long and contented life in his hometown of Boiling Springs. He never married, despite his best intentions to meet girls, but was a devoted brother to his sisters. Stanley passed away on January 29th, 1996, at the age of 90.

ABOUT THE AUTHOR/EDITOR

Joe Sledge is the author of several books on North Carolina, including his four book series, *Did You See That?*, a collection of hidden history and roadside attractions across the state. He has penned a growing collection of ghost tales across the coast and over North Carolina. Additionally, he has written a novel under the pseudonym John Martell, *The Unmerciful Sea*, a paranormal thriller novel taking place in Ocracoke. Joe is the author of a series of young adult books, starting with *Bess Truly And Her Zap-Gun Rangers*. He has republished *Nag's Head*, a book originally written in 1850, by Gregory Seaworthy, which was the first book to describe vacation life on the coast at a contemporary time.

Joe is from the Outer Banks, and attended the University of North Carolina Chapel Hill. He traveled frequently, going from coast to coast, as well as visiting other countries. Joe is happily married with a family that likes to share in his adventures and travels across the state, but they all prefer to find time to be at the beach whenever possible.

Joe is also the owner of his publishing company, Gravity Well Books.

PHOTO CREDITS

All photos are used with permission or through public domain. Permission is granted for this book only. Photos may not be duplicated without permission of the rights holders.

Bodie Island -- Joe Sledge

Live Oak -- Joe Sledge

Carroll A. Deering -- public domain

Ash Wednesday Storm -- Aycock Brown, courtesy of the Outer Banks History Center

Hatteras Map -- North Carolina Maps, State Library of North Carolina

Schooner Iowa -- public domain

Manteo-Hatteras Bus Line (2 photos) -- courtesy the Outer Banks History Center, David Stick Papers

Bridge -- Joe Sledge

Old Christmas Old Buck, Drum -- public domain

Old Christmas Drum and Santa -- John Griffin, Chicamacomico Lifesaving Station

Stanley Green -- from the original printing of his book

SPECIAL THANKS

Kinnakeet Adventure had the benefit of already being written. I just needed to copy it down. But all the stories it opened up, from finding the ownership of the book to getting all the little details for the appendixes took a lot of help, from old and new sources. I'd like to thank them all here.

My dear "aunt" Annie Mae Bridges gave me permission to republish this great book. That was the start I had to have, and I thank her profusely for letting a whole new world read *Kinnakeet Adventure*. My mom, Joyce Sledge filled in the family stories. My cousin Elizabeth Pack answered my emails and got me in touch with Stanley's family. Their help was immense.

Danny Couch, John Griffin, and Lois Gray Miller, all from the Outer Banks coast, all historians and storytellers in their own right, helped fill in so many blanks as far as the minutiae of Kinnakeet and the shores of Hatteras. Gee Gee Rosell of Buxton Village Books encouraged me to get the book back in print, and has been a long time supporter of books about the Outer Banks. I encourage everyone to stop by her store and pick up a great read.

And of course, Stanley Green himself, who did the real heavy lifting by preserving the history of his memoirs in this book, as well as living it all in the first place.

My appreciation to all of you is tremendous. Thank you so much!

www.ingramcontent.com/pod-product-compliance
Lightning Source LLC
Chambersburg PA
CBHW071137130626
46553CB00004B/1415